D0123317

THE RISE OF MODERN RELIGIOUS IDEAS IN AMERICA

— Editorial Director —

SYDNEY E. AHLSTROM, American Studies Program, Yale University

JOSIAH STRONG

The New Era, or
The Coming Kingdom

Reprint Edition
with a New Introduction

THE REGINA PRESS

Reprint Edition 1975

THE REGINA PRESS
7 Midland Avenue
Hicksville, New York 11801

New Introduction © 1975 by The Regina Press

Library of Congress Catalog Number: 74-78273
International Standard Book Number: 0-88271-011-7

HN
31
S87
1975

This volume is reprinted according to the standards
established in 1972 by the Rare Book Libraries' Conference on Facsimiles.

Manufactured in the United States of America.

INTRODUCTION TO THE REPRINT EDITION
by Sydney E. Ahlstrom,
American Studies Program,
Yale University

JOSIAH STRONG (1847-1916) has become a legend in American history, as both a religious and a secular figure. As one would expect, therefore, characterizations of the man have run to extremes. Historians of American foreign policy and critics of imperialism have depicted him as an unrestrained advocate of military conquest, especially in connection with the War with Spain of 1898. Other critics have seen him as a racist, a nativist, and a bigot who saw immigration and immigrants as a national peril. To champions of ethnicity, cultural pluralists, lovers of the world's diversity, critics of Christianity, and members of other faiths his advocacy of the Church's "universal conquest" has been regarded as cultural imperialism at its worst. By conservative Evangelicals Strong has been denounced as one who betrayed biblical teaching on the Kingdom of God and put millenial doctrines at the service of social reform and foreign policy. To those many Protestants in almost all denominations who think of the churches as essentially spiritual institutions which should be concerned primarily with reaching and converting individuals, Strong was seen as a meddler in secular affairs which are not the proper concern of organized Christianity; in addition he was blamed for subverting the aims of the Evangelical Alliance by making it an engine of theological liberalism and social activism. Finally, thinkers who regard themselves as realists have constantly used any number of Strong's statements to prove that the Protestant establishment in general and religious liberals in particular tended to be fatuously optimistic and totally unaware of the propensities of human beings and nation-states to behave in terms of their own short term interests and not philanthropically. Typical of the kind of statements Strong would make are his observations on the military made in 1900: "As the world is being gradually civilized and civilization is gradually being Christianized, armies are finding new occupations. As *The Outlook* says, 'The army among Anglo-Saxon peoples is no longer a mere instrument of destruction. It is a great reconstructive organization.'"

Given the present state of the evidence and the lack of a thorough and evenhanded biography it is difficult to make a very good case in Josiah Strong's behalf. He did reflect a major tendency in American thinking about the nation and its future. Beyond this, he was given to strong and effusive utterance. Furthermore he did come very close to identifying Christianity and American or Anglo-Saxon civilization. Beyond any doubt he did espouse and preach a strong but semi-secularized postmillenialism that strengthened the American's old propensity to regard the United States as an Elect Nation.

On the other hand there are some grounds for mitigating some of these harsh judgments. First and most generally it must be said that he was criticized in his own time by only a very small minority, whereas his positive proposals were echoed and applauded in all quarters, in the election campaigns of both parties, and by most occupants of the White House. In this same sense his use of the term "Anglo-Saxon" and "race" would have to be interpreted as typical of a prevailing way of thinking; thus they reflect the nation's racism and do not stand out as especially malignant instances. Perhaps the most important thing that needs to be said in Strong's behalf is that he saw the blight of the cities and the vast ranges of social injustice which industrialism and exploitation were creating. If the Social Gospel and its secular corollary, Progressivism, deserve any credit, then so does Josiah Strong. Indeed he more than any other made it possible to speak of the Social Gospel as a *movement*.

Strong was born in Naperville, Illinois, but his parents moved to Ohio, where he attended Western Reserve College, graduating in 1869. He then attended Lane Theological Seminary in Cincinnati and began his ministerial career with a two year's pastorate in the Congregational Church of Cheyenne, Wyoming, after which he returned to Western Reserve for three years as a chaplain and instructor in religion. Then followed a ministry in Sandusky, Ohio, a term as Secretary of the Home Missionary Society for his region. During this long period Strong was outwardly successful but he remained inwardly dissatisfied until he became minister of the Central Congregational Church in Cincinnati in 1884. In the following year he published the book that made him famous, *Our Country: Its Possible Future and Its Present Crisis* (1885). To implement this book's program for action, he then convened a great interdenominational congress of social reformers, and later followed up these efforts with three other influential conferences, in 1887, 1889 and 1893. Becoming general secretary of the Evangelical Alliance in 1886, he also gave an organized ecumenical structure to the movement he was trying to galvanize. And it was to further this aim and to provide a broad and inspiring manifesto for the conference of 1893 that he wrote the present book: *The New Era, or The Coming Kingdom*, (1893). This meeting was linked with the great Columbian Exposition in Chicago and the book was therefore published simultaneously in England and America. In it his intense preoccupation with the church's responsibilities for the city was restated, and he quoted extensively from *Our Country* to underline the nation's worldwide responsibilities. The conference was an immense success and the book took its place in American history, and not only as a monument to Josiah Strong's zeal but as a great representative statement of a movement and an era.

Bibliographical Suggestions:

The spirit and context of Strong's labors are best seen in Charles H. Hopkins, *The Rise of the Social Gospel in American Protestantism, 1865-1915* (New Haven: Yale University Press, 1940) and Robert T. Handy, *A Christian America: Protestant Hopes and Historical Realities* (New York: Oxford University Press, 1971. On Strong's thought see Dorothea R. Muller, "The Social Philosophy of Josiah Strong: Social Christianity and American Progressivism," *Church History*, XXVIII (1959), pp. 183-201.

THE NEW ERA

OR

THE COMING KINGDOM

BY

Rev. JOSIAH STRONG, D.D.

General Secretary of the Evangelical Alliance for the United States;
Author of " Our Country "

FORTY-FIRST THOUSAND.

" The Present Time—youngest born of Eternity, child and heir of all the Past Times with their good and evil, and parent of all the Future—is ever a ' New Era ' to the thinking man. . . . To *know* it, and what it bids us do, is ever the sum of knowledge for all of us."
—Thomas Carlyle.

" Lift up your eyes, and you may see another stadium of history advancing. Its aim will be to realize the Christianity of Christ himself, which is about to renew its youth by taking to heart the Sermon on the Mount. He that sitteth on the throne is saying : ' Behold, I make all things new.' This earth is yet to be redeemed, soul and body, with all its peoples, occupations, and interests."
—Roswell D. Hitchcock.

NEW YORK

THE BAKER & TAYLOR CO.

5 AND 7 EAST SIXTEENTH ST.

PREFACE.

It is a common observation that we are living in a period of transition. Such periods are always characterized by uncertainty and anxiety, by difficult problems and by great opportunities. Of these we hear much; but I know of no one who has attempted to show *why* this is a period of transition, or to point out its relations to the past and future and thus interpret its meaning. This volume is such an attempt. I have tried to lay hold of fundamental laws and principles and to apply them to the explanation of existing conditions and to the solution of the great problems of the age.

The reader will see that the treatment of subjects has been suggestive rather than exhaustive; to have done them full justice each chapter should have been a volume.

Considerable portions of addresses made before a meeting of the Evangelical Alliance for the United States in Boston, a meeting of the Canadian Evangelical Alliance in Montreal, a union meeting of the Congregational and Presbyterian clubs of Minneapolis and St. Paul, and the International Convention of Christian Workers in New York, have been used. Also, with the kind permission of editors or publishers, I have made some use of articles written for the *Review of Reviews*, the *Chautauquan*, *Our Day*, the *New York Observer*, the *Christian at Work*, the *Independent*, and for a volume entitled "Parish Problems," published by the Century Company.

I am indebted to Rev. D. W. Waldron of Boston, Dr. A. Ritchie of Cincinnati, Rev. J. C. Armstrong of Chi- cago, and Mr. George D. Kellogg of St. Louis for infor- mation concerning their respective cities; and especially to Mr. William E. Dodge and Rev. Horace G. Hoadley for helpful documents and references. I desire also to acknowledge my obligations to Mr. Thomas D. Seymour of Yale University, a former fellow-student, and to Dr. Carroll Cutler, a former instructor, for kindly listening to the reading of a considerable portion of the manu- script and for the benefit of their valuable judgment.

J. S.

NEW YORK, June, 1898.

CONTENTS.

CHAPTER I.

THE NINETEENTH CENTURY ONE OF PREPARATION.

CHAPTER II.

THE DESTINY OF THE RACE.

confirmed by man's constitution, by Revelation, by history, by science.

Progress toward a perfected society to be much more rapid in future. Tendency to sacrifice the development of the individual to the organization of society, or *vice versa*. The former characterizes the civilizations of Asia, the latter those of Europe. China and Greece. Same tendency in religion. Romanism and Protestantism. The development of the individual and the organization of society not conflicting but correlative. Now, for the first time, conditions favorable to the one are favorable to the other, hence unprecedented progress.

Time has come for men to aid the development of these two principles intelligently. Development of individual must be harmonious. Dignity and worth of the body. Depreciation of the body among Christians. Christian civilization preserves defective classes. Cultivation reduces fecundity. The New England stock "dying out." The survival of the unfittest. The remedy. The more perfect organization of society. This also must be harmonious. The physical. The intellectual. The spiritual. The final unity in diversity. P. 17.

CHAPTER III.

THE CONTRIBUTION MADE BY THE THREE GREAT RACES OF ANTIQUITY.

Preparation of the world for the inauguration of the kingdom of God. Threefold—physical, intellectual, spiritual.

Spiritual preparation by the Hebrew. Monotheism the germinal principle of the nation. Meaning of Egyptian bondage. Occupation. Exclusiveness. Spirit of the nation. Captivity. Conception of Jehovah. Compared with that of surrounding peoples. Dispersion. A prepared soil for the seed of Christianity.

Intellectual preparation by the Greeks. Their home. Coastline. Mountain system. Mixed origin of tribes. Climate. Openair life. Love of the beautiful. Perfection of language. Centrifugal tendency. Dissemination of language.

Physical preparation by the Romans. Universal empire. Roads. Lines of preparation centred in Judæa.

Further preparation. Three great failures. The Hebrews and ritualism. The Greeks and culture. The Romans and law.

Essential difference between morality and true religion. The "fulness of time." P. 41.

CHAPTER IV.

THE CONTRIBUTION MADE BY THE ANGLO-SAXON.

The qualities which made the Hebrews, Greeks, and Romans supreme in their respective spheres *all* unite in the Anglo-Saxon race.

Religious life. Missionary ardor. Representation of races at World's Missionary Conference, London, 1888. As the Hebrew carried his pure monotheism around the Mediterranean, so the Anglo-Saxon is carrying a spiritual Christianity around the world.

Intellectual life. English literature. Statesmanship. Language. Schaff, Candolle, Weisse, and Grimm quoted. Tables showing progress of English language. Causes of rapid extension. As the Greek carried his language and civilization around the Mediterranean, so the Anglo-Saxon is carrying his around the world.

Mastery of physical conditions. Inventive power. Control of the world's communications. Wealth. Growth of Anglo-Saxon race. Its extension. Superiority of Anglo-Saxon empire to Roman.

This race unites the individualism of the Greeks with the organizing genius of the Romans. Union of culture and religion. The three essential elements of a perfect civilization, each in an eminent degree, unite in Anglo-Saxon civilization.

The home of the Anglo-Saxon compared with those of the Hebrew, Greek, and Roman. Necessity of adequate physical basis for national greatness in the future. The United States a hundred years hence. We co-ordinate the two principles of individualism and organization in their application to government better than any other people. Conditions more favorable here than elsewhere for solving social problems. Interpretation of these facts. Corollaries. P. 52.

CHAPTER V.

THE AUTHORITATIVE TEACHER.

If the character and life presented in the Gospels are genuine, the teachings of Jesus are authoritative. Those who reject their

CHAPTER VI.

THE TWO FUNDAMENTAL LAWS.

Man sustains relations to God and to his fellow-men ; hence
the two lines of progress, already traced, along which civilization

CHAPTER VII.

POPULAR DISCONTENT.

CHAPTER X.

THE SEPARATION OF THE MASSES FROM THE CHURCH.

The fact of separation. The fact that the churches are gaining on the population no evidence against such separation. Less than half the people profess to attend church. Vermont. Maine. New York. The South. The West. Means of estimating non-church-goers where canvass has not been made.

Generally workingmen and farmers on whom the churches have lost their hold. Situation much the same in England.

Causes. 1. Ideas of duty less strict than formerly. 2. Continental ideas of the Sabbath. 3. Rush of modern life. 4. Rivals of the pulpit. 5. "The Sunday-school the children's church." 6. Nomadic habits of life. 7. Lay inactivity; pastors' hands full. 8. Ownership of church pews. 9. Church dress. 10. Indifference both of church-goers and non-church-goers. 11. "Total depravity." None of these causes the cause, viz., the fact that the churches have failed to teach and to exemplify the gospel of human brotherhood.

Christian work has become largely institutional instead of personal, and, therefore, largely mechanical instead of vital. Self-giving the proof of love. Church habits and methods signally fail to manifest a personal love for non-church-goers.

Significance of this separation. The discontented class and the non-church-going class substantially the same. It is the masses who are discontented; the masses who rule; the masses on whom the church has lost her hold. P. 203.

CHAPTER XI.

THE MISSION OF THE CHURCH.

A vicious dualism, the "sacred" and the "secular." The church accepts the "sacred" as her sphere. Were thirty of Christ's years "secular" and only three "sacred"? His teaching. His example All things sacred or *unholy*. God's kingdom one. Importance of the physical. Natural laws expressions of the divine will. They are laws of the Kingdom. *All* of God's laws will be obeyed when his will is "done on earth as it is in heaven."

CHAPTER XII.

THE NECESSITY OF NEW METHODS.

CHAPTER XIII.

THE NECESSITY OF PERSONAL CONTACT.

CHAPTER XV.

THE TWO GREAT PRINCIPLES APPLIED TO THE TWO GREAT PROBLEMS.

substitute for morals. Remedy must be found in *men.* Municipal elections must be emancipated from politics. Co-operation of
good citizens. 2. The peculiar difficultities of city evangelization
and the two great principles. Two cities in one. The residence
portion ; the business portion. Difference of treatment required.
For the business and tenement portion the methods of the McAll
Mission and of the institutional church. Wide difference between these methods and those commonly in use. Marvels
wrought by the McAll Mission. How to provide down-town districts with institutional churches. The city missionary society.
House-to-house visitation. Trained visitors, nurses, and kinder-
garteners. Deaconesses ; a training-school and home for them.
Dr. Chalmers's work in Edinburgh. P. 318.

CHAPTER XVI.

AN ENTHUSIASM FOR HUMANITY.

The sense of humanity. The oneness of the race. The age of
homespun. The influence of industrial changes. Illustrations.

The race united in its succeeding generations. Heredity. Margaret, the mother of criminals. A new sense in which the race is
becoming one. An enlightened selfishness compels us to care for
others. The higher social organization of the future demands a
nobler bond. An enthusiasm for humanity.

A recapitulation shows that the church must make the Kingdom the object of endeavor, and enter on the work with a burning
enthusiam.

How is such enthusiasm to be kindled and sustained ?

The enthusiasm for humanity shown by the early Christians
was kindled by a new valuation of human nature. By the revelation of human nature seen in Christ. By the teaching that debased human nature was savable. By the passion of love which
they felt for Christ. By the revelation of the brotherhood of the
race, and the preaching of the kingdom of God.

All of these sources of enthusiasm save one opened afresh in
modern times. Special reasons why this generation should show
an enthusiasm for humanity. Anglo-Saxons. Americans. Need
of divine quickening. Conviction on fire. Judson.

An enthusiasm for humanity would move the American church,
to discharge her duty to China and Africa.

THE NEW ERA.

CHAPTER I.

THE NINETEENTH CENTURY ONE OF PREPARATION.

WE are entering on a new era of which the twentieth century will be the beginning and for which the nineteenth century has been a preparation.

The great movements and events which mark the centuries have very commonly come to a definite close, as did the Crusades and the French Revolution. Though their results may be lasting, they are the results of spent forces. But the great movements which characterize the nineteenth century generally suggest, not finality or completeness, but rather beginnings. Many and great as have been the changes of this century, there is reason to expect that those of the next will be even more and greater. It is not proposed to call on the imagination to anticipate them. This work is not speculative. It does, however, attempt to trace some of the general lines of development in the past, to note their present trend, and, within certain limits, to project them into the future. It is quite true, as Lowell remarks, that "the course of events is apt to show itself humorously careless of the reputation of prophets." But surely one may study discerningly the signs of the times, which are only the shadows of coming events cast before, without attempting the prophetic *rôle*.

If events were simply strung together in orderly fashion on the thread of time, like beads on a string, without any relation of cause and effect, there could be no signs of the times. But because to-morrow is folded within to-day, because human nature and its development are under laws which remain constant from age to age, because, as Carlyle says, "the centuries are all lineal children of one another" and bound by the law of heredity like other offspring, it becomes possible, in a measure, to forecast coming events, to draw from the study of past experiences and present conditions reasonable inferences concerning the future.

Let us glance hastily at some of the more significant changes which have taken place during the past century and note their meaning.

1st. Changes which may be called physical. There is nothing more fundamental touching the circumstances which affect all human beings than time and space. They condition all human activities and relationships, and hence to change them is to affect all human activities and relationships. This is the reason that steam and electricity have had so profound an influence on modern civilization. They have materially changed these two great factors that enter into all lives. It is as if the earth had been, in two or three generations, reduced to a much smaller scale and set spinning on its axis at a far greater speed. As a result, men have been brought into much closer relations and the world's rate of progress has been wonderfully quickened. Time-saving methods and appliances now crowd into a day business which a generation ago would have occupied a week or more. The passage of the Atlantic which once required weeks is now a matter of days. It is possible to be in the United States one week and before the close of the next in Asia. A little time suffices to compass great events as well as great distances. We read of the "Thirty Years' War" in the seventeenth century; the Franco-Prussian war, which destroyed one empire and created another, was begun and *practically* ended in

thirty days.[1] By reason of the increased ease of communication new ideas are more speedily popularized,
public opinion more quickly formed and more readily
expressed; both thought and action are stimulated; reforms are sooner accomplished, and great changes of
every sort are crowded into as many years as once they
would have required generations or even centuries.

And it must be remembered that these quickening
processes are not yet completed or their results fully
apparent. Science is daily making easier the conquest
of space; and there is reason to believe that the victories of electricity are only well begun.

Thus these changing physical conditions will continue
to render the isolation of any people increasingly difficult—a fact of the utmost importance to the world's
progress, for isolation results in stagnation, and we
accordingly find that the *civilization of all peoples is
inversely as their isolation.* The conformation of
Europe and the exceeding irregularity of her coast-line
are favorable to the intercourse of her various nations
with each other and the world, and Europe has developed the highest civilization. Moreover those of her
peoples who are most favorably located for intercourse
with their neighbors have made the most progress.
The great mountain ranges of Asia, her vast plains, together with oceans so broad as to discourage the timid
navigators of earlier centuries are much less favorable
to intercourse, and the civilization of Asia is much
lower than that of Europe. That part of Africa which
lies on the Mediterranean has been in contact with the
world and has had at times a high civilization. But
the remainder of the continent has been for the most
part a *terra incognita.* Her people have looked out,
not upon the highway of narrow seas or straits, but
upon the barriers of boundless oceans. The location

---

[1] The hostile armies first came into collision Aug. 2, 1870, and the battle
of Sedan, which was decisive of the final result and was followed next day
by the surrender of the emperor with an army of more than 80,000 men, was
fought Sept. 1.

of Africa and her coast-line are much less fávorable to intercourse than those of Asia, her people have been much more isolated, and there we find a lower barbarism than any in Asia.

The world is entering on an era in which the isolation of any people will become impossible and then will the world's barbarism disappear.

2d. Notice briefly the political changes of the past century. The explanation of most of them is found in the growth of democracy.

During the eighteenth century the spirit of free inquiry became universal in Europe, but it was purely speculative. Though England enjoyed a measure of liberty, absolutism still reigned on the Continent. For sixty years of that century Louis XV. disgraced the throne of France. He regarded the people of his domain as his personal property. Their lives and substance were at his disposal. But wretched and enslaved as was the condition of the French, that of other Continental nations is shown by De Tocqueville to have been even worse.

The French Revolution made the people conscious of their power, and hence prepared the way for liberty as soon as the people should become capable of it. Napoleon in accomplishing his own selfish and despotic purposes did inestimable service to popular rights, and though, upon his fall, the old order of things was re-established for a season, at least in form, absolutism from that time on must needs reckon with the growing spirit of democracy.

Says Robert Mackenzie[1]: "Sixty years ago Europe was an aggregate of despotic powers, disposing at their own pleasure of the lives and property of their subjects; . . . to-day the men of Western Europe govern themselves. Popular suffrage, more or less closely approaching universal, chooses the governing power, and by methods more or less effective dictates its policy.

---

[1] The Nineteenth Century, p. 459.

One hundred and eighty million Europeans have risen from a degraded and ever dissatisfied vassalage to the rank of free and self-governing men." When we remember that freedom is the most favorable condition for a natural, healthful development, we see the significance of the growth of modern democracy. This great political change is prophetic of progress because it has removed the barriers which most seriously obstruct progress.

3d. Consider now certain social changes. Since the middle of the century there has sprung up and spread well-nigh throughout Christendom a deep discontent on the part of workingmen. Its causes and its significance will furnish the subject of a later chapter (VII), in which it will be shown that this popular discontent foreshadows important changes in our civilization. Suffice it now to remark that a condition of *political* equality having been achieved, it is short-sighted to suppose that society has, therefore, arrived at a state of stable equilibrium. Democracy necessitates popular education, and popular education multiplies popular wants. If the many have the same wants as the few, they will demand the same means of gratifying those wants. To give to the poor like tastes with the rich is to create an inevitable demand for substantial equality of condition and to stimulate discontent until such equality is secured.

The discontent of labor has gained such a hearing that there has been awakened within a few years an unprecedented interest in industrial and all sociological questions. Books treating these subjects have had an astonishing circulation. A large number of periodicals devoted to social economy and advocating industrial, economic, or social reforms have sprung into existence. Labor organizations, whose avowed object it is to effect important changes in the laws and in the whole status of labor, have appeared and grown powerful. Advocates of the reorganization of industry on a co-operative instead of a competitive basis have made many disciples.

The word Socialism is growing less obnoxious to Americans. It is, as Dr. Gladden says, being "fumigated." And it has needed it, for some foul meanings have infested it. Socialism, separated from all adventitious doctrines, has been accepted by many Christian men and women of the American stock, and among them are many of the younger clergy.

The growth of socialism in Germany during the past twenty years has been surprising. The socialist vcte for members of the Reichstag in 1871 was 124,655; in 1890 it was 1,341,587. Schmoller well remarks: "A social movement of thousands is possible only when thousands of thousands have become doubters."

The German government has taken an important step toward state socialism by insuring German workingmen against illness, accident, and old age, making such insurance compulsory. Like measures have been proposed in France, Hungary, and Denmark. "The question at issue among most Continental statesmen and students to-day concerns the details rather than the principle of such state help. The era of full reaction against *laissez-faire* theory and practice has come and Emperor William II. is its prophet." [1]

Taken in connection with the discontent of workingmen and an increasing readiness on the part of society to listen to their demands for change, there is great significance in the tendency toward organization and centralization which is seen everywhere.

The progress of the race has been along two lines, viz., the development of the individual and the organization of society, the kind of organization of which society is capable being dependent on the measure or type of development attained by the individual. In the history of Europe, for centuries together, progress seems to have been along only one of these lines at a time—a development of the individual at the expense of social organization, followed by a closer organization

---

[1] G. W. Hinman, in *The Social Economist*, April, 1891.

of society, a centralization of power at the expense of personal liberty. Thus when society began to emerge from the lawless individualism of the barbarians it was organized under the aristocratic form and then passed into the more centralized form of absolutism, which culminated in the seventeenth century and under which individual rights were ruthlessly sacrificed. In the next century the reaction toward individualism came with the French Revolution. The remarkable growth of democracy during the past one hundred years, which of course meant the development of individualism, has already been noticed. And now we see unmistakable evidence that the pendulum of the ages has again begun to swing in the direction of a closer organization of society, which movement is greatly facilitated by the increased ease of communication afforded by steam and electricity.

Look at some of the evidence of this reaction. In the commercial world the tendency toward consolidation is most striking. First, many independent railway corporations were united into a system, and now great systems are being consolidated under one management. The same is true of telegraph lines. A like tendency is seen in all kinds of production. In various lines of manufactures there appear an increasing output and a *decreasing* number of factories, showing of course consolidation. This tendency must continue so long as production on a large scale is cheaper than production on a small scale. "The following statements have recently been made in California, on what is claimed to be good authority (*Overland Monthly*), of the comparative cost of growing wheat in that State on ranches, or farms of different sizes. On ranches of 1,000 acres, the average cost is reported at 92½ cents per 100 pounds; on 2,000 acres, 85 cents; on 6,000 acres, 75 cents; on 15,000 acres, 60 cents; on 30,000 acres, 50 cents; and on 50,000 acres, 40 cents." [1]

---

[1] D. A. Wells' Recent Economic Changes, p. 99.

One of the most striking features of the modern business world is the growth of powerful corporations and more powerful combinations in the form of "pools," "trusts," and "syndicates." The conditions of production and transportation have largely ceased to be democratic; and the question may be reasonably asked, Can our government remain democratic and our industries continue aristocratic or monarchic—that is, controlled by the corporation or the industrial "king"? Mr. Alexander Johnston says[1]: "The great American republic seems to be entering upon a new era, in which it must meet and solve a new problem—the reconciliation of democracy with the modern conditions of production."

Ever since our civil war there has been a marked tendency toward the centralization of the government of the United States. Justice Miller, in an address at Philadelphia on the occasion of the centennial celebration of the adoption of the Constitution, said: "While the pendulum of public opinion has swung with much force away from the extreme point of states-rights doctrine, there may be danger of its reaching an extreme point on the other side."

This centripetal tendency of the times is further illustrated by the creation of the Kingdom of Italy and the Empire of Germany out of political fragments. In the latter part of the eighteenth century there were in Germany nearly three hundred independent powers.

Another manifestation of the same tendency is seen in the wonderful drift of population to the cities, which seems to be a world-phenomenon.

So general a tendency toward the centralization of population, of political power, of capital, and of production, manifested in ways so various, can indicate nothing less than a great movement toward a closer organization of society, a new development of civilization.

Thoughtful men everywhere have become expectant

---

[1] Encyclopædia Britannica, Vol. XXIII. p. 787.

of great social changes. Says President Andrews of
Brown University[1]: "If anything has been made certain by the economic revolution of the last twenty-five
years, it is that society cannot much longer get on
upon the old libertarian, competitive, go-as-you-please
system to which so many sensible persons seem ad-
dicted. The population of the great nations is becoming too condensed for that."

Bishop Westcott, while professor at Cambridge,
wrote[2]: "On every side imperious voices trouble the
repose which our indolence would wish to keep undis-
turbed. We can no longer dwell apart in secure isolation. The main interests of men are once again passing
through a great change. They are most surely turning
from the individual to the society." The author of
"God in His World" remarks[3]: "We are now approaching such a crisis. No human wisdom can pre-
dict its shaping any more than it can prevent the
issue. The air is full of auguries, and even our fiction has become very precisely apocalyptic. It is
theoretic prophecy, anticipating the realization of perfect scientific and social economics—the Paradise of
Outward Comfortableness." *The Westminster Review*
says[4]: "It is felt by every student and every statesman that some movement vast and momentous,
though indefinite, is passing like a great wave over
the civilized world." And *The Churchman* says[5]:
"It is idle to refuse to admit the fact that modern
civilization is in a transition state. . . . There are a
thousand evidences that the present state of things is
drawing to a close, and that some new development of
social organization is at hand." Says Mr. William T.
Stead[6]: "Everywhere the old order is changing and
giving place unto the new. The human race is now at
one of the crucial periods in its history when the fountains of the great deep are broken up, and the flood of

---

[1] *The Congregationalist*, Jan. 22, 1891. [2] Social Aspects of Christianity, p. 4.
[3] Page xxv. [4] London, May, 1890.
[5] New York, Jan. 17, 1891. [6] The Pope and the New Era, p. 20.

change submerges all the old-established institutions and conventions in the midst of which preceding generations have lived and died." Such citations might be indefinitely multiplied.

Many expect violent revolution. Whether such expectations are realized will depend probably on the Christian church, whether she is sufficiently awake to see and to seize her opportunity. The church is not yet adequately aroused, but I believe that she can be, and therefore do not deem revolution probable. We *may* have social *revolution*, we *must* have social *evolution*. Social systems are never invented, they are evolved, they grow out of what has preceded. A revolution may suddenly sweep away existing institutions as a fire destroys a forest, but the new forest which rises out of the ashes is a growth. Surely it is too late for the world—or at least the Anglo-Saxon part of it—to fall into the "French fallacy that a new system of government" or a new social organization "can be ordered like a new suit of clothes."[1] The social changes which are sure to come will doubtless be great, but they will be natural—the effects of causes long antecedent ; hence the importance of comprehending, as far as possible, existing conditions and tendencies.

4th. Consider now briefly a few suggestions touching the changes of which the progress of science is prophetic.

Most of our scientific knowledge is the growth of the past century. It would be idle to attempt even to enumerate its practical applications to life. By making communication easy and swift science has affected all human relations and conditions: by perfecting the press it has popularized knowledge and powerfully stimulated the mind; by means of labor-saving appliances it has revolutionized the industrial world and added enormously to the world's wealth, awakened new aspirations on the part of the multitude

---

[1] James Russell Lowell's " Democracy," p. 23.

and created new problems and possibilities of life. If all that science has done for the world during this century were suddenly struck out, it would leave our civilization in ruins; so universal and profound would be the changes wrought that we should hardly know whether we were living on this planet or had been mysteriously transferred to some other. And we must remember that much of the progress of science is so recent that as yet we have seen scarcely a beginning of its endless applications to life. Moreover some of the most practical sciences are still in their infancy; the field of knowledge is boundless, and each new acquisition makes others more easy. We must remember also that a great body of men are making it their business to extend science; and while discovery and invention were once accidental, they have now become the specialty of many. Science is certainly destined to make great progress during the next century and, therefore, to work great additional changes in civilization.

What if it could be certainly known that during the twentieth century there would be a new revelation of God's will, another table of the divine law given to men to meet new needs of civilization and to hasten the coming of the kingdom of heaven upon earth; and so given as to authenticate itself and carry conviction of its truth to all the world? With what profound and eager expectation would it be awaited! What supreme blessings should we expect it to bestow on mankind, and what a mighty upward impetus would it give the race!

Just such a revelation has been made during the past century and is to be continued in the next. Its truth is evident, but all do not yet perceive that the truths of science are God's truths, that its laws are God's laws. The church has even looked askance at it. It has been regarded not only as secular but as actually hostile to religion. Books have been written and professorships established to "reconcile," if possible, these two "foes." But Clement of Alexandria was quite right when he refused to make any distinction "between what man discovers and what God reveals." Science discovers natural laws and processes; and if God is really the ruler of the universe, the laws and processes of nature are only the divine purposes and methods. Science is therefore as truly a revelation from God and of God as are the Scriptures, as really a revelation of his will as was the Decalogue, and one which is to have as real a part in the coming of his kingdom among men as the New Testament. God's will expressed in what we call natural law is as benevolent and as sacred as his will expressed in what we call moral law. The more perfectly his law, whether natural or moral, is known and obeyed, the better is it for the race. This new evangel of science means new blessings to mankind, a new extension of the kingdom. The church ought to leap for joy that in modern times God has raised up these new prophets of his truth. It will be shown later that this modern revelation of his will means a mighty hastening of the day when his will is to be done on earth as it is in heaven.

One of the great services which science has rendered has been to clear the world of an immense amount of rubbish which lay in the path of progress. The scientific habit of mind is fatal to credulity and superstition; it rests not on opinions, but facts; it is loyal, not to authority, but truth. This means that as the scientific habit of mind obtains, men will break away from the superstitions of heathenism and from the superstitious forms of Christianity. Scientific knowledge is rapidly becoming a necessity to all civilized peoples. Commerce is bringing the nations into an ever closer contact, which means increasing competition, and however cheap flesh and blood may be, they cannot compete with steam and steel. The Bureau of Statistics at Berlin estimated in 1887 that the steam-engines then at work in the world represented approximately 1,000,000,-000 men, or three times the working population of the earth. This mighty force is at work for the *Christian* nations. What are all the millions of China and India compared with it? Cheap labor cannot compete with machinery which enables one man to do the work of ten or twenty or a hundred men. Labor-saving machinery is destined to go wherever men toil, and with it will go an increasing knowledge of science.

Moreover China, hating foreigners, wishes to become independent of them. She has been compelled to employ them to build her navy, to arm her soldiers and make her munitions of war. In order to become independent of them she must needs introduce the study of the sciences into her schools. Thus science is destined to become the great iconoclast of the heathen world. What then? Men react from superstition into infidelity, which has already become the great peril of Japan and is becoming the peril of India. The greatest of modern Hindoos, Keshub Chunder Sen, once said: "I fear for my countrymen that they will sink from the hell of heathenism into the deeper hell of infidelity." The prospect is that in the course of a few generations the heathen world will become either Christian or agnostic. Which it will become will depend on the church.

In this connection we may not inappropriately remind ourselves of the familiar and significant changes which have already taken place during the past century among heathen and Mohammedan peoples.[1]

A hundred years ago the Japanese were so separated from the remainder of mankind that so far as any intercourse is concerned they might almost as well have inhabited the moon. There was then in force a law providing that "no ship or native of Japan should quit the country under pain of forfeiture and death; that any Japanese returning from a foreign country should be put to death; that no nobleman or soldier should be suffered to purchase anything from a foreigner; that any person bringing a letter from abroad . . . should die

---

[1] For a full and able discussion of these changes see that missionary classic, "The Crisis of Missions," by Rev. A. T. Pierson, D.D.

together with all his family and any who might pre-
sume to intercede for him."

Until within a few years the following royal rescript,
issued on the extirpation of the Jesuits, remained
posted up through all the kingdom: "So long as the
sun shall warm the earth let no Christian be so bold as
to come to Japan; and let all know that the king of
Spain himself, or the Christian's God, or the great God
of all, if he violate this command, shall pay for it with
his head." To-day there is a new civilization in Japan.
As a Japanese lecturer said, there is nothing left as it
was thirty years ago, "except the natural scenery." [1]
The nation is now eager to place itself in the forefront
of progress.

China has for centuries been separated from the
world by a barrier far more effectual than her famous
"Myriad-Mile Wall"—a wall of pride and prejudice,
more immovable, more impenetrable, more insurmount-
able than any possible wall of stone and mortar.

But a trial of arms with Great Britain and France
taught China a wholesome respect for Western Powers;
and her pride was sufficiently humbled to employ foreigners to teach her sons ship-building and navigation,
together with the military science by which her armies
had been beaten.

The war of 1856 resulted in the Treaty of Tientsin,
which guarantees the protection of the Chinese authorities to all persons teaching or professing the Christian
religion, thus opening the door to Christian civilization.

At the beginning of this century the gates of India
were locked to Christian missions and the East India
Company held the key. That company was hostile to
missions because it received large revenues from native
idolatries, and "as late as 1852 $3,750,000 were paid
from public funds to repair temples, provide new idols
and idol-cars, and support a pagan priesthood." [2]

The East India Company was abolished in 1858, and

---

[1] The Crisis of Missions, p. 100.   [2] Ibid. p. 48.

the British Government is in hearty sympathy with Christian missions in India. Its officials there annually contribute many thousands of pounds for their maintenance. Moreover social caste, which in India separates classes as oceans separate continents, and which has served to maintain isolation and stagnation, is giving way before modern civilization, which is every where bringing men into closer relations.

At the opening of the nineteenth century the Ottoman Empire was characterized by the same spirit which had once rendered it a terror to Christian nations. To-day the Protestants of Turkey, like the other religionists of the empire, have their recognized rights and a representative at the imperial city, religious liberty having been assured by the Treaty of Berlin.

Only a few years ago the vast interior of the Dark Continent was a mystery. Now the great "open sore of the world" has been thoroughly probed—a long step toward its healing.

The changes which have been very briefly recited have a significance which is simply boundless. During this century the barriers which separated more than 800,000,000 heathen from the transforming influences of modern and Christian civilization have been broken down. The prison-pens which condemned more than one half of the human family to isolation and, therefore, stagnation have been thrown open. The contact of the Occident and the Orient has already produced in the latter unwonted signs of life. The dead crust of fossil faiths is beginning to be shattered by the movements of new life underneath. "In every corner of the world," says Mr. Froude,[1] "there is the same phenomenon of the decay of established religions. . . . Among the Mohammedans, Jews, Buddhists, Brahmins, traditionary creeds are loosing their hold. An intellectual revolution is sweeping over the world, breaking down

---

[1] *North American Review*, December, 1879.

established opinions, dissolving foundations on which historical faiths have been built up." And it should not be forgotten that religious beliefs underlie and determine social and political institutions.

The door " great and effectual " which is thus opened to the Christian church has been only partially entered. Noble as has been the work of modern missions, it must be regarded chiefly as one of preparation. The languages of savage peoples have been reduced to writing, the Bible and a Christian literature have been translated into tongues spoken by hundreds of millions, schools and seminaries for training up a native ministry have been established, missionaries have learned much of native character and of the necessary conditions of success. A foothold has been secured, a fulcrum found, the gospel lever put in place, and the near future will see the mighty uplift.

We have cast a hasty glance over Christendom and heathendom, and have sought to interpret briefly, though not superficially, the great changes of the century. They seem to me to point unmistakably to one conclusion. The drawing of the peoples of the earth into ever closer relations, which will render isolation and, therefore, barbarism impossible and will operate as a constant stimulus; the growth of freedom which removes the greatest barriers to progress; the social ferment and the evident tendency toward a new social organization; the progress of science, destroying superstition, thus clearing the way for truth; the opening of the heathen world to the power of the Gospel and the quickening forces of modern life; the evident crumbling of heathen religions, which means the loosening of the foundations of heathen society—surely all these indicate that the world is about to enter on a new era, for which the nineteenth century has been the John the Baptist.

> "Out of the shadow of night
> The world moves into light ;
> It is daybreak everywhere !"
> LONGFELLOW

CHAPTER II.

IT is evidence of a narrow and thoughtless mind to imagine that the existing condition of things is final. Certainly no condition of society that has ever existed has been final, and none ever can be until perfection is reached; and no one surely will contend that society as now organized is perfect; no one will imagine that man has already attained the highest development of which he is capable.

Obviously the body was intended to serve the intelligence. Limbs and bodily organs are the instruments of the higher nature. Evidently, then, so long as the great mass of mankind are chiefly concerned from morning till night to obtain the necessaries of life, so long as the intelligence plans and the will strives above all things to find covering for limbs and bread for mouth, there is manifest perversion, the higher nature has become the slave of its own servant. Such inversion is unnatural; such a condition of things cannot be final. It is not what God intended for the race when he gave man a spiritual nature.

> " If life's to be filled with drudgery, what need
> of a human soul ?"

When we think of what man is capable—that he may search out the secrets of nature and "think God's thoughts after him;" that he may become sensitive to all beauty and delight himself in the harmonies of sound, of color, of form, of numbers, of laws; that he is capable of a self-forgetting love even unto death for his fellow-men; that he is capable of high aspirations, of

17

spiritual struggle and victory, of entering into God's great plans for the race and attaining a divine harmony of thought and feeling and purpose with the Highest;— when we think of the high plane on which he is capable of living and then remember where he is, and consider that to most of the race, even as to the brutes, life is one long, weary struggle to supply *animal wants*, surely we must look upon the race as in a low and early stage of development.

Have we any means of judging of the future development of the race and of its destiny? If we find that its progress thus far has been along certain lines from the beginning, we may reasonably infer that it will continue to move along those same lines in the future, and we may rest in this conclusion with the greater confidence if these projected lines lead up to a consummation foretold both by revelation and science, the agreement of which is an evidence that the interpretation of both is correct.

Science has discovered that underlying the wonderful complexity of nature there is a no less wonderful unity, and confirms that highest of all generalizations expressed in the word *universe*, which declares that all creation is a whole. The scope of Humboldt's great work, the *Kosmos*, was to show the unity which exists amid the complexity of nature. There would be no propriety in speaking of the mineral, vegetable, and animal *kingdoms*, were not their endless varieties brought under the sceptre of unifying laws. *Unity in diversity seems to be the fundamental law of the universe.* Broader than the law of gravitation, which embraces only the physical creation; broader than the laws of thought, which are confined to the intellectual world; and broader than the law of love, which is binding only in the moral realm, this basal law unites these several spheres in one infinite whole, including, as it seems, all created existence, and finds its highest illustration in the highest of all existences, even the Creator himself, who has revealed himself to us as the triune God.

But many who see that unity in diversity is the great
law of nature fail to perceive that it is also the great
law of history, that

"Through the ages one increasing purpose runs."[1]

There could be no philosophy of history if there were
no laws, no purpose or plan running through the whole,
bringing into relations with each other events which
seem wholly disconnected and sporadic. The atheist is
unable to account for such unity, if he perceives it,
and the agnostic does not attempt to account for it;
but the theist finds this profound fact in perfect harmony with his belief in an Infinite Intelligence who
created and now governs the universe, and governs it
with reference to a definite and benevolent outcome.

In the history of civilization this great law of unity in
diversity manifests itself in two fundamental principles, viz., the development of the individual (diversity), and the organization of society (unity). All the
progress of the race has been along one of these two
lines, the higher development of the individual or the
higher organization of society.

Unity in diversity, which finds perfect illustration in
the material universe, only imperfectly describes the
condition of the moral world. There it represents not
the actual but the ideal, the goal toward which the race
has thus far slowly moved. The harmony of the physical universe has not been marred since the morningstars first sang together, for *things* have no will power
and cannot disobey. But God gave to men will and
liberty that they might have moral character and that
their obedience might mean something more than the
unerring movements of the stars. Harmony in diversity where there is no liberty is devoid of moral beauty;
and liberty and diversity where there is no harmony
mean anarchy, while diversity is the inevitable result
of liberty and a necessary condition of harmony. It
appears, then, that the highest conceivable society, one

---

[1] Locksley Hall.

perfectly illustrating this most comprehensive of all laws, would be composed of persons of perfect individuality, each enjoying perfect liberty and yet all in perfect harmony with the divine will and therefore in perfect harmony with each other. The development of such a society would seem to be the divine ideal for the race.

Revelation certainly teaches that final earthly society is to be perfect. By a perfect society I do not mean a changeless society, for intelligence demands endless growth, but one free from all taint of evil, "without spot or wrinkle or any such thing"—"a new earth," [1] "which shall remain," [2] "wherein dwelleth righteousness," [3] where sin and sorrow shall be unknown, for these "former things shall have passed away." [4] We are apt to understand the twenty-first and twenty-second chapters of the Revelation as a description of heaven. And so they are, but it is heaven on earth, the new Jerusalem come down to the new earth "from God *out of* heaven." [5] It is a glorious vision of the kingdom of God fully come. Every one who believes in heaven at all believes that *there* is realized a perfect society; but we are told that the kingdoms of "*this world*" are to become the kingdoms of our Lord,[6] that when the fulness of time is come there are to be gathered together "in one all things in Christ, both which are in heaven *and which are on earth.*" [7] This promise of all things "gathered together in one" is a prophecy that the law of unity in diversity is yet to find perfect exemplification in the moral world.

History shows that man has already travelled a long way in this direction. To be sure there is still a vast amount of corruption and meanness in the world, much of injustice and inhumanity, much of tyranny and brutality and beastliness. One does not need a wide acquaintance with the world in order to understand Madame de Staël's declaration that the more she saw of

---

[1] Isa. lxv. 17 ; 2 Pet. iii. 13; Rev. xxi. 1.   [2] Isa. lxvi. 22.
[3] 2 Pet. iii. 13.   [4] Rev. xxi. 1, 4, 27.   [5] Rev. xxi. 2, 10.
[6] Rev. xi. 15.   [7] Eph. i. 10.

men the more she liked dogs. Dogs are not capable of
such degradation as are men. Human nature may fall
as much below brute nature as it is capable of rising
above it. Surely the race is low enough, but the question is not simply Where are we? but Whence come we?
and In what direction is our face set? In historic times
there has been a vast change for the better. Progress
has not been uniform or constant, but no one can question that civilization is on a higher plane now than formerly. We have better laws, better institutions, higher
moral standards, more of liberty and less of lawlessness
and violence; and these changes show a change in man
himself. The world's sensibilities have become more
tender, there is greater respect for the rights of others,
there is more of self-control, there has been progress in
men's ideas, there are higher conceptions of life, there
is spiritual growth. All who hold with Browning that

" . . . man was born to grow, not stop,"

will agree that his growth is the promise of a perfected
humanity. And this prophecy of history and Revelation is also uttered by science.

Many who would not accept the testimony of Darwinism as to the origin of man will listen to its prophecy
concerning his destiny. Mr. John Fiske says[1]: "According to Darwinism, the creation of man is still the goal
toward which nature tended from the beginning. Not
the production of any higher creature, but the perfecting of humanity is to be the glorious consummation of
nature's long and tedious work." "The most essential
feature of man is his improvableness, and since his first
appearance on the earth the changes that have gone on
in him have been enormous, though they have continued to run along in the lines of development that were
then marked out."[2] And again he says[3]: "The future
is lighted for us with the radiant colors of hope. Strife
and sorrow shall disappear. Peace and love shall reign
supreme. The dream of poets, the lesson of priest and

[1] The Destiny of Man, p. 31.   [2] Ibid. p. 71.   [3] Ibid. pp. 119, 108.

prophet, the inspiration of the great musician, is confirmed in the light of modern knowledge." "The modern prophet, employing the methods of science, may again proclaim that the kingdom of heaven is at hand."

Thus we have seen that the constitution of man—his high capabilities afford a presumption which is confirmed by Revelation, history, and science that humanity is to be perfected.

There are reasons for believing that the world's progress toward a perfect society is to be much more rapid in the future than it has been in the past.

It was pointed out above that the development of the individual and the organization of society were the two fundamental principles in the history of civilization, the two lines along which the progress of the race could be traced.[1] Until recent times the conditions most favorable to the development of one of these principles were unfavorable to the development of the other. There has, therefore, been a constant tendency to sacrifice the one to the other. And the general character of the civilization of a nation or of an age has depended on which of these two principles was dominant.

A low form of individualism with little or no organization marks the savage. A low form of individualism with a degree more of social organization characterizes the barbarian. The sacrifice of individuality to an extended and comparatively high social organization results in a civilization like that of ancient Egypt, Assyria, India, and China. There is a good degree of permanence, but with it stagnation. On the other hand, the sacrifice of organization to a high degree of individualism produced the wonderful civilization of the Greeks—strangely brilliant and as strangely brief.

---

[1] These two principles spring from the very constitution of man (as will be shown in a later chapter), and are, therefore, permanent. They not only help us to interpret the past, but should aid us in some measure to anticipate and shape the future. Indeed, they seem to afford the true key to history, though I find no recognition of them in Hegel, Guizot, Buckle, Draper, or any other writer on the philosophy of history.

The principle of individualism is progressive, that of organization is conservative. The former introduces the new, achieves liberty, and insures growth. The latter is needed to adjust the new to the old, to preserve order and insure permanence.

Here we see the fundamental difference between the civilizations of Asia and those of Europe. In Asia there have been vast organizations of society, but the development of the individual was early arrested, hence the stagnation of everything. Oriental civilization manifests unity with but little diversity, hence-the dead uniformity of many centuries. Occidental civilization illustrates diversity with but little unity, and its history records revolutions and progress. In Europe there has been a marked development of the individual, while the various organizations of society have been much less extended and much less permanent than those of Asia, though of a higher type because of the higher development of the individual, which has made western civilization progressive.

The high table-lands of the East, unfavorable to agriculture, produced pastoral peoples whose wandering habits prevented any organization of government or society more extended than those of the tribe. And with a low development of the individual, they have remained fixed for centuries in a rude barbarism.

The great civilizations of Asia have arisen in the fertile valleys of great rivers like the Euphrates and the Tigris, the Indus and the Ganges, the Hoang-Ho and the Yang-tse-Kiang. The Nile afforded similar conditions which were attended with like results, viz., the production of a numerous and *homogeneous* people. Agriculture produced fixed habits and a local habitation favorable to an extended organization of society. But the growth of a tribe into a numerous people of the same blood, having the same traditions and religion, the same habits and ideas, living under the same laws and conditions, though most favorable to the development of organization, was least favorable to the development of individuality. There were lacking the stimulating contact and conflict of different ideas, institutions, and customs.

European civilization has been produced by the commingling and conflict of many diverse elements.

> " Mountains interposed make enemies of mankind
> That else, like kindred drops, had mingled into one."

Mountain ranges and seas have separated peoples sufficiently to favor the development of different characteristics and institutions, but have been unfavorable to extended empires like those of the East, though they have not forbidden that intercourse between nations which is necessary to stimulate them.

Of all European countries Russia is the most Asiatic in its physical conditions and is least European in its civilization. Here we find the extended plain and a great population which is nearly homogeneous; for although the Czar rules over many races, the vast majority of his subjects are Slavs. As in Asia, there is a most extended and centralized organization to which the development of the individual is sacrificed, making civil and religious liberty impossible.

On the other hand, the conditions which have produced modern European civilization have been most fully realized in Great Britain, and there we find the highest civilization, the largest liberty of the individual, and the noblest literature, which is the natural flower of a high individuality.

Greece and China afford the best possible illustrations of the high development of one of these principles at the expense of the other. The former cultivated the bodily and intellectual powers of the individual to the highest degree. But the competition and rivalry between tribes and cities and citizens of the same city which contributed so much to Grecian individualism created a spirit of independence and jealousy which made impossible that organization of government and society which are essential to strength and permanence. On the other hand, it would seem as if the Chinese were all run in the same mould, and each generation were a weary repetition of the preceding. There is a uniformity which is favorable to far-reaching organization but fatal to individuality; and where there is no individuality there can be no progress. China has stood for many centuries with her back to the future. A patent of nobility elevates not the unborn descendants but the dead ancestors. As Hegel says: "The Chinaman first counts for something when he is dead." Such a civilization furnishes the most striking example of conservatism and permanence.

Pericles, who lived some sixty-five or seventy years, was contemporary with Æschylus, Miltiades, Themistocles, Aristides, Zeno, Anaxagoras, Protagoras, Antiphon, Sophocles, Eupolis, Euripides, Phidias, Myron, Thucydides, Socrates, Hippocrates, Lysias, Xenophon, Isocrates, Aristophanes, and Cratinus, half of whom were born in Athens and all of whom at some time made Athens their home. And of this wonderful galaxy of statesmen, generals, orators, philosophers, poets, historians, and artists, whose names will remain forever luminous, at least ten, and possibly fourteen, were living at one and the same time in this little city of about 30,000 citizens.

The population of China to-day is sufficient to furnish inhabitants for some thousands of cities like the Athens of Pericles; and there have lived and died Chinese enough to people the whole earth over and over again, and yet all of these thousands of millions have not given to the world as many great men as were living in this Grecian city at one time. But the civilization of ancient Greece is now only a glorious memory, while China, still a power, reckons her life by millenniums.

This same disposition to sacrifice one of these two fundamental principles to the other asserts itself in the religious as well as in the political and social world. And as the dominance of the one principle over the other marks the essential difference between the civilization of Europe and that of Asia, it also constitutes the fundamental difference between Protestantism and Romanism. The latter gathers its more than 200,000,000 souls, scattered over all lands, into one vast and centralized organization, whose head exercises absolute authority, or, in the language of the Vatican Council, is possessed of " all the fulness of supreme power " over all " things which belong to faith and morals " · and " that pertain to the discipline and government of the church." [1] This of course disallows the right of private judgment, denies the liberty of conscience, and to a great degree suppresses individuality.

Protestantism was a reaction against the absolutism of Rome, and at length achieved religious liberty. It was a development of individualism accompanied with more or less of disorganization. Evidently Roman Catholics are the Chinese, and Protestants are the Greeks, of the religious world. On the one hand there is the sacrifice of individuality and with it the loss of liberty, but there is the strength and permanence which spring from a consummate organization. On the other hand we find the progress, the liberty, the originality, the noble literature[2] which always accompany a highly-developed individuality, but there is also the weakness of disorganization and of rival sects.

Luther had vindicated the one principle. Loyola, seeking to counteract the influence of the Reformation, emphasized the correlative principle. Accordingly in the order of the Jesuits there is the highest organization and a complete centralization of power in the hands of the general of the order, who is absolute. The individual will is as nearly as possible extinguished.

Thus Protestantism and Romanism, European and

---

[1] See the First Dogmatic Constitution of the Church of Christ, Chap. III.

[2] Poetry is probably the most perfect expression of a well-grown individuality. It is, therefore, significant that the Roman Catholic world with its vast numbers has produced but one poet of the first rank; and Dante was in spirit a Protestant. He dared to do his own thinking.

There was a singular dearth of poets in the world for 1000 years until the Renaissance, which was a revolt from the long bondage of ecclesiastical and political despotism.

Asiatic civilization and the various periods in the development of European civilization (see Chap. I) have all been shown to illustrate the tendency to sacrifice one of these two principles to the other, both of which are alike necessary. The progress of civilization has been slow because the conditions most favorable to the development of one of these principles have been least favorable to the development of the other. *It is of the utmost significance that now for the first time in the history of the race the same causes are favorable to the development of both.* I refer to *steam* and *electricity*. These are the forces which in recent years have so prodigiously stimulated organization in all directions. They make the social organization and government of 65,000,000 people inhabiting a continent to-day far easier and simpler than the social organization and government of 4,000,000 people occupying one tenth the present area a hundred years ago. At the same time these forces operating through the press and commerce are bringing all civilizations into touch and creating a universal rivalry, are making the world a forum, thus producing the stimulus of a perpetual conflict of ideas, which constitute the most favorable conditions for the development of the individual. In a word, these great forces which are now exerting so profound an influence on civilization are far more favorable to organization than the conditions which produced the vast organizations of Asia, and at the same time much more stimulating to the individual than those conditions which produced the individualism of Europe. Surely such a change, harnessing together to the chariot of the world's progress these two principles which for thousands of years have drawn, now one and then the other, but never together, and often against each other, is so profoundly significant that it marks nothing less than the beginning of a NEW ERA in the history of the race.

Thus far the race has been, like Mephibosheth, lame in both its feet. It has hobbled along now on one foot and now on the other. It shall yet *run* in the way of

God's commandments, which is the path of swiftest progress.

From the fact that the one principle has heretofore been sacrificed to the other we might hastily infer that a highly-developed social organization is inconsistent with highly-developed individuality. Indeed, socialists and individualists are apt to assume that the two are mutually exclusive. But there is no necessary conflict between these two principles; instead, the perfect development of the one is dependent on the perfect development of the other, and an absolutely perfect society would exhibit the two working together in absolute harmony. The great problem of civilization, therefore, toward the solution of which our progress in the future is to be so much more rapid than it has been in the past is the entire co-ordination of these two principles. Of such co-ordination nature furnishes abundant examples. Organization implies a difference of parts, and the higher the organization the greater that difference. The higher the rank of an organism in the animal world the more specialized are its separate organs. The like ought to be true and may be true in society; the more individualized its members the higher may be its organization. This is happily illustrated by President Seth Low from the art of printing: "Only when the type had been individualized, only when each type came to represent a single letter, was the era of combination reached. So now, as I conceive, we have reached in human society, and in this country in its highest form, the era of combination."[1]

Of a tribe of Indians in the savage state, all the men have the same attainments. There is little difference except of degree. Each can make his own clothes, his wigwam and his weapons, can procure his food and cook it. He is independent, but of no service to the tribe except that he counts one more fighting man. The civilized man, to clothe, house, and feed himself, em-

[1] Address on "The Relation of the Church to the Capital and Labor Question" at the Conference of the Evangelical Alliance. Washington, Dec. 1887.

ploys the labor of many hundreds or thousands. The
more individualized he is the more dependent upon
society he becomes and the more important to society.
In an organization each part increases the effectiveness
of all the other parts. All parts, therefore, become more
or less dependent on each; and the greater the dependence of these parts on each other the greater, of course,
is their importance to each other. Thus civilization has
increased both the dependence and the importance of
the individual. And the more highly society becomes
organized the greater should be the individuality and
the importance of every being composing it.

I have tried to show that the organization of society
and the development of the individual are not conflicting, but correlative, principles; and that the world's
progress is likely to be much more rapid than it has
been because the great forces of modern civilization are
calculated to stimulate the development of both of
these principles. But this is not all. The time has
fully come when men should intelligently aid this development.

The world's progress is neither fortuitous nor arbitrary, but subject to the laws of growth. It does not
follow, therefore, as some have supposed, that the
progress of the race cannot be helped forward by
human intelligence. In the vegetable and animal kingdoms we have ten thousand proofs that men can stimulate and direct growth through a knowledge of its laws.
It is precisely because the development of humanity is
subject to laws that it may be in some measure understood and quickened. The world's progress, while unquestionably real, has heretofore been slow because men
have failed to discover and obey the laws of progress.
The race has stumbled along in the dark. Its upward
movement has been too much like that of the brute
creation, unintelligent, unintended, the unforeseen results of conflicting forces, and attended with measure-
less suffering.

The intelligent and benevolent Governor of the universe must have a plan of life for the race and for every
member of it; the best possible plan, not one that is
absolute, because man is a free agent, but conditioned
—a plan that will be wrought out as far and as fast as
men co-operate with God. Thus far men have generally worked out the divine plan blindly. The great
forward steps of the race have been taken unintelli-
gently. When the flood of barbarians swept down
upon Southern Europe it wrought both devastation and
purification. The former was the object of the barbarians, the latter was in the plan of God. This letting
of fresh and healthy blood into the veins of an effete
civilization, without which modern Europe and America
would have been impossible, was not intended by man.
The object of the Crusades, which for two hundred
years emptied Europe upon Asia, was puerile and its
attainment of no consequence to civilization; but their
results, which no man foresaw, were profound and
beneficent. The triumph of monarchy over the feudal
system, which by centralizing power made possible the
better organization of society and thus gave an impetus
to civilization, sprang not from a love of humanity on
the part of a few great nobles, but from the love of
power which circumstances made it possible to gratify.
The policy of the East India Company was dictated by
the most sordid selfishness, but it was providentially
used to introduce Christianity and western civilization
into the heart of Asia. Thus men in all ages have
builded for the race more wisely than they knew, after
the unseen plan of the divine Architect. And if God
can thus make the ignorance and selfishness and wrath
of men to praise him, how much more their glad and
intelligent obedience of his laws? Science, which is a
revelation of God's laws and methods, enables us to fall
into his plans intentionally and to co-operate with him
intelligently for the perfecting of mankind, thus hastening forward the coming of the kingdom. It is true that
the goal of our desires and endeavors is very remote,

but if the way is so long, that is only the more reason why we should mend our pace.

The progress of the race in the future as in the past must be along these same two lines, the development of the individual and the organization of society. Let us dwell for a moment on each.[1]

The development of the individual should be harmonious; that is, the physical, mental, and moral or spiritual growths should keep pace with each other. The growth of the higher seems to be limited by that of the lower. A great mental or spiritual development is impossible where there is a low cerebral development. The cranial capacity of the Australian is forty cubic inches less than that of the European. It would be impossible to raise the intellectual life of the former to that of the latter until his brain had been equally developed.

Brain power is indicated not only by the size of the organ but also by the extent of cerebral surface, which by means of furrows may be enormously increased. "The cerebral surface of a human infant is like that of an ape. In an adult savage, or in a European peasant, the furrowing is somewhat marked and complicated. In the brain of a great scholar the furrows are very deep and crooked, and hundreds of creases appear which are not found at all in the brains of ordinary men."[2] These facts illustrate the closeness of the relations between mind and body, and show that if we desire a large superstructure we must have a correspondingly large foundation.

Science is constantly giving us new data for a higher estimate of the dignity and worth of the human body. It is the most marvellous product in the material world. "All creative processes from the beginning looked forward to this result. The gradual unfolding of life from

---

[1] Practical methods of quickening the movement of the race along these two lines of progress, thus co-operating intelligently with the divine plans, will be presented in later chapters.

[2] Fiske's Destiny of Man, p. 49

its beginnings through the whole series of its structures had reference to this wondrous fabric which was to crown the series. Each one has contributed something to its beauty and perfection. The human body is a microcosm of the universe. The more minutely it is studied, the more its hidden depths are penetrated by the microscope, the greater are the wonders revealed. It is now known that the human soul within it dominates not only a life, but a whole kingdom of lives—an empire with provinces and principalities and powers, with armies and hosts of sentient creatures, each holding some position of service and performing some useful function in the organization." [1]

The race can never be perfected until there is much greater respect for the human body. Many who do not lack self-respect hold their bodies, or at least the laws which govern them, almost in contempt. This is an inheritance from many centuries. There early appeared a disposition on the part of Christians to depreciate the body, due probably to a misunderstanding of the word "flesh," which occurs so often in the New Testament. It has been supposed that there is an antipathy between the spiritual and the physical—that if the former is to be cultivated the latter must be depressed and depleted. Hence the mortification of the Roman Catholic saints.

Of course the pampering of bodily appetites is fatal to spirituality; and this having been discovered it was not strange that Christians in the midst of animalism should go to the opposite extreme of asceticism. The depletion of the body is doubtless conducive to that nervous state in which men see visions and experience ecstasies, which have been so long mistaken for evidence of exalted piety. But if the true Christian aim is service, not ecstasy, then that is the most Christian treatment of the body which fits it for the most perfect, the most abounding, the longest-continued service in upbuilding the kingdom of God.

[1] L. C. Baker.

Ever since Christ dignified our human nature by assuming it, man's body has been the temple of God. Surely we cannot honor God by dishonoring his temple; and surely it is a desecration of that temple to disregard the laws which God has laid down for its government and preservation. Yet multitudes who would shudder at the thought of committing sacrilege do not hesitate to desecrate this living temple of God.

In every age men have lavished treasure, toil, and genius on their temples. It is a far nobler ambition and a more acceptable service to strive for the perfecting of God's living temple. I do not refer simply to the perfecting of an individual, but to the perfecting of the race.

Christians as such ought to have a great longing to see man perfected in body and soul. To see a human being stunted by overwork or lack of food, or one blotched and bloated by sin, ought to hurt like a blow. It is a wrong inflicted on the race, against which every member of it has a right to protest.

Many sin against their own bodies, saying, "I will take the consequences." But the matter does not end there. He who wrongs his own body has no monopoly of the consequences. Every sin against the body by one who is ever to become a parent is a sin against the race which postpones the day of its perfection, and so prolongs its period of sin and suffering.

Among those for whom I write it goes without saying that the training of mind and heart are essential to the development of the race. I have dwelt on the importance of perfecting the body because its training is much more apt to be neglected. We devote laborious years to informing and strengthening the mind, but not one in a hundred of our population has been given a course of physical training. The state insists on the intelligence of the child, but good health is not made compulsory, though well-formed bodies are no less important to the public weal than well-informed minds, and as surely result from intelligent training.

It is easy to make the mistake of cultivating only a fraction of our nature. The Greeks developed the most perfect intellect and the most perfect body; but their civilization failed because there was no corre⋅ sponding development of the spiritual nature. On the other hand, there have been centuries when, excepting ecclesiastics who had some learning, all training was addressed to the spiritual nature, to the total neglect of mind and body. Says Dr. Schaff:[1] "The Renaissance drew its inspiration from the poets and philosophers of ancient Greece and Rome; the Reformation, from the apostles and evangelists. The Renaissance aimed at the development of the natural man; the Reformation, at the renewal of the spiritual man. The Renaissance looked down upon earth, the Reformation looked up to heaven." We need a Reformation and Renaissance combined, which shall draw its inspiration from Christ himself, the perfect man, which shall aim at perfecting the entire nature, "body, soul, and spirit," and which in order to look up to heaven will not have to look away from earth, but which will bring heaven down to earth by making the will of God the joyfully-accepted law of the one even as it is of the other.

Christian civilization, though on the whole the most powerful force for uplifting humanity, in some respects tends directly toward the enfeeblement of the stock. Says Mr. Darwin[2]: "With savages, the weak in body or mind are soon eliminated; and those that survive commonly exhibit a vigorous state of health. We civ⋅ ilized men, on the other hand, do our utmost to check the progress of elimination; we build asylums for the imbecile, the maimed, and the sick; we institute poor- laws; and our medical men exert their greatest skill to save the life of every one to the last moment. There is reason to believe that vaccination has preserved thou- sands who, from a weak constitution, would formerly

---

[1] "Renaissance and Reformation." A paper read at the Florence Confer⋅ ence of the Evangelical Alliance, April, 1891.
[2] Descent of Man, Vol. I. p. 168.

have succumbed to small-pox. Thus the weak members of civilized societies propagate their kind. No one who has attended to the breeding of domestic animals will doubt that this must be highly injurious to the race. It is surprising how soon a want of care, or care wrongly directed, leads to the degeneration of a domestic race; but, excepting in the case of man himself, hardly any one is so ignorant as to allow his worst animals to breed."

And civilization not only preserves the defective classes and permits them to propagate their kind, it also tends to reduce the fecundity of the more highly cultivated. The poor are apt to have large families, the rich small. "Cherry Street" (New York) has been shown to be much more prolific than "Fifth Avenue." It is in the "East End" and not among the palaces of West London that children swarm. The Mountain Whites of the South, who are little more than semi-civilized, do not count a family of a dozen or fourteen members large; and sometimes there are found twenty or more children of one mother. On the other hand, we hear laments that the old New England stock is dying out. Certainly the families of that stock are much smaller than they were a few generations ago and afford a painful contrast to those of alien blood who are transforming New England into a New Ireland or New France. Whatever subordinate causes may be operative, a sufficient explanation is found in the fact that the stock referred to is highly civilized and becoming more so with each generation. It seems to be a general law of life from the lowest forms[1] to the highest that as the scale of being rises fecundity decreases. Speaking of the increasing brain power of the race, Herbert Spencer says[2]: "We must conceive the type

---

[1] Bacteria are capable of an increase which fairly " shames the multiplication-table." It has been estimated that a single germ, under favorable conditions, may in two days produce 281,500,000,000 bacteria—nearly 200 times as many as the population of the globe.

[2] Principles of Biology, Vol. II. p. 520.

gradually so modified that the more developed nervous system irresistibly draws off, for its normal and enforced activities, a larger proportion of the common stock of nutriment, and while thus increasing the intensity, completeness, and length of the individual life, necessarily diminishing the reserve applicable to the setting up of new lives."

Now it is evident that the race cannot afford to have itself propagated by its poorest representatives. This is the survival of the unfittest. The replenishing of populations by the more ignorant and degraded does much to counterbalance all of the efforts to uplift the race made by the better and smaller elements of society. But so long as the greater fecundity of the lower is a general law of nature, *the only way to obviate this evil is to elevate the lower classes.* And, it may be remarked in passing, this seems to be the only escape from the gloomy conclusions of the Malthusian theory. Elevate the masses, and the rate of increase of the race will be correspondingly reduced.

Moreover this greater fruitfulness of the lower strata of society (lower as to brain development) will gain added significance as democracy triumphs more and more widely in the world. If, therefore, from no higher or more Christian motive, the better elements of society, the "higher classes," *must in self-defence level up the lower*.

The organization of society, like the development of the individual, should be harmonious. There should be a certain parity of growth or balance preserved in the physical, the intellectual, and the spiritual development of society. The order of development is like that of the individual; as St. Paul said, first that which is natural and afterward that which is spiritual. The progress of material civilization during this century has been beyond all comparison. The multiplication of inventions, the control of natural forces, the utilization of nature's resources, in short, the mastery of physical conditions within the memory of some still living, has no doubt been greater than that during the entire preceding history of the race. Massachusetts may with ease and dispatch exchange her manufactures for the coal of Pennsylvania, the fruits of Florida, the sugar of Louisiana, the cotton of Texas, the beef of Nebraska, the wheat of the Dakotas, and the gold of California. We seem to have mastered the physical conditions necessary for a perfectly organized social life.

In nature, from the lowest forms of life to the highest, the higher organization is accompanied with a higher intelligence; so in society, as relations are multiplied, become more delicate and farther-reaching, there must be a corresponding increase of intelligence to preserve and direct the more complex organization. There is now a rapidly growing interest in the "science of society," though when Robert Owen invented the phrase it was regarded as absurd and many thought it actually wicked. We are beginning to see that God's methods are scientific, and, if we would co-operate intelligently with him, our methods must be scientific also. Good intentions are not enough, as the English poor-laws and their results clearly show. Purity of motive can no more absolve from the penalties of violated sociological laws than it can suspend the operation of gravitation. It has been said with some truth and more wit that "in this world a large part of the business of the wise is to counteract the efforts of the good." Ignorant and blundering goodness is often as mischievous as well-schooled villainy. A big heart is not all that is necessary to make a successful philanthropist.

The progress of science is disseminating a knowledge of the laws of life and of social well-being, thus making it easier for "the good" to become "the wise." Progress in the science of statistics is most encouraging. The government census, when properly taken, is an invaluable contribution to the progress of society. For lack of it, until recent times, much of the experience of the race has been wasted. Generation after generation has repeated the mistakes of its predecessors, at a dreadful cost of suffering and loss, which was as need-less as it would be for ships, in clear weather, to split on rocks known to sailors for centuries. How much progress would navigation ever have made if navi-gators had kept no log and made no charts? The national census is the log-book of the ship of state. The various labor bureaus, national and state, together with the census bureau, which should by all means be made permanent, are preparing the way for scientific legislation and scientific philanthropy.

But a well-grown and healthy moral and spiritual life is as essential to a noble and enduring social organiza-tion as is a high degree of intelligence. In a noble social organization there must be liberty as well as law. As we have seen, among the Chinese personal liberty is sacrificed to organization, while among the Greeks organization was largely sacrificed to personal liberty. Yet the two are by no means inconsistent with each other. As Professor Peabody of Harvard happily says: "True liberty is the discovery of one's place in the universal organism." But the *acceptance* of our place in the universal organism involves our entering into right relations with our fellow-men and with God, which is the acceptance of all moral and spiritual obli-gations and which indicates a healthy moral and spir-itual nature. This was the great and fatal lack of Grecian character and civilization. If there had been a harmonious development of the individual, if the moral and spiritual life had been as vigorous as the intellect-ual and physical, they would doubtless have been able to perfect their organization and render their civiliza-tion permanent.

We have seen that physical conditions seem favorable to the highest organization of society. We have also seen that there is increasing intelligence in regard to the laws of social life. We seem to possess all the means which the intellectual life of a perfect social organization would require for its exercise and expres-sion. Here are the telegraph for communication, the press for discussion, and the ballot-box through which intelligence is brought to bear on government—or at least may be. But what of the moral and religious life of society? The church is the especial guardian of those interests, but it is shattered into scores of fragments. Its body is dismembered, and the eye says to the hand, "I have no need of thee;" and the head says to the feet, "I have no need of you." The church among us has no organized life. The social conscience should control the entire life of the social organism, but there is no organization through which it can express itself. Assuredly the great need of society to-day, and the most essential condition on which it can rise to a higher organization, is a larger development of its moral and spiritual life, together with some means by which this highest and rightfully regnant part of the social organism—the social conscience—may be brought into vital and controlling touch with the entire intellectual and physical life of society.

When the social conscience, properly enlightened, thus actually rules the organized life of men, social wrongs will disappear, the strifes of classes and of races will cease, and wars will be no more. "When such states are formed and compacted, as incorporeal complex persons, under the governing Christian law of justice and of charity, then shall be accomplished what the Roman Empire grossly prefigured when, in the amazing development of its force—as under some brooding Providence above—it flung forth its avenues toward the ends of the earth, and sought to bind all peoples together under the power which ruled from the Tiber: what Charlemagne perhaps dimly contemplated, in the splendid rashness of his colossal and impracticable plan, when he sought to re-establish the Western Empire with more august sanctions and in a richer religious life, over the Europe which had replaced the old: what Napoleon the First sketched in a sort of lurid caricature on the canvas of history when he rushed abroad with what appeared irresistible legions, for the

conquest of the Continent and the combination of its
several kingdoms under the sovereign leadership of
France. A plan surpassing all of these, as the bending
sky surpasses the clouds which drift across it—even
that will have been realized when the different nations,
each on its untroubled territory, each with its idioms of
custom, law, as well as language, and each with its
peculiar life, shall be united in the bonds of a peace
which knows no suspicion and admits no suspension,
because it results from the voluntary subjection of each
and all to a Law universal: whose authority is conceded
because a Divine majesty and charm are recognized in
it." [1]   Then will be realized amid the diversity of earth's
peoples and kindreds and tongues a blessed unity more
glorious than that which binds the suns and systems of
countless constellations into one harmonious whole.
Then will come the glad consummation for which the
ages have waited, which prophets have foreseen and
poets sung, for which the good have longed and labored
and martyrs bled, for which nature has served and the
" whole creation groaned and travailed in pain together
until now," for which, over all and through all, the
infinite God has wrought the

" . . . one far-off divine event,
To which the whole creation moves " [2]

—even the final, triumphant coming of the kingdom of
Him who is to gather together in *one* all things, both
which are in heaven and which are on earth.

[1] Dr. R. S. Storrs' Divine Origin of Christianity, p. 207.
[2] Closing words of Tennyson's "In Memoriam.'

CHAPTER III.

Of all the great peoples of antiquity only three made
large contributions to modern civilization. Of these
three each was supreme in a different sphere, one in the
physical, one in the intellectual, and one in the religious
or spiritual world.

Because these three elements, the spiritual, the intellectual, and the physical, enter into man's nature, they
also enter as factors into all the great practical problems of the race—a fact too often forgotten. We cannot deal with man as if he were pure spirit or intellect.
We must reckon also with flesh and blood, and remember that man's physical nature subjects him to the laws
of the physical world. Nor can we elevate him physically if we ignore his higher nature.

It will serve several purposes to study briefly the
divine method of preparing the world for the inauguration of the kingdom of God among men.

The question may be asked, If Christ was to inaugurate that kingdom, why was his coming so long delayed? The objection is as old as Celsus. Human
limitations in a sense limit God. He cannot deal with
us, cannot reveal himself to us as if we were arch-
angels. He can reveal no more of himself or of his
truth to any generation of men than their capacity can
measure. Both nature and history show that he
accomplishes his purposes, as he requires us to do, by
the use of means. The kingdom of heaven could be
inaugurated in the world only when the world, after

41

long ages of preparation, had been made ready for it. Because man's nature is what it is this preparation must needs be spiritual, intellectual, and physical. To work out these three lines of development God chose three nations, the Hebrews, the Greeks, and the Romans.[1] The meeting of these lines in the fulness of time was the world's preparation for the advent of the Christ, and hence became the great focal point of the world's history—the fruit of its past, the seed of its future.

A people's conception of deity profoundly influences the national character and life. In the time of Abraham the world was polytheistic. Idolatry degraded mankind. In order to the elevation of the race men must be led to a knowledge of the one true God. To be instrumental of this was the high mission of

The Hebrews.

They had what the younger Humboldt would call a "talent for religion." The germinal principle, which gave birth to the nation, directed its growth and moulded its character, was monotheism. A virgin soil was needed in which to plant this truth. Such a soil could not be found in any idolatrous people whose institutions, laws, and habits of national life had grown and hardened for hundreds of years. The chosen family is, therefore, led into Egypt, where in bondage they might grow into a nation's numbers without having developed national institutions or even a national life, until, born in a day, the nation was led apart into the wilderness to receive its religious institutions.

Ignorant and undisciplined as children, debased by many generations of slavery, and holding the grossest conceptions of Jehovah, they were given the Mosaic ceremonial, which was a great object-lesson, adapted with wondrous wisdom and skill to the minds of these

---

[1] On this subject see Conybeare and Howson's St. Paul, Chap. I.

orientals and calculated to awaken in them new conceptions of holiness, justice, and mercy and then to transfer these attributes to Jehovah.

As they were to be surrounded by idolatrous nations, their religion would be liable to lose its purity by heathen admixture. Their occupation therefore must be such as to bring them as little as possible into contact with heathen peoples. Had they been traders like the Phœnicians or the modern Jews, doubtless there would have resulted a fatal contamination. They were shepherds and agriculturists, and these forms of industry were conserved by the fact that family lands could not be wholly alienated. As an additional safeguard against foreign influence there must be developed in them a peculiar exclusiveness. And this we find to have been a distinguishing characteristic of the Hebrews, dating back doubtless to the Egyptian servitude. In common sorrow they had learned a common sympathy. They had been thrust into the fires of slavery and welded by the blows of oppression. Thus the circumstances under which they grew to be a nation, as well as their subsequent history and the Mosaic law against foreign marriages, served to develop this national trait of exclusiveness, which indeed proved none too strong, as they lapsed many times into idolatry through the influence of surrounding tribes.

Their government was a theocracy, their ruler was Jehovah, and when they set a king over themselves, Saul and all of his successors held the sceptre only as representatives of the invisible King. Greater even than their kings were their prophets, because they were the direct messengers of Jehovah. Their literature was religious, and like the name of their deity has become sacred to hundreds of millions of the most enlightened moderns. Their national festivals were all of a religious character. That the spirit of the nation was essentially religious and monotheistic appears from the fact that it was during periods of religious declension that they suffered themselves to be enslaved and oppressed by their enemies, and a revival of the worship of Jehovah was always accompanied by a revival of patriotism and a renewed assertion of the national life.

They were taught by their prophets that all of their national calamities were suffered as penalties of their disloyalty to Jehovah. At length from the discipline of the seventy years' captivity the Jews effectively learned the lesson of monotheism. From that day to this who has ever heard of an idolatrous Jew?

For many ages their conception of Jehovah was narrow and low, but through the training of their national institutions, through providential lessons, and through the teachings of the prophets their ideas were elevated and enlarged until at length the nation conceived of God as one, eternal, self-existent, holy, and perfect in every attribute. Such a conception of God, which is the richest possession of the world to-day and which underlies every blessing of a Christian civilization, came to the world through the Hebrews; and to have been the medium of such a benediction was worth the thousand years of national training which it cost.

When we compare the Jews' conception of God with that of surrounding tribes, whether of the Canaanites, who laid their children in the burning arms of Moloch, or of the Egyptians, who worshipped life and whom Juvenal satirized in the line, "O sacred nation, whose gods grow in gardens," or with the Persian "fire-worshippers," or with any of the other surrounding peoples, we find the contrast like that between light and darkness. There could be no more striking proof of the incomparable superiority of the Hebrew conception of deity over that of all other ancient peoples than the fact that to-day the most civilized nations of the earth designate the Supreme Being of the universe, not by a Greek or Roman or Egyptian or Persian or Assyrian or Babylonian name, but by JEHOVAH, the name of the God of the Hebrews—a people, apart from their religious character and influence, quite insignificant.

Of all the ancient nations such a conception of God was lodged in the mind of the Jew alone; and this conception constituted the Jewish mind a fit soil for the truths which the Christ taught and exemplified.

Observe now that as soon as the great lesson of the nation was learned—not before—the Jews were scattered over the civilized world to furnish in every land a prepared soil for the seed of Christian truth. After the Babylonian captivity, from which their pure monotheism dates, they commenced to colonize. They went eastward to the shores of the Caspian. A large and flourishing colony remained on the banks of the Euphrates. They scattered up and down Phœnicia and Syria. Antiochus the Great planted 2000 Jewish families in Lydia and Phrygia, which spread over Asia Minor. They went in large numbers to Egypt, settling in Alexandria and in "parts of Libya about Cyrene," and even penetrating Ethiopia. They colonized all along the southern coast of Europe. They became numerous and influential in Rome. They scattered into other parts of Italy and crossed over into Sardinia. And wherever the Jew went, there were found the synagogue and the proselyte. We are told by one authority that the great majority of the women of Damascus had become proselytes to the Jewish faith. We notice as we follow the apostles through the Acts that, wherever they went, at almost every point they found a congregation of Jews and "devout strangers." Thus for 500 years B.C. a pure doctrine concerning God was being taught to the nations preparatory to the preaching of Christianity.

But there was to be an intellectual as well as a spiritual preparation. The scattering of men and their subsequent isolation produced at length divergences of speech so great that peoples of the same origin, now separated, could no longer understand each other. Thus languages and dialects were multiplied until the whole earth became a Babel. If the good news of the kingdom of God was to be widely published and men

generally invited to citizenship, there must be some
common medium of communication, a language generally understood.

And this tongue must be a fit vessel in which to bear
to the nations the water of life—a language rich in spiritual power and capable of still further enrichment.
No adequate language existed. The Hebrew, though
rich in religious terms, is not adapted to the expression
of deep and abstract thought.[1] There must be developed not only an adequate tongue, but also a civilization
capable of diffusing it throughout the civilized world.
This preparation was to be wrought by

The Greeks.

In the production of their civilization perhaps their
land was no less influential than the stock from which
they originally sprung.

The two striking features of Greece are its mountain
system and its coast-line. No part of the land is forty
miles from the sea or ten miles from the hills. Though
not much more than half the size of Portugal, it has a
coast-line greater than that of Spain and Portugal together.[2] Of the numberless bays some are "narrow
enough for the butterflies to cross and yet navigable
for the largest vessels." With a rocky and reluctant
soil, the sea penetrating the land by a thousand inlets
was always inviting the Greeks to a seafaring life; and
islands, scattered over the Ægean like seed from the
hand of a sower, enticed them on from one to another
until they learned to visit other lands. They became
adventurers, travellers, traders, pirates, ravaging the
surrounding coasts, bringing back new treasures and
new ideas. The Peloponnesus is like a mighty hand
with extended fingers, stretched by Greece down into
the Mediterranean to grasp its commerce. Becoming

---

[1] See Hardwick's Christ and Other Masters, p. 75.
[2] Encyclopædia Britannica, *in loco.*

masters of the sea, the Greeks were brought into quickening contact with all the civilizations of the Mediterranean world, thus stimulating their intellectual life and sharpening their wits.

The heterogeneous character of the original elements of the Grecian tribes should be noted. "No nation," says Hegel,[1] "that has played a weighty and active part in the world's history has ever issued from the simple development of a single race along unmodified lines of blood-relationship; there must be differences, conflict, a composition of opposed forces." The mountain-ranges of Greece were high enough to favor a separate development of the Grecian tribes, but not high enough to isolate them and prevent a vigorous rivalry or the contagion of ideas. Thus sea and mountain conspired to establish conditions precisely opposite to those which exist where great homogeneous populations occupy vast and fertile valleys like those of the Nile, the Euphrates, and the Indus. Such conditions produce powerful empires but do not develop the individual, to do which was the mission and the glory of Greece.

The Greeks regarded their climate, which was free from great extremes, as a gift of the gods. An intensely blue sky, a transparent atmosphere, a landscape of mountain and valley, of river and sea, the beauty of the tropics without their debilitating air or their unearned and pauperizing bounty, so little winter as to permit them to live out of doors with light clothing, allowing the freest movement and constant contact with nature—such were the conditions which favored a perfectly healthy development of body and mind.

Living in the open air amid such scenes, an alert and sensitive mind must be awakened to a love of the beautiful. Moreover, dwelling among enemies, the Greeks were trained to war. The safety of their homes and their own lives in the hand-to-hand conflict of battle

---

[1] Philosophy of History, p. 181. Griggs' Philosophical Classics.

depended on their skill at arms and on the strength
and endurance of their bodies. Accordingly, supported
as they were by the toil of their slaves, physical culture early became the business of the Greeks. Among
the Spartans the bodily training of girl as well as boy
began as soon as the child could walk. It is not strange
that a race neither stunted by excessive toil nor rendered effeminate by luxury, having the highest possible
incentives to develop the body, should in the course of
generations produce as nearly as possible the ideal
human form. This highest type of beauty in the material world conspired with the charms of sea and earth
and air to develop their love of the beautiful and to
perfect their artistic sense, until at length beauty became the great informing idea of Greek civilization,
expressing itself in sculpture, painting, music, architecture, and literature.

In the age of Pericles Grecian civilization had become
the highest the world had ever seen, and Grecian commerce was bearing it to all the ports of the Mediterranean. Moreover the Greeks had developed a strong
centrifugal tendency. They were great colonizers. The
single city of Miletus had become the mother of three
hundred towns, colonizing the entire coast of the Black
Sea. They planted their arts, sciences, philosophy, and
literature in Asia Minor and in Italy. Then Alexander
arose to press the die of Grecian civilization on one half
the people of the globe. He built new cities from Alexandria in Egypt eastward, which became new centres
of civilization and which perpetuated Grecian influence
when Grecian arms had long since lost their power.
Thus "gradually," says the historian Kurtz,[1] "the
Greek language, which when the Gospel was first
preached was understood and spoken throughout the
Roman Empire, obtained universal dominion — as it
were a temporary suspension, this, of the judgment
by which languages were confounded." So that the

---

[1] Church History, Vol. I. p. 50.

writings of the apostles, whether addressed to Roman, Grecian, or Asiatic Christians, might all be in Greek. And even the epistle to the Hebrews, scattered abroad, was probably written, not in their own language, but in this perfected and cosmopolitan tongue.

But equally necessary with the preparation of a fit medium for the Gospel was the work to be accomplished by

The Roman.

He was to supply the necessary physical conditions, to level the barriers between different peoples by bringing them under one government, and to cast up the great highways which would facilitate the intercourse of the nations. One of their own writers thus states the mission of his race : " It is for others to work brass into breathing shape—others may be more eloquent or describe the circling movements of the heavens and tell the rising of the stars. Thy work, O Roman ! is to rule the nations; these be thine acts, to impose the conditions- of the world's peace, to show mercy to the fallen and to crush the proud."

Imagine the Roman work of preparation undone, that empire broken into petty and jealous principalities. Ignorance of each other and attending prejudice and suspicion would cut off intercommunication, and frequent wars would prevent the spread of the Gospel of peace.

God foresaw this necessity, and seven and a half centuries before he " sent forth his Son " he planted on the banks of the Tiber a power which should stretch its arm over all nations and, grasping the world's fragments, unite them under universal empire.

The Roman roads were the world's great arteries radiating from the Eternal City as its heart. Every pulsation of that heart was felt at the finger-tips of civilization. Men of every race flowed into Rome; and the torch of the Gospel flaming there might cast its light into every land.

Thus the three great lines of preparation were developed, each of which was necessary. Without the preparatory work of the Jew, Christianity could not have arisen; without that of the Greek and Roman, its two wings would have been clipped and it must have fallen where it arose, to become provincial, a phase of Judaism instead of the religion of the world.

These lines of preparation centred in Judæa. There was the home of the Jews, there was Grecian civilization, there was Roman power. The coins of the Jews bore the "image and superscription" of the Cæsars, their sacred writings circulated in the Greek of the Septuagint. An illustration of this triple civilization has been remarked in the fact that Herod the Great rebuilt the temple for the Jews and within the walls of the sacred city erected a theatre and amphitheatre for the Greeks and Romans. And there in Palestine, where these three civilizations met in most perfect conjunction, appeared He whose advent Hegel calls "the goal of all previous history and the starting-point for all history to come." [1]

But this was not the only preparation to be made. In addition to the vast work of a positive character which has been outlined, each of these three great races was to exhibit a great failure which would further prepare mankind for a Saviour. Man has many methods by which he attempts to save himself. If I mistake not, they are all reducible to three great classes or genera, viz., ritualism, culture, and law. All these are found in varying proportions in some of the great religions of the world, but ritualism is usually the basis of heathen religions and it has entered largely into corrupted forms of Christianity. If ritualism had had any saving power, it should have manifested itself in Judaism. Ritualists in the Christian church will generally concede a divine origin and authority to the rites and ceremonies of the Jewish church which they would

---

[1] Philosophy of History, p. 227, Griggs' Philosophical Classics.

hardly claim for their own; and Jewish ritualism produced not national righteousness but Rabbinism, which
"strained out a gnat and swallowed a camel," and
Pharisaism, which "devoured widows' houses and for a
pretence made long prayers."

There is perhaps at the present time an increasing
number who rely on culture to save the world. I once
heard Bayard Taylor say that what society needed to
purge its vice was "more of art." Had he forgotten or
had he never learned the great lesson of Greek civilization ? The love of the beautiful did for the Greeks all it
could do for any people. As we have already seen, it
became the informing idea of their civilization. It can
never again so profoundly influence another civilization, because modern life has become so complex. The
different classes of society are now dominated, not by
one supreme motive, but by many and conflicting motives. A single idea cannot now take possession of a
nation and mould its life for generations. That is, the
experiment can never again be repeated under so favorable conditions. And what was its success ? The culture of the Greeks not only could not save them from
vice, but helped to plunge them into its most loathsome
depths. The utter failure of that experiment was a
demonstration for all time that mere culture has no
saving power.

The dominating and formative idea of Roman civilization was that of law. The central idea of Judaism
and of Christianity is one and the same, viz., loyalty to
a personal God; that of the Roman was loyalty to law,
not as the expression of a personal will, but as *abstract
law*, or, at best, as representing the state; it was wholly
impersonal.

Precisely here do we find the essential difference between morality and true religion. The laws of morality
are abstractions, they are wholly impersonal; those of
Christianity are the expressions of a personal will.
Morality fashions the life by rules, that is, from without; Christianity by love to Him whose will the laws

of life express, that is, from within. The former is mechanical and bound, the latter is vital and free. The one affords light without heat; the other heat with light. A moral character is made; a Christian character grows. The former is beautiful, but its beauty is that of the statue, wrought from without and lifeless; the beauty of the latter is that of the living form, created by a vital principle within. Says Dr. H. J. Van Dyke with nice discrimination : " A Christian life is not an imitation, but a reproduction, of the life of Christ."

Roman genius for law could develop great national strength and create a vast organization, could produce legions whose disciplined and resistless might planted the Roman eagle in every capital, it could bring all nations under Roman law and furnish a code for the courts of subsequent ages, but it could not produce a human brotherhood. It could develop a strength of character equal to thrusting the hand into a flame and holding it there until consumed, or to leaping into a bottomless chasm for the good or glory of the state; it could produce a few such stoics as Seneca, Marcus Aurelius, and Epictetus, but it could not save society from sinking into the foulest corruption or give relief to the millions of slaves who writhed under the heel of Rome. Says the author of "Ecce Homo"[1]: "Never did men live under such a crushing sense of degradation, never did they look back with more bitter regret, never were the vices that spring out of despair so rife, never was sensuality cultivated more methodically, never did poetry curdle so readily into satire, never was genius so much soured by cynicism, and never was calumny so abundant or so gross or so easily believed. If morality depended on laws, . . . this would have been the most glorious era in the past history of mankind. It was in fact one of the meanest and foulest." " What a society was this of Rome, . . . where the most monstrous cruelty was allied with the most shameless libertinism ! "[2]

---

[1] Pp. 144, 145.   [2] Schmidt's Social Results of Early Christianity, p. 95.

Thus while the spiritual, intellectual, and physical conditions were being made ready for Him who was to inaugurate the kingdom of God among men, the world was being taught her need of Him by her own decisive failures.

And now "when the fulness of time was come, God sent forth his Son,"

> " Of wedded maid and Virgin-Mother born."

> " No war, or battle's sound
> Was heard the world around;
> The idle spear and shield were high up hung,
> The hooked chariot stood
> Unstain'd with hostile blood." [1]

And upon the world's stillness broke the angel's song: "Glory to God in the highest, and on earth peace, good will toward men."

In that birth at Bethlehem the dying forces of Judaism, Greece, and Rome were born again, for Christ was to redeem their failures, to substitute life for the forms of Judaism, to exemplify in his own character and impart to his followers a perfection of beauty of which the Greeks had never dreamed, and to found a kingdom broader than the empire of mighty Rome, established in the hearts of men whose loving loyalty to him, as the giver of every law, would make them at once obedient and free—a kingdom whose citizens would be brothers.

---

[1] Milton's Christmas Hymn.

CHAPTER IV.

THE CONTRIBUTION MADE BY THE ANGLO-SAXON.

THE traveller at Rome sees many magnificent columns and capitals which were brought from heathen temples to sustain and beautify Christian churches. Thus we find in the temple of Christian civilization Hebrew and Greek and Roman pillars.

In the preceding chapter we have glanced hurriedly at these three greatest nations of antiquity, partly because they made the deepest and most lasting impression on modern civilization, partly as an example of the threefold character of the great problem of the race, partly as an evidence of the divine mission of Christ for whose coming they were used to prepare the world, and partly as an illustration of the divine method of preparing nations to do a specific work and guiding them to its completion.

It should be observed that it was precisely because these three nations were supreme, one in each of the three spheres pointed out, that they could be used as they were, and that they and they alone of ancient peoples left a permanent and profound impress on modern and western civilization. It is, therefore, of the utmost significance that of these characteristics, each of which singly sufficed to make a nation supremely important in the world's history, *all three* unite in the one Anglo-Saxon race.

1. The religious life of this race is more vigorous, more spiritual, more Christian than that of any other. Not that Anglo-Saxons are righteous overmuch. They will have to answer for many sins against weaker races

54

and against the weaker of their own race. They produce as worldly, as gross, as selfish and beastly men
and women as do any other people, but for all that they
exemplify a purer Christianity and are to-day a mightier power for righteousness on the earth than any other
race. Speaking of England, Montalembert says: "She
is the one which has best preserved the three fundamental bases of every society which is worthy of man
—the spirit of freedom, the domestic character, and *the
religious mind*." This utterance is the more significant
coming from an eminent Frenchman and an ardent
Roman Catholic.

"With beautiful and important exceptions, Protestantism on the Continent has degenerated into mere
formalism. By confirmation at a certain age, the state
churches are filled with members who very commonly
know little or nothing of a personal religious experience. In obedience to a military order, a regiment of
German soldiers files into church and partakes of the
sacrament, just as it would shoulder arms or obey any
other word of command. Protestantism on the Continent seems to be nearly as poor in spiritual life and
power as Romanism. That means that most of the
spiritual Christianity in the world is found among
Anglo-Saxons and their converts; for this is the great
missionary race. If we take all the German missionary
societies together, we find that, in the number of
workers and the amount of contributions, they do not
equal the smallest of the three great English missionary societies. The year that the Congregationalists
in the United States gave one dollar and thirty-seven
cents per caput to foreign missions, the members of the
great German State Church gave only three quarters of
a cent per caput to the same cause." [1]

No race has ever shown such philanthropy, no race is
so easily moved by great moral ideas, none is so capable
of a moral enthusiasm, none is so quick to accept re-

---

[1] The Author's "Our Country," p. 209.

sponsibility for the ignorant, the degraded, the suffering, or to make generous self-sacrifice in their behalf as the Anglo-Saxon. None is so capable of disinterested endeavor. This race is forever organizing a society to help some one. No doubt it sacrifices more lives and more treasure for the uplifting of mankind than all other races combined.

Of the one hundred and thirty-nine missionary societies represented at the General Conference of Foreign Missions in London in 1888, eighteen represented all Continental races and one hundred and twenty-one represented the Anglo-Saxon race (I use the term Anglo-Saxon broadly to include all English-speaking peoples). That foreign missionary societies were very generally represented appears from the statement of the programme committee, that "while the entire revenue of all Protestant missions of the world does not amount to £2,250,000 per annum, the societies taking part in the conference have an aggregate annual income of more than £2,000,000." Moreover a large proportion of the £250,000 not represented passes through the treasury of an English society which declined to participate in the conference. Evidently it is chiefly to the Anglo-Saxon race that we must look for the evangelization of the world. And to show that this is pre-eminently the missionary race is to show that it is the most Christian race, for the missionary spirit is the essential spirit of Christianity.

As the Hebrew carried his pure monotheism around the Mediterranean, so the Anglo-Saxon is carrying a spiritual Christianity around the world.

2. I do not forget that comparisons are odious, and especially so when the subjects of comparison are such as do not admit of exact measurement and the result must, therefore, be a matter of opinion. The argument, however, requires a comparison of the intellectual powers of the Anglo-Saxon with those of other races.

The highest expression of the intellectual life of a people is to be found in their literature and more especially in their poetry. Surely no one would be so bold as to attempt to match English poetry in any modern literature, and it may be questioned whether even the Greek affords its equal, all things considered. Edmund Gosse names a dozen poets "as the manifest immortals of the British Parnassus ;" [1] viz., Chaucer, Spenser, Shakespeare, Milton, Dryden, Pope, Burns, Wordsworth, Coleridge, Byron, Shelley, Keats. Of course other great names might be mentioned whom many would deem better entitled than some of these to a place in the first rank; but take simply these twelve, and in what skies does such a constellation blaze save in the British heavens? Speaking of the brightest lights of English literature, Emerson says : " I find the great masters out of all rivalry and reach." [2]

And the lesser lights are almost as the stars for multitude. English literature is hardly less remarkable for its volume than for its quality. Taine, whose aim was to show that a people's psychology is to be found in its literature, explains why he chose the English for discussion. "If I have chosen this one in particular," he says, "it is not without a reason. I had to find a people with a grand and complete literature, and this is rare; there are few nations who have, during their whole existence, really thought and written. Among the ancients, the Latin literature is worth nothing at the outset, then borrowed and imitative. Among the moderns, German literature is almost wanting for two centuries [1550–1750]. Italian literature and Spanish literature end at the middle of the seventeenth century. Only ancient Greece, modern France and England, offer a complete series of great significant monuments." [3]

During the reign of Elizabeth no less than two hundred and thirty-three English writers appeared, nearly all of whom possessed some unusual excellence. And

---

[1] *The Forum*, April, 1889, p. 178.   [2] Prose Works, Vol. II. p. 273.
[3] Taine's English Literature, pp. 20, 21.

now for three hundred years since that age of unri-
valled splendor there has been a wonderful succession
of poets, essayists, historians, novelists, philosophers,
orators, scientists, and scholars. Thinkers of every
description have enriched the language with a wealth
which has made all later generations their debtors.

America's interest in this wealth of thought is not
wholly that of inheritance. She has produced a fair
share of it. Sydney Smith's contemptuous question,
"Who reads an American book?" is no longer pertinent
enough to provoke answer or indeed to be asked. Still
the intellectual vigor of the American branch of the
Anglo-Saxon race has displayed itself less in the pursuit
of literature than in the mastery of the physical conditions involved in the conquest, for civilization, of three
million square miles of territory. With nations as with
individuals physical development precedes intellectual.
"First that which is natural, and afterward that which
is spiritual." When the energies of the nation are less
absorbed in the development of our matchless physical
resources, there will appear no doubt a higher intellectual life.

We do not forget the precious contributions to letters,
philosophy, science, and every department of scholarship made by the Germans, the French, and other races,
but to the Anglo-Saxon race must be credited the greatest poet and the greatest cluster of poets, the greatest
modern philosopher and the two greatest scientists.
When Prof. Tyndall was in the United States, he said
something to this effect: "If a horizontal line were
drawn from the top of Sir Isaac Newton's genius,
stretching to our own day, it would leave immeasurably
below it every head that has since appeared excepting
that of Thomas Young; and if it declined at all to reach
his, the declination would be very slight." And Prof.
Helmholtz has said: "The greatest discovery I ever
made was that of the genius and writings of Thomas
Young; I consider him the greatest man of science that
has appeared in the history of this planet."

Inventive genius, which especially characterizes Anglo-Saxons and is a pre-eminent triumph of mind over matter, is surely an evidence of intellectual power, and might be appropriately noticed in this connection, but it will be considered later.

Comparing the entire product of the Anglo-Saxon mind as preserved in the English language with that of all other races, can any one question that the destruction of these treasures would be a greater loss to the world than would the destruction of all the thought embodied in any other language? And if this be so, may we not correctly infer that, on the whole, the Anglo-Saxons are the intellectual leaders of the world?

Again, another high expression of the intellectual life of a people is found in their statesmanship, and their statesmanship is to be seen crystallized in their laws and institutions. "The institutions of a people," says Hamilton W. Mabie, "are its solution of the problem of life." Surely there is no greater problem, and the best solution of the greatest problem implies the best powers of mind.

Anglo-Saxon institutions show a skilful adjustment of powers, a harmonization of conflicting claims, a combination of apparently opposite principles, a balance of rights and duties, a union of liberty and law, an example of unity in diversity such as cannot be found in any other civilization, eastern or western, ancient or modern. The American constitution is doubtless the highest example of constructive statesmanship in history. Mr. Gladstone pronounces it "the most wonderful work ever struck off at a given time by the brain and purpose of man." [1] The growth of the English Constitution is a living monument to the practical statesmanship of the English race; and the recent Australian Federation affords a new illustration of Anglo-Saxon political genius.

That ability which enables a people so to adjust itself

[1] " Kin Beyond Sea "—*North American Review*, Oct. 1878.

to the conditions imposed by nature, to establish such
relations with other peoples and so arrange its internal
economy as to secure the largest liberty, the greatest
progress, the most general intelligence and prosperity,
may be despised in certain quarters as "grossly practical," but this accurate perception of conditions, this
sagacious judgment, and this nice power of adjustment,
whether called statesmanship when applied to national
concerns or plain common-sense when exercised in
every-day affairs, seem to me nothing less than a
genius for living. This characteristic is pre-eminently
Anglo-Saxon, distinguishing the American even more,
if possible, than the Englishman. Said Montesquieu :
"No people have true common-sense but those who are
born in England." "A strong common-sense," observes
a discerning critic, "which it is not easy to unseat or
disturb, marks the English mind for a thousand years."[1]
Common-sense adjusts men to their environment,
which in the struggle for life is an immense advantage.

Several Continental races are superior to the Anglo-
Saxon in speculative thought, in scholarship, in music,
and in art. But these are the flowers, not the roots, of
life; they adorn civilizations, but do not create them.
The Anglo-Saxon, like the ancient Greek, has the rare
power of propagating his civilization, which together
with his language he is carrying around the world.

"The progress of humanity and of Christianity," says
Dr. Schaff, "requires the preponderance of one language as a common medium of international intercourse and a connecting link between the various members of the civilized world."[2] English is better fitted
than any other language to render this service. The
characteristics of a people appear in their language.
The English tongue, like the English race, has a wonderful power of assimilation and expansion, is the most
intellectual and at the same time the most direct and

---

[1] Emerson's Prose Works, Vol. II. p. 271.
[2] The English Language, p. 54.

practical. It is said by an eminent scholar, a German-American, to be the "most easily acquired and most easily used." Concerning the English language let me cite the testimony of men whose blood and birth preclude the suspicion of any bias in its favor. M. Alphonse de Candolle says (Histoire des Sciences): "English is the most forcible, the most succinct, as well as the most assimilative." "Its composite character," says Dr. Schaff, "imparts to it a pliability, expansiveness, and perfectibility which no other language possesses."[1] "Dr. John A. Weisse, in a work on the English language, says that he was an utter stranger to it up to his thirtieth year. Convinced of its inferiority, he studied it with a view to demonstrating that inferiority. His investigations convinced him that 'English contains the cream and essence of its predecessors and contemporaries.' He is not content to class it *among* the best; it is *the best*, the most flexible, the one language of all that have ever existed most suitable to become a world-language."[2] Another German declares that while in it has been written the richest and greatest literature, it is also the most practical language; clear, concise, pre-eminently the language of business and of telegraphic communication. Mr. Orton, late president of the Western Union Telegraph Company, says English is twenty-five per cent cheaper for telegraphic purposes than any other. I must be permitted one more citation. It shall be from the founder of scientific German philology, the eminent Jacob Grimm. "Among all the modern languages," he says, "none has, by giving up and confounding all the laws of sound, and by cutting off nearly all the inflections, acquired greater strength and vigor than the English. Its fulness of free middle sounds which cannot be taught, but only learned, is the cause of an essential force of expression such as perhaps never stood at the command of any other language of men. Its entire, highly intellectual and won-

---

[1] The English Language, p. 53.
[2] *Methodist Review*, Nov.–Dec. 1890, p. 861.

derfully happy structure and development are the result of a surprisingly intimate marriage of the two noblest languages in modern Europe, the Germanic and the Romance; the former (as is well known) supplying in far larger proportion the material groundwork, the latter the intellectual conceptions. As to wealth, intellectuality, and closeness of structure, none of all the living languages can be compared with it. In truth, the English language, which, by no mere accident, has produced and upborne the greatest and most commanding poet of modern times as distinguished from the ancient classics—I can, of course, only mean Shakespeare—may with full propriety be called a world-language; and like the English people it seems destined hereafter to prevail even more extensively than at present in all the ends of the earth." [1]

The anticipations of the great scholar are being fully realized. The following table [2] shows by how many people the seven leading languages of civilization were spoken at the beginning of this century and in 1890.

1801.

Rank.	Language.	Number by whom Spoken.	Per cent.
1	French......................	31,450,000	19.4
2	Russian	30,770,000	19.0
3	German	30,320,000	18.7
4	Spanish	26,190,000	16.2
5	English....................	20,520,000	12.7
6	Italian..............	15,070,000	9.3
7	Portuguese.................	7,480,000	4.7

1890.

Rank.	Language.	Number by whom Spoken.	Per cent.
1	English.............	111,100,000	27.7
2	German........	75,200,000	18.7
3	Russian	75,090,000	18.7
4	French	51,200,000	12.7
5	Spanish	42,800,000	10.7
6	Italian.....................	33,400,000	8.3
7	Portuguese.................	13,000,000	3.2

[1] Ueber den Ursprung der Sprache (Berlin, 1852), p. 50. Quoted by Dr. Schaff, The English Language, pp. 8, 9.

[2] Mulhall.

Here it appears that English has risen from the fifth place to the first. In 1801 German was spoken by 10,000,000 more people than English; now English is spoken by 36,000,000 more than German. Then French was spoken by 11,000,000 more than English; now English is spoken by 60,000,000 more than French. In 1801 these seven languages were spoken by 161,800,000 people, in 1890 by 401,700,000. The proportion of the whole speaking German and Russian remains unchanged, but each of the other tongues except the English is spoken by a smaller percentage of the whole now than it was in 1801; while English-speaking peoples have risen from less than thirteen per cent of the whole to more than twenty-seven—from less than thirteen per cent of 161,800,000 to more than twenty-seven per cent of 401,700,000—and are now more than five times as numerous as they were at the beginning of the century.

The marvellous spread of the English language is due very largely to the wonderful growth of the Anglo-Saxon race, but not wholly by any means. Bishop Taylor said, a dozen years ago, that there were then in India a million natives who spoke English, and the desire to learn the language was constantly growing.[1] Julius Seelye and Joseph Cook a few years ago addressed large audiences of Brahmins without an interpreter. This language is the principal vehicle of modern and western civilization; and wherever the currents of new life touch in the Old World there are nations eager to learn English. It is taught as a regular branch of instruction in the best universities and colleges of Continental Europe. Wherever English, Scotch, and American missionaries go—and where do they not go?—they plant schools and colleges, in which English soon becomes almost or quite a necessity. When a young Asiatic has been taught to think and has been acquainted in some measure with the world's his-

---

[1] *Methodist Review*, Nov.—Dec. 1890, p. 866.

tory and modern science, there has been developed in
him an intellectual life which demands food. He has
acquired literary tastes and an appetite for knowledge
which the vernacular cannot possibly satisfy. He
must know a European language, and that of his in-
structors is the one naturally chosen. The study of
English in the colleges carries it for purposes of preparation into the lower schools, so that the English language and with it English ideas naturally work their
way wherever the English-speaking missionary goes.
And now it has come to pass, as Dr. Schaff says, that
" the English classics are daily read in countries of
which Shakespeare and Milton never heard, and by
millions who but recently were ignorant of the very
existence of England."

Travel also and commerce as well as the missionary
are disseminating a knowledge of this tongue. It is
said that three fifths of all the railroad tickets sold in
the world are used by English-speaking peoples. And
two thirds of the tonnage of all the merchant navies
afloat belong to Anglo-Saxons. Thus in all the ports of
the world and along all routes of travel you find English taking root. An intelligent traveller [1] estimates
that out of every thousand persons whom he met in a
recent tour around the world seven spoke French,
thirty-three German, and one hundred and seventy-
eight English.

We have seen that the English language is better
fitted than any other to become, and that it is actually
becoming more and more, a world-language. Now the
language of a race is a wonderfully truthful expression
of its thoughts, its feelings, its habits, its life, its character, its institutions, its civilization. The English language is no more pervasive than English civilization.
Evidently the Anglo-Saxon is doing for the modern
world what the Greek did for the ancient. They each
produced a civilization characterized by a high develop-

---

[1] Rev. E. G. Porter.

ment of the individual, they each produced an unequalled language and literature; and as the restless Greek carried his language and civilization around the Mediterranean, so the more restless Anglo-Saxon is carrying his language and civilization around the globe.[1]

3. We have seen (Chap. III) that the Roman possessed a mastery of physical conditions and a genius for law, organization, and government unequalled in the ancient world. A glance suffices to show that in the modern world the Anglo-Saxon occupies a position of like pre-eminence.

Nothing so well illustrates man's triumph over nature and his control of the physical conditions of life as invention, and in this sphere the Anglo-Saxon has no rival. Of important inventions doubtless the mariner's compass, gunpowder, printing, the steam-engine, the electric telegraph, the application of steam to the printing-press, the locomotive, and the steamship are those which have exerted the most profound and far-reaching influence on civilization and the destiny of nations. The first two originated in the far East and the remote past. Of the last seven, six were Anglo-Saxon in origin. Only less important than these were the invention or discovery of the power-loom, the mule-jenny, the cotton-gin, illuminating gas, the Bessemer-steel process, the sewing-machine, the reaper, and the thrashing-machine, all of which are Anglo-Saxon. Almost never is the world indebted to a single brain for a great invention. It is usually a development, dependent on principles or discoveries made known perhaps by men of

---

[1] It is not claimed that the Anglo-Saxons are the modern Greeks. In subtilty of thought the Germans, and in temperament the French, resemble the Greeks much more than the Anglo-Saxons do. On the whole, probably both of these races are more Grecian than is the Anglo-Saxon, but here is the point of my contention: in those particulars wherein the Greeks rendered supreme service to the world, viz., in the development of individualism, in the production of the noblest language and literature, in the centrifugal or colonizing tendency, in power to impress their civilization on the world, the Anglo-Saxons are certainly the modern representatives of the Greeks.

other races and other ages. Many such discoveries have been made by the Italians, French, and Germans, but it is very apt to be an Anglo-Saxon who seizes on the new knowledge and applies it to practical use.

Electricity is the great power of the future and is, no doubt, destined greatly to extend man's dominion over nature; and in its application the Anglo-Saxon is likely to keep the lead. At the International Electrical Expo- sition in Paris, a few years since, five gold medals were given for the greatest inventions or discoveries, all of which were conferred on Americans. "Yankee ingenu- ity" has become proverbial. The English are by far the most inventive people of the Old World, and the United States government issues four times as many patents as the English. In fifty-three years, from 1837 to 1889, our Patent Office issued 449,928 patents, and in the one year of 1889 over 21,000. Herbert Spencer says that "beyond question, in respect of mechanical appliances, the Americans are ahead of all nations."

More than all other races taken together the Anglo- Saxons control the world's communications. Fifty- eight per cent of all railway mileage is in lands governed by them, and they own and control a much larger percentage. Of every hundred miles of railway lines in the world forty-one are in the United States; and this country has thirty per cent of all the tele- graph lines, while forty-six per cent of the world's lines are in Anglo-Saxon territory. This race sends more than one half of all the telegraph messages of mankind, and the people of the United States send several million more in a year than the French, Ger- mans, Austrians, Russians, Italians, and Spaniards combined. We have already seen that two thirds of the tonnage of the world's merchant-ships is Anglo- Saxon. And England commands the gateways of many seas and most of the great gulfs of the world.

It is not strange that a race which has gained such mastery of physical conditions should be the richest among men. Great Britain is the richest nation of

Europe, and the United States is richer than Great Britain. In 1880 the Anglo-Saxon race possessed nearly two thirds as much wealth as all Continental Europe, and the proportion is much larger now. The time will soon come when this one race will hold more than one half of the wealth of the world.[1]

The most significant part of the physical power of this race is its unparalleled increase and extension, especially during the last century. In 1700 it numbered less than 6,000,000; in 1800 it had increased to about 20,500,000; and in 1890 it could claim more than 111,000,000. Here is an increase of more than 90,000,000 within the memory of living men. This has been due in large measure to the assimilating power of this race, which is wholly exceptional. Conditions are much more favorable for an increasing rate of growth in Anglo-Saxon countries than in Continental Europe, but if we reckon the growth of European population for the next century at its rate of increase from 1870 to 1880 and the Anglo-Saxon at much less than its rate of increase during the same ten years, a hundred years hence this one race will outnumber all the peoples of Continental Europe by 100,000,000 souls.[2]

No less remarkable than the increase of this race has been its extension. From its little island home it has expanded until now it is in possession of a third portion of the earth, and rules over some 400,000,000 of its inhabitants—an empire several times more vast than the Roman world when its eagles flew the farthest.

And Anglo-Saxon empire is not only more vast than Roman ever was, but possesses elements of strength and permanence which Rome always lacked. Doubtless there never was a time in its history when the eventual destruction of that empire was not sure. Its very structure necessitated ruin. Conquered peoples

full

---

[1] For a discussion of the wealth of the United States see Chap. X of the author's "Our Country."

[2] For a fuller discussion of this subject see the Author's "Our Country," Chap. XIV.

were not coherent because they were not assimilated. The unity of the empire was artificial. Its uniting bond was external, and whenever it was sufficiently weakened, as with the vicissitudes of ages it must be, the unity was lost and the empire was again resolved into its constituent elements. This has not been the method of English greatness. It is the glory of England, not that her arms have been victorious in every clime, not that every great circle of the earth must cross her empire, but that she is extending her civilization around the globe. True, she has empire which she holds by force and which she might lose by force, but North America, South Africa, and Australia are hers by a different tenure. She has conquered these lands by giving to them her sons and daughters, her free institutions, her noble civilization. England might be sunk in the sea and these vast areas would remain her glory, loyal to the essential principles which she has given to them.

Commenting on this genius for propagating their civilization which characterizes the Anglo-Saxons, a French writer [1] says: "The world will not be Russian, nor German, nor French, alas! nor Spanish. For it can be asserted that, since the great navigation has given the whole world to the enterprise of the European races, three nations were tried, one after the other, by fate, to play the first part in the fortune of mankind, by everywhere propagating their tongue and blood, by means of durable colonies, and by transforming, so to say, the whole world to their own likeness. During the sixteenth century it was rational to believe that Spanish civilization would spread all over the world; but irremediable vices soon dispersed that colonial power, the vestiges of which, still covering a vast space, tell of its ephemeral grandeur. Then came the turn of France; and Louisiana and Canada have preserved the sad remembrance of it. Lastly, England came for-

---

[1] M. Prévost-Paradol. Quoted in "Our Race," p. 11.

ward; she definitely accomplished the great work: and England can disappear from the world without taking her work with her—without the Anglo-Saxon future of the world being sensibly changed."

Each of the three great races of antiquity developed a remarkable centrifugal tendency, a movement outward, which was essential to the fulfilment of its high mission. This same tendency has made the Anglo-Saxon the great colonizing race of the ages; and in fulfilment of its mission this race is carrying its civilization, like a ring of Saturn—a girdle of light,—around the globe.

To prepare the world for the coming of Him who should inaugurate among men the kingdom of God three races wrought through many centuries until the necessary spiritual, intellectual, and physical conditions were made ready. These three spheres all belong to that kingdom....It cannot fully prevail until men are brought into glad obedience to the harmonious laws of these three spheres. Now when we find the most essential characteristics of these three races, the very ones which enabled them to fulfil their mission of preparation, all united in one race, does it not look as if that race were especially commissioned to prepare the way for the full coming of God's kingdom in the earth?

The great marvel of the Anglo-Saxon race is not that it has attained the highest religious development of any, or that it has achieved as great individualism and freedom as the Greeks, or that it has shown a mightier mastery of physical conditions, a profounder genius for organization and government, than the Romans. *The miracle is that these three supreme characteristics are all united in one and the same race....*A high development of the individual and a powerful, far-reaching organization of society have *seemed* incompatible. A hundred civilizations have illustrated the sacrifice of the one to the other, but here is a civilization which combines the two, each in a pre-eminent degree. Here is a race which unites the Greek individualism with the Roman

genius for organization—the only race in history which
has emphasized either of these two great principles
without, in large degree, sacrificing to it the other.[1]

And many would deem it as difficult or impossible to
unite in the same people the fundamental characteristic of the Hebrew with that of the Greek as to unite
the Grecian with that of the Roman. Here, says Mr.
Butcher[2] of Edinburgh University, is one of the problems of modern civilization, ". . . how we are to unite
the dominant Hebrew idea of a divine law of righteousness and of a supreme spiritual faculty with the Hel-
lenic conception of human energies, manifold and expansive, each of which claims for itself unimpeded play;
how life may gain unity without incurring the reproach
of onesidedness; how, in a word, Religion may be combined with culture." The two are often and perhaps
commonly regarded as irreconcilable. I would not say
as some do that these two principles can be harmonized,
for that would concede the existence of a discord,
whereas they are so entirely accordant that each is
essential to the perfect development of the other. If
we take a sufficiently broad view of both, there will be
seen no semblance of conflict. The application of the
great law of unity in diversity makes it obvious that
these two principles are correlative and necessary to
each other. No solution is to be found in compromise
and partition. We may not mark off a part of the life
and say, This is the proper domain of religion and
that of culture. This is that old and pernicious blunder
of dividing life into the "sacred" and the "secular."
If culture means the development of the "manifold
and expansive energies" of man, let culture have the

---

[1] The Romans did not wholly sacrifice individualism to their genius for
organization. They gave play to the two principles more than any other
ancient people, hence the superior greatness of their civilization. There was
a measure of liberty under Roman law, and they developed a sufficient
individuality to produce many great men and a valuable literature, while
their wonderful organizing power gave long life to the empire. "It took
Rome a thousand years to die."

[2] Some Aspects of the Greek Genius, p. 45.

whole field, for the entire man should be fully developed. This is demanded by a true individualism. And if religion means bringing the life under "the divine law of righteousness," then let religion have the *whole* field, for mind and body belong to God as truly as the spiritual nature. And when the entire man is developed by a complete culture which embraces the spiritual, the intellectual, and the physical, and the entire man is brought into perfect obedience to God under the divine law of righteousness, then is perfectly exemplified the fundamental law of unity in diversity.

When such religion and such culture are thus united in every member of the human family the race will have been perfected, and there will then be a perfect organization of society as well as perfect individuality; for when men are brought into perfect harmony with God they will be in perfect harmony with each other.

Because man has a spiritual, intellectual, and physical nature, the final and complete civilization must exhibit a normal development of the spiritual, intellectual, and physical life. These three elements of civilization perfected would constitute a perfect civilization. As we have seen, the Hebrews, Greeks, and Romans each afforded an illustration of one of these elements developed to a remarkable degree. The world needs three such civilizations in one, or rather it needs the three elements which made those peoples great united in a single race. And now for the first time in the history of mankind these three great strands pass through the fingers of one predominant race to be braided into a single supreme civilization in the new era, the perfection of which will be the Kingdom fully come.

A hasty comparison of the leading characteristics of the three great races of antiquity with those of the Anglo-Saxon indicates somewhat the mission of the latter. Let us also compare very briefly the homes of these several races. That of the Hebrew was about the size of our state of New Hampshire; that of the Greek was not as large as the state of Maine; that of the Roman was smaller than the state of Montana. The home of the Anglo-Saxon has served well its purpose in the past, but it too is small and is now outgrown. The home of this great race of the future must be that which Prof. Bryce calls "the Land of the Future." Scattered as is this race over the earth, more than one half of its members are already found in the United States; and more and more will this land become the centre of its influence, the seat of its power.

Probably many Englishmen think of our states as about equal in size to their counties. But of our fifty-one states and territories twenty-seven are each larger than all England, while our entire territory would contain England sixty-nine times. Ten of our states and territories are each larger than England, Wales, and Scotland; while five are each larger than the United Kingdom of Great Britain and Ireland. A German newspaper points out the fact that a person may walk through seven German states in seven hours. Thirteen of the smaller German states might all find room in our Connecticut, and Connecticut might be laid down in the state of Colorado a score of times; and Montana is larger than Colorado by 42,000 square miles. Make Montana the Mecca of the world. Gather into it the 125,000,000 [1] of North and South America, the 380,-000,000 of Europe, the 850,000,000 of Asia, the more than 100,000,000 of Africa, and all the dwellers in the islands of the sea—in short, the nearly 1,500,000,000 of mankind, and when we have gathered within the bounds of this one state the entire human family there will be but fifteen souls to each acre. And California is larger than Montana by 12,000 square miles. Reference has been made to the homes of the three great races among the ancients. Italy, Greece, and Palestine might all be

[1] These estimates of population are from Proceedings of the Royal Geo graphical Society for January, 1891.

gathered into California and then leave ample room for a fair-sized kingdom. And Texas is larger than California by 107,000 square miles. Lay Texas on Europe and it might be placed so as to include the capitals of England, France, Belgium, Switzerland, Germany, and Austria. And Alaska is more than twice as large as Texas. The United Kingdom of Great Britain and Ireland, the Empire of Germany with its twenty-six states, the Republic of France with its eighty-six departments, the kingdom of Greece with its thirteen nomarchies, and the Republic of Switzerland with its twenty-two cantons might all be carved out of this one territory of Alaska.[1]

Great Britain is to-day the home of less than one third of the Anglo-Saxons. And when this race has multiplied tenfold, only an insignificant fraction can occupy the mother-country. Australia and South Africa will both have large populations then, but those countries suffer great natural disadvantages compared with North America. This continent constitutes seven twelfths of the possessions of this race, and here its empire is unsevered, while the remaining five twelfths are fragmentary and scattered over the earth. Our continent lies in the pathway of the nations and belongs to the zone of power; it has room and resources. It can be shown that the agricultural resources of the United States are equal to supporting a population of 1,000,000,000. And the resources of Canada are only less opulent. According to Hon. James W. Taylor, American consul at Winnipeg, "whose knowledge of

---

[1] Of course it is not pretended that Alaska equals in resources these countries which it equals in area. It must not be imagined, however, that this territory is monopolized by Arctic ice and polar bears. The climate is so modified by the Pacific "gulf stream" that at Sitka, the capital, the temperature rarely falls as low as $0°$ F. and the lowest record for forty-five years is $-4°$. Besides her rich fisheries Alaska has great resources in timber, grazing, and mining lands. Mr. William H. Dall of the Smithsonian Institution says: "I come back convinced, from personal inspection, that Alaska is a far better country than much of Great Britain and Norway, or even part of Prussia."

the great Northwest has been for many years a national possession,"[1] the western half of Canada together with Alaska are equal in area to England, Ireland, Scotland, Denmark, Norway, Sweden, Belgium, Holland, and most of Germany and Russia in Europe. "And the productiveness of the American area," he adds, "would surpass that of the European one... There are in these sections of North America fully 200,000,000 acres well adapted to wheat culture." Surely this majestic continent with its unequalled resources is worthy and destined to be the home of this majestic race. Is there no significance in the fact that while the great races of antiquity occupied insignificant homes, and many inferior races have possessed superior lands, *now for the first time in the record of history the greatest race occupies the greatest home?* What a conjunction, big with universal blessings: the greatest race, the greatest civilization, the greatest numbers, the greatest wealth, the greatest physical basis for empire! • • •

No nation can now become or remain a first-class power without an adequate physical basis. The time has not yet come when the nations will consent to be controlled wholly by considerations of right and reason. It is still true that the argument is on the side of the heaviest battalions; still true among nations that the weight of an opinion depends much on the fighting weight of the government which utters it. Before the machinery of war was invented the strength, skill, and bravery of the individual soldier were everything. Now they count for comparatively little. The wars of the future will be won or lost by the national treasury, the patent office, and the census department. It is devoutly to be hoped that the various branches of the Anglo-Saxon race will sustain such relations to each other in the future that their overwhelming superiority of power will be able to compel the world's peace and deliver the nations from the vampire of militarism.

---

[1] See *Harper's Weekly*, Feb. 20, 1892.

Imagine all the races of Europe transformed into one blood, their babel of sixty tongues hushed, and the custom-houses of a score of frontiers closed. Imagine these many lands occupied by 380,000,000 Anglo-Saxons, speaking one language, having common institutions and interests, and all under one government. The mightiest empire that ever existed would be but a faint suggestion of the resistless power of such a people. But this is only a picture of what the United States will be one century hence. All Europe, including the vast plains of Russia, may be laid down within our national bounds, and by a conservative estimate we shall have a population of 373,000,000 in 1990. "A hundred years hence," says the late Émile de Laveleye,[1] "leaving China out of the question, there will be two colossal powers in the world, beside which Germany, England, France, and Italy will be as pygmies—the United States and Russia." But Russia is scarcely worthy to be named in this connection. She will be great in numbers, but can hardly become a rival to Anglo-Saxondom in any other respect. Her civilization is Asiatic rather than European. It suppresses the individual. Such an empire can never excel in the arts of peace without which she must remain poor, and lacking wealth her military power will be insignificant when compared with that of the Anglo-Saxon race.

North America, the future home of this great race, is twice as large as all Europe and is capable of sustaining the present population of the globe. Such a country, with its resources fully developed; such numbers, homogeneous in their civilization; such a race, thrice fitted to prepare the way for the full coming of the kingdom, must, under God, control the world's future.

The overwhelming numbers and the amazing wealth of the future are not the only considerations which will make this continent the great centre of Anglo-Saxondom. As was said by Archbishop Ireland in his

---

[1] *The Forum*, October, 1889.

noble discourse at the Centennial Conference of American Catholics at Baltimore: "We cannot but believe that a singular mission is assigned to America, glorious for ourselves and beneficent to the whole race—that of bringing forth a new social and political order based, more than any other that has theretofore existed, upon the common brotherhood of man, and more than any other securing to the multitude of the people social happiness and equality of rights." As we have already seen, Anglo-Saxons, far better than any other race, have solved the problem of uniting individualism with organization; and Americans, far better than Englishmen, are working out the co-ordination of these two principles as applied to government. Parliament governs the United Kingdom in a sense that Congress does not govern the United States. There authority is centralized at Westminster; here it is distributed throughout the land. Parliament deals with a thousand local matters. Edward Everett Hale says that when he was in London, a member of Parliament asked the government what they were going to do in the case of a school-teacher in Ireland on whose head, four years before, a blackboard had fallen. "The proper officer replied. Notice had been given in advance of this question. The incident took five or ten minutes of a busy night. It was all in good faith. It was not a bit of obstruction. Imagine a question like that in Washington! Strictly speaking, it ought to make a rebellion if anybody in Washington presumed to ask what had become of a school-mistress's head in Oregon." Congress is concerned only with national affairs. Not only have the states of the Union each its separate government, but the counties of each state, the townships of each county, and even the school-districts of each township, within certain limits, control their own affairs. We have local self-government which affords the largest individual liberty, while the general government unites all in the harmony and strength of a mighty nation. "One from many" perfectly illustrates in the sphere of government the most fundamental law of the universe, viz., unity in diversity. In adopting *E Pluribus Unum* as the motto of the United States our political fathers unconsciously adopted what seems to be God's motto of the universe; and it will be the motto of the perfected society toward which the world is moving.

Every one who reads the signs of the times sees a strong tendency toward a closer and more complete social organization. The local self-government in the United States, just mentioned, is eminently favorable to the development of the most perfect social order, because experiments in government can be made under such conditions with far greater ease and safety than where the sovereign power is centralized. When the action of Parliament touches social questions it affects many millions. If an experiment is disastrous, its evil effects are far-reaching. With us one state may try experimental legislation without involving the others. If results are disastrous, only a small fraction of the nation suffers in consequence and the other states may profit by the experience of the one. If a chemist could experiment only on an immense scale, his experiments would doubtless be very costly, perhaps very dangerous, and certainly very infrequent. Another chemist who could use ounces instead of tons would be much less conservative and much more likely to make valuable discoveries. Because of the above characteristics, in which our government differs so widely from that of Great Britain, we are more likely than the English to make progress in social science which depends mainly on experiment.

Moreover the meeting of many races here as nowhere else in the world, with equal rights before the law, with like educational, social, political, and industrial opportunities open to them, is peculiarly favorable to the eradication of race prejudice and the cultivation of a broad sympathy which must precede the coming brotherhood of man. Political equality and brotherhood by no means imply each other, but the true spirit of democracy, which, as Theodore Parker said, means not that " I'm as good as you are " but that " you're as good as I am," is a long step toward fraternity. And doubtless there is among all classes in the United States such a measure of true self-respect united with proper regard for the rights of others as is hardly possible among any people having aristocratic institutions. The new social order based on the brotherhood of man, which we believe ourselves destined to bring forth in the new era, implies the intelligence, well-being, and happiness of the many. That these have been already achieved among us to so exceptional a degree is a favorable comment on our institutions and a justification of our noble hope. In the closing words of his great work, "The American Commonwealth," Mr. Bryce of Cambridge, our most generous yet discriminating critic, says: " America has still a long vista of years stretching before her in which she will enjoy conditions far more auspicious than England can count upon. And that America marks the highest level, not only of material well-being, but of intelligence and happiness, which the race has yet attained, will be the judgment of those who look, not at the favored few for whose benefit the world seems hitherto to have framed its institutions, but at the whole body of the people."

In other important characteristics of the Anglo-Saxon race have Americans outgrown the English. Referring to individualism the eminent author just quoted says[1]: "Everything tended to make the United States in this respect more English than England, for the circumstances of colonial life, the process of settling the western wilderness, the feelings evoked by the struggle against George III., all went to intensify individualism, the love of enterprise, the pride in personal freedom." Many causes have here operated to intensify Anglo-Saxon energy and aggressiveness. A stimulating climate, the undeveloped resources of a continent, our

---

[1] American Commonwealth, Vol. II. pp. 406, 407.

social and political institutions, have all united to produce the most forceful and tremendous energy in the world. Archdeacon Farrar said in 1885: "In America I have been most struck with the enormous power, vivacity, and speed in every department of exertion." Moreover the colonizing tendency of this race is here intensified. It was those in whom this tendency was strongest who settled this country, and this inherited tendency has been further developed by the westward sweep of successive generations across the continent.

Now what is the interpretation of these facts? "It seems to me that God, with infinite wisdom and skill, is here training the Anglo-Saxon race for an hour sure to come in the world's future. Heretofore in the history of mankind there has always been a comparatively unoccupied land westward into which the crowded countries of the East have poured their surplus populations. But the widening waves of migration, which millenniums ago rolled east and west from the valley of the Euphrates, meet to-day on our Pacific coast. There are no more new worlds. The unoccupied arable lands of the earth are limited, and will soon be taken. The time is coming when the pressure of population on the means of subsistence will be felt here as it is now felt in Europe and Asia. Then will the world enter on a new stage of its history—*the final competition of races, for which the Anglo-Saxon is being schooled.* Long before the thousand millions are here, the mighty centrifugal tendency inherent in this stock and strengthened in the United States will assert itself. Then this race of unequalled energy, with all the majesty of numbers and the might of wealth behind it—the representative, let us hope, of the largest liberty, the purest Christianity, the highest civilization—having developed peculiarly aggressive traits calculated to impress its institutions upon mankind, will spread itself over the earth. And can any one doubt that the result of this competition of races will be the survival of the fittest?"[1] Is it

---

[1] The Author's "Our Country," p. 222.

not reasonable to believe that this race is destined to dispossess many weaker ones, assimilate others, and mould the remainder, until, in a very true and important sense, it has Anglo-Saxonized mankind ?

I have only to add in conclusion a few corollaries.

1. Both good and evil have a longer leverage in the United States than anywhere else in the world.

2. The importance to mankind and to the coming Kingdom of guarding against the deterioration of the Anglo-Saxon stock in the United States by immigration. There is now being injected into the veins of the nation a large amount of inferior blood every day of every year.

3. The importance of annihilating the saloon and every other agency which is devitalizing and corrupting our population.

4. He does most to Christianize the world and to hasten the coming of the Kingdom who does most to make thoroughly Christian the United States. I do not imagine that an Anglo Saxon is any dearer to God than a Mongolian or an African. My plea is not, Save America for America's sake, but, Save America for the world's sake.

CHAPTER V.

WE have seen that the world is evidently about to enter on a new era, that in this new era mankind is to come more and more under Anglo-Saxon influence, and that Anglo-Saxon civilization is more favorable than any other to the spread of those principles whose universal triumph is necessary to that perfection of the race to which it is destined; the entire realization of which will be the kingdom of heaven fully come on earth. We have seen that the Anglo-Saxon is accumulating irresistible power with which to press the die of his civilization upon the world. But this die is by no means completely cut as yet and fit for its work. Our civilization is only partially Christianized. And it is this fact which accounts for the existence of the great problems which vex modern society and shame our best wisdom.

If, as many believe, we are entering on a transition state, it is criticall; important that our plastic institutions be brought under the moulding hand of Christ, and that his teachings be recognized as binding on all men, not only in their relations with God, but also in their daily relations one with another.

Of course the church accepts Christ's teachings as authoritative, though we shall see later that it explains away an important part of them. But I am writing for a large class outside the church as well as for those in it, for men who are deeply interested in social and industrial reform, but who look for no help from the church or its Founder; who do not see that the most

81

reasonable hope of gaining industrial peace is through
Him who came to bring " peace on earth," and who do
not know that the only hope of realizing their dreams
of a brotherhood of man is through Him who revealed
the fatherhood of God.   Indeed, many of this class
believe that we know too little of Jesus to be able to
determine whether the character attributed to him in
the Gospels is real or ideal and whether the words
ascribed to him were actually uttered by him or not.
For such I wish to show that the character and life
portrayed in the Gospels is beyond a peradventure
genuine.

Moreover, it will do no harm to confirm the faith of
the churches, for we live in an age of doubt.   The
growth of science has created the scientific habit of
mind which accepts nothing on mere authority.   Beliefs are no longer sacred simply because they were
held by the fathers.   The application of the scientific
method to history has dissipated into myth or legend
much that the fathers held as substantial reality.   Furthermore, it has been a mischievous mistake on the
part of many Christians to build their faith not solely
on Christ, the Rock of Ages, but partly and largely on
the shifting sands of human theories; and as the progress of knowledge has destroyed these human foundations, the faith of many has perished with them.   Not
a few are saying to-day that if they are compelled to
surrender their belief in the inerrancy of Scripture,
their faith in Christianity will have to go with it.   That
would be a sacrifice as gratuitous as sad.   Nothing can
shake my confidence in Christianity which does not
shake my confidence in the genuineness of the life and
character of Christ, for he is the only true foundation
of the Christian faith.   It has been said that Romanism
is the religion of a church, and that Protestantism is the
religion of a book.   Both church and Bible are necessary, but all true Christianity, whether Protestant
or Roman Catholic, is the religion of a *person*, centred
in Christ and drawing its life and power from him.

There are many, in the church as well as out of it, who need to learn that Christianity is neither a creed nor a ceremonial, but a life vitally connected with the living Christ.

For all, therefore, who base their hope of eternal life on the truth of Christianity, for those who see in it the great uplifting power for perfecting the race, and for those who are raising the question whether it has spent its force and exhausted its vitality, there can be no more fundamental inquiry than this: Are the character and life presented in the Gospels genuine?

No one questions that in the time of Tiberius there was a man called Jesus, who was put to death by the procurator Pontius Pilate, whose doctrines spread rapidly throughout the Roman world, whose followers worshipped him as God and lived lives of remarkable purity. Thus much is not a matter of inference or faith, but of established fact. Had the Gospels never been written, we should know as much as this from Tacitus, Suetonius, Juvenal, Adrian, Pliny, and others. But all this being beyond doubt, there is still room for the questions, Is the character ascribed to Jesus in the Gospels genuine? Was the life there recorded really lived?

Those who answer these questions in the negative must resort to one of two theories or to both in part to account for the character and life presented in the Gospels, viz., either that additions to the truth were invented with intention to deceive, or that they grew up unconsciously out of the ideals of the people and were gradually crystallized in the form of myths around the historical facts in the life of Jesus. We will consider the latter first.

I. This theory assumes that Jesus was a great man, but holds that the character and life depicted in the Gospels are seen through the mists of legend or myth and, like all objects seen through a fog, are magnified. Let us judge whether the men of Christ's age and nation were capable of magnifying even a great man into

the incomparable character before us—the most masterful of history.

Every people and ev ry generation has its own
"climate of opinion." Popular standards and the atmosphere in which we live have become Christianized
to such an extent that we now take for granted, or
regard as the normal outgrowth of human nature,
many things of which the world before Christ had no
conception. Ideas of right and noble sentiments are
now become commonplace and are regarded as elementary which the greates minds before Christ had
perceived only dimly or not at ll. It is, therefore,
very difficult for us to appreciate how entirely strange
and even contrary to all preconceived ideas were many
of the teachings of Christ to the men of his generation,
and how incapable were such minds of originating the
utterances attributed to him.

Christ belonged to a narrow age. No people found
much to admire in the world beyond th ir own national
horizon. The Greeks had one word f r stranger and
barbarian. Plato divided mankind into "Barbarians
and Hellenes," which reminds us of a similar division
into "Jews and Gentiles." Among the Romans the
same word meant stranger and enemy. The Jews were
the most intensely narrow and intolerant of all races.
They entertained a supreme contempt for everything
non-Jewish and a bitter hatred toward all Gentiles.
Every Gentile child was regarded unclean as soon as
born. All heathen and their belongings were polluted
and held in abhorrence and were to be altogether
avoided except in cases of necessity or for the sake of
business. Heathen were not to be delivered from peril.
The Mishna forbids aid to a mother in the hour of her
need, or nourishment to her babe.[1] It was held that
even the good deeds of the Gentiles were reckoned to
them as sins. According to a rabbinical proverb, they
looked coolly upon their own proselytes until the

---

[1] Edersheim's *Life and Times of Jesus*, Vol. I. p. 91.

twenty-fourth generation. "If a heretic returned to the true faith, he should die at once—partly, probably, to expiate his guilt, and partly for fear of relapse." [1] Such were the people whom we are asked to believe originated the legends which enlarged and rounded out the figure of Jesus into a generic character as broad as the race and as comprehensive as the ages.

The conception, the teachings, the plans of the character found in the Gospels were as wide as the world. God so loved not the Jews only but "*the world*" that he sent his Son. "Go ye into *all the world*, and preach the gospel to *every creature.*" "Whosoever," "all," "every one," "any man," "all nations," "all men," "the earth," "the world," are frequently-recurring words.

This character is represented as singularly tolerant. When Christ's disciples said to him, "Master, we saw one casting out devils in thy name; and we forbade him, because he followeth not with us," he answered, "Forbid him not; for he that is not against us is for us." [2] He said to the Samaritan, "Woman, believe me, the hour cometh, when ye shall neither in this mountain, nor yet at Jerusalem, worship the Father; . . . when the true worshippers shall worship the Father in spirit and in truth: for the Father seeketh such to worship him." [3] Dr. Schenkel, a rationalistic theologian, calls these words "the grandest of all speeches in defence of tolerance." [4]

Christ did not fiercely denounce those who persecuted him or his disciples, but said "the time cometh, that whosoever killeth you will think that he doeth God service." [5] Many men treat a difference of opinion as if it were intended as a personal affront, but in this passage Christ attributed the best of motives to those who should martyr his followers. He recognized their sincerity and put the most generous and charitable con-

---

[1] Edersheim's Life and Times of Jesus, Vol. I. p. 91.   [2] Luke ix. 49, 50.
[3] John iv. 21-23.   [4] Quoted by Prof. Christlieb, Modern Doubt, p. 357.
[5] John xvi. 2.

struction on their persecutions. In such charity, how many centuries was Christ in advance of his age! Indeed, it would seem that our own times have not as yet altogether overtaken his teaching. The "odium theologicum" still finds common illustration. It is not many generations since good men burned good men and saintly women for honest difference of opinion. And it is only about thirty years since a Calvinist in New England, a man of undoubted piety and of great reputed learning and ability, when asked if any of the Methodists (or Arminians, as they were then called) could be saved, replied with the utmost solemnity, " Not *one!*"

This generation is more charitable, but many a man in this day lays the flattering unction to his soul that he is " tolerant," "liberal-minded," when in point of fact he is so shallow-souled as to be simply indifferent to all truth, and perhaps indifferent to wickedness as well—a more dangerous state of mind than that of the bigot, and a more contemptible character. The bigot is narrow, but intense. He believes something firmly enough to sacrifice for it—other people, at least, and very likely himself.

Now, Christ was so far from being indifferent to the truth that under the shadow of the cross he exclaimed, " To this end was I born, and for this cause came I into the world, that I should bear witness unto the truth." [1] He was absolutely loyal to the truth and at the same time tolerant of the opinions of others and of their conduct also, provided it seemed conscientious. Whence came such exalted character? Anything like a large tolerance has never been general until recent times, and even now good men follow their Master afar off and limpingly. Can we believe that in a far more intolerant age the most bigoted of races, on whom intense narrowness had been inculcated as a *religious duty*, originated conceptions of tolerance so far in advance not of that age only but also of this?

---

[1] John xviii. 37.

The love which Christ inculcated and manifested was far more wonderful than his tolerance. The Pharisees taught that every enemy was to be hated, and that every one who was not a Jew was an enemy. To be guilty of belonging to any Gentile race was to be worthy of hatred, but to be a Roman was to be abhorred. No thought was sweeter to the Jew than that of vengeance on his Roman oppressor. Nothing could have been more impossible to the nation while under that yoke than such a popular state of mind or heart as would give rise and currency to legends which taught the possibility and duty of loving their Roman masters.

The love of man as man implies an estimate of humanity which was not held by any ancient people before Christ. The Jew respected Jewish nature, but not human nature. The highest Greek philosophy had no respect for man as such. Not only were foreigners despised, but the common people of their own race also. The Romans were broader than the Jews or Greeks and admitted many aliens to citizenship, but their treatment of slaves and of their own children shows that they saw in human nature no intrinsic grandeur or worth. "Individual right and respect for human personality found no place in Greece or Rome." [1] Slaves were mutilated and maimed, and their flesh was sometimes used to fatten the fish of their Roman lords. Captured in war or purchased of pirates for a few sesterces, a slave might be of noble blood, might have more learning or rarer accomplishments than his master, he might even possess genius, but because he lacked power he was entitled to no respect. He had no more right to a will than a dead man or a brute.

It was common for Roman parents to expose their new-born infants to wild beasts and birds of prey or to the more horrible fate of being rescued for the vilest purposes. Quintilian says that "to kill a man is often held to be a crime, but to kill one's own children is

---

[1] Schmidt's Social Results of Early Christianity, p. 76.

sometimes considered a beautiful action among the Romans." [1] And Seneca writes: "Monstrous offspring we destroy; children too, if weak and unnaturally formed from birth, we drown. It is not anger, but reason, thus to separate the useless from the sound." [2] Thus it appears that use, not inherent worth, was the criterion by which the value of human nature was measured. The famous apothegm of Terence, "I am a man, and nothing of man is foreign to me," might seem to indicate a broad humanity, but the admirable things said of man by the Greek and Roman sages were spoken only of the freeman. "He who was neither a freeman nor a citizen was not looked upon by them as a man at all, but only as a chattel." [3] The utter emptiness of this beautiful sentiment of Terence is shown by the fact which has often been pointed out, that the man who utters it is the very father who earlier in the play had rebuked his wife for exposing their child instead of killing it as he had previously commanded.

The Roman father had unlimited power over his children. He could put them in chains, sell them into slavery, or kill them. And he frequently exercised this power. Nor were such practices at all peculiar to the Romans. The same powers, modified by Mosaic legislation, were possessed by the Hebrew father. The prevalence of such customs and the universality of slavery indicate that men had not yet conceived of the inherent dignity and worth of human nature taught by Christ.

Until modern times, few things have been as cheap as human life. We hardly need to remind ourselves of the countless numbers, during centuries, "butchered to make a Roman holiday." Trajan in a hundred and twenty-three days forced 10,000 prisoners and gladiators to fight to the death in the amphitheatre. We are told [4] that in "Christian" England 72,000 thieves and robbers

---

[1] Quoted in Gesta Christi, p. 73.
[2] De Ira, I. 15. Quoted by Brace in Gesta Christi.
[3] Schmidt's Social Results of Early Christianity, p. 76.
[4] Hume, Chap. XXXIII.

suffered the death penalty during the reign of Henry
VIII., when the population was only about one seventh
of what it is now; and in one year 300 beggars were
executed for soliciting alms. Late in the eighteenth
century the value of human life was so small that
Edmund Burke said he could obtain the assent of the
House of Commons to any bill imposing the punishment
of death. "It seems, at first, that there can scarcely be
two hundred and twenty-three human actions worthy
even of the mildest censure. But our stern fathers
found that number worthy of death. If a man injured
Westminster Bridge, he was hanged. If he appeared
disguised on a public road, he was hanged. If he cut
down young trees; if he shot at rabbits; if he stole
property valued at five shillings; if he stole anything at
all from a bleachfield; if he wrote a threatening letter
to extort money; if he returned prematurely from
transportation,—for any of these offences he was immediately hanged." [1] Early in the present century, coun-
terfeiting the stamps that were used for the sale of
perfumery or hair-powder was punishable with death.
In colonial times, the laws of Virginia made absence
from church services a crime, and for the third offence
prescribed the death penalty. So slow has the world
been to learn the sacredness of human life. But see
how Christ appraised every human being, not simply
the physical life but the essential man, whose worth is
such as to give dignity and value to all that pertains to
him. He taught that God numbered every hair of the
head,[2] and that a whole world would not compensate for
the loss of a single soul.[3] He restored the sick and
withheld not his healing touch from the loathsome
leper. He identified himself with the obscurest of his
followers.[4] He paid a beautiful tribute to human nature
in the respect which he showed to little children.[5] His
treatment of them was "utterly contrary to all Jewish

---

[1] Mackenzie's Hist. Nineteenth Century, pp. 77, 78.   [2] Matt. x. 30.
[3] Matt. xvi. 26.   [4] Matt. xxv. 40.   [5] Mark x. 13-16.

notions and incompatible with the supposed dignity of a rabbi." [1] But his interest in men when ruined and depraved placed a still higher estimate on the worth of every man. The return of one such to a righteous life was an event of sufficient consequence to be celebrated in heaven. [2] He represents the Good Shepherd as seeking the one wandering sheep until he finds it and brings it home with joy. His estimate of the value of every human being is strikingly shown by his interview with the woman of Samaria. According to Jewish ideas there should be no needless conversation with a woman, and to instruct a woman in the law was forbidden. [3] Not only did this woman belong to a people held in peculiar contempt by the Jews, but she was a woman of bad character—a member of a class despised among a despised people. This woman, who in the eyes of the Jews was superlatively worthless and altogether contemptible, Christ instructed and reclaimed, and, by declaring to her his Messiahship, conspicuously honored.

By his teachings and death Christ has given to the world a new conception of man. He has been called the discoverer of the individual. [4] In harmony with the high estimate which he placed on human nature was his respect for the poor. "The poor represent man stripped of all extrinsic attributes of honor, and reduced to that which is common to all mankind. On this naked humanity the world has ever set little value. It begins to interest itself in a man when he is clothed with some outward distinction of wealth or birth or station. A mere man is a social nobody. Christ, on the other hand, highly valued in man only his humanity, accounting nothing he could possess of such importance as what he himself was or might become." [5] In founding his kingdom Christ sought his adherents and chose his dis-

---

[1] Edersheim's Life and Times of Jesus, Vol. II. p. 336.
[2] Luke xv. 10.
[3] Edersheim's Life and Times of Jesus, Vol. II. p. 418.
[4] Stalker's Imago Christi, p. 58.
[5] Bruce's Kingdom of God, p. 130.

ciples from among the poor. Men who seek kingdoms or think to transform society aim to acquire influence in the high places of the earth. Christ began with the lowly, not as the partisan of a class, but because he saw what men are only now beginning to see, that in order to uplift society we must commence at the bottom. He perceived what the world did not discover until nearly two thousand years later, that the so-called "common people" are the most important to the nation and to the world. It is because Christ recognized the value of human nature, aside from position or possession, that Lowell called him "the first true democrat that ever breathed." [1]

The breadth of the character presented in the Gospels has been briefly illustrated by its tolerance, its all-inclusive love, its high estimate of human nature, and its respect for the poor. These conceptions are as much broader than were the ideas of the Jews as the world is broader than Palestine.

Let us now glance at the spiritual elevation of this character.

The religion of the Jews had degenerated into mere externalism. The rabbis had prescribed an enormous number of rules to cover the entire field of human conduct, providing for every possible and impossible case. Religion had become ritualistic, and consisted in the observance of forms and ceremonies. There was here and there a devout soul, but the nation had lost its spiritual life and of course its spiritual perception.

The Messiah, for whose coming the nation looked with passionate longing, was not thought of as a saviour from sin, but as a king who should bring deliverance from the galling yoke of the hated Roman and accomplish the national restoration. Much less was he thought of as the saviour of other peoples. Whatever differences may have existed on other points among the Jews scattered over the world, all agreed on this, that

---

[1] Democracy, p. 21.

the Messiah was to come as the king and deliverer of their nation and the conqueror of all others. He was to be a typical Israelite. Not only the predictions but also the history and institutions of the nation were to find their consummate flower and fruitage in him. He was to be "alike the crown, the completion, and the representative of Israel." [1] The popular mind was so steeped in the conviction that the Messiah was to bring, not a spiritual salvation for the world, but a political salvation for the nation, that even those who had been for three years under Christ's tuition failed to perceive the spiritual character of the kingdom which he had come to establish, and only a short time before his death his disciples, like so many spoilsmen, quarrelled over the division of the expected prize. [2]

Instead of resorting to arms as the nation expected and desired, Jesus foretold that he would conquer his kingdom by the *cross !* [3] Nothing could be more inconceivable to the Jews. It is perhaps impossible for us to dissociate from the cross the meaning which has gathered to it during these nineteen Christian centuries. It is inseparably associated with that which is deepest in Christian experience and most sacred in religious feeling. It has entered into poetry, architecture, and art, has become the most beautiful and significant of all symbols, and is recognized as the invincible standard of an all-conquering faith. But to the ancient Jew it was only hideous. It meant to him all that the gallows means to us, with the added horror of prolonged torture. It was the sign of helpless and suffering ignominy. Cicero somewhere says the cross was not to be mentioned in polite society. The idea of a king's winning his kingdom by means of death, and death on the cross, must have struck men as superlatively absurd. The cross and the Messianic glory were farther apart in the Jewish mind than the East and the West. The spiritual significance of the cross was at an impossible height

---

[1] Edersheim, Vol. I. p. 161.   [2] Matt. xx. 20-24.   [3] John xii. 32.

above the Jewish imagination. So far were the disciples from originating the conception that they could not comprehend it when Christ unfolded it to them.

The dignity and blessedness of service is another truth which was above the comprehension of that generation. It contradicted custom, opinion, and inclination. To serve was menial; slavery degraded labor. Power existed for the gratification of its possessor. The emperor was servant of none and was served by all. "But it shall not be so among you; but whosoever will be great among you, let him be your minister; and whosoever will be chief among you, let him be your servant." [1] This generation acknowledges that service is one of the fundamental laws of society; the ruler of England is her first *minister*, and president, king, and emperor profess themselves the servants of the people.

Christ uttered other spiritual truths which have been only very partially apprehended and accepted as yet and which anticipate the perfect society of the future.

The principles of his teachings are believed by the best modern thinkers to furnish the solution of the great problems of modern society. Says Mr. Gladstone: "Talk about the questions of the day; there is but one question, and that is the Gospel. It can and will correct everything needing correction." Prince Bismarck asks for social well-being nothing more than "Christianity without phrases." The Hon. Carroll D. Wright, Chief of the National Bureau of Labor, says: "I believe that in the adoption of the philosophy of the religion of Jesus Christ as a practical creed for the conduct of business lies the surest and speediest solution of those industrial difficulties which are exciting the minds of men to-day, and leading many to think that the crisis of government is at hand." Prof. R. T. Ely declares that from the study of political economy he has come to the conclusion that "the remedy for social discontent and dynamite bombs is Christianity as

---

[1] Matt. xx. 26, 27,

taught in the New Testament." [1]   And Herbert Spencer, "the most distinguished living sociologist, studying human beings in their social relations, and interrogating experience to find the right rule for their guidance, reaches, after much careful study, the very law laid down by Jesus Christ nineteen hundred years ago." [2]

How are we to account for the fact that the utterances ascribed to Christ have such a forward reach that, stretching over the heads of nearly threescore generations, they anticipate the loftiest moral and spiritual conceptions of our own day and are echoed in the ripest conclusions of modern social science ? Which is the more reasonable, to ascribe these sayings to a wholly unique person, whom we *know* to be historic, or to the unconscious wisdom, the legendary growths of a generation which could not comprehend their meaning ? Were men who had become spiritually blind, whose religion consisted in forms, who tithed mint, anise, and cummin and omitted judgment, mercy, and faith, who piously strained out the gnat of ceremonial uncleanness and calmly swallowed camels of moral depravity, men whose lives had been emptied of principles and smothered with rules—were such the men to give to the world the organic laws of human society and to reveal the fundamental moral truths of the ages ?

Much of the doctrine of Jesus was above the comprehension of his countrymen, and much which they understood contradicted teachings which they had held sacred for ages, so that they repeatedly declared that he was possessed of a devil and mad.   Edersheim says that "Jesus fundamentally separated himself from all the ideas of his time." [3]   There was absolute contrariety between his teachings and rabbinism, which was regarded by the people with profound reverence.

We should remember that it is difficult to convince

---

[1] *The Home Missionary*, Oct. 1884, p. 227.
[2] Dr. Washington Gladden's Applied Christianity, p. 232.
[3] Life and Times of Jesus, Vol. I. p. 104

men of anything which they do not wish to believe. They demand evidence, and what would afford proof to an unbiassed mind is often quite insufficient to convince men against their will; while that which harmonizes with preconceived opinion is often accepted with little or no evidence. Hence it is that myths and legends which are believed gain credence because they flatter national pride, like the story of William Tell, or embody national ideals, or are for some other reason pleasant to believe. Distasteful legends do not gain currency as true. And the narrower men are the more difficult is it to convince them of anything which runs counter to their prejudices.

Now the Jews are characterized by a peculiar tenacity. In contact with all the races of the world, they still cling to their traditional beliefs. Carlyle remarks on their tenacity and obstinacy as "clinging to the same belief, probable or improbable, or even impossible." [1] Such was the race, steeped in their religious convictions, among whom we are asked to believe that legends sprung up which taught original conceptions of religious truth in absolute conflict with the most sacred beliefs of the nation.

If it be said that these legends originated, not among Jews who still adhered to Judaism, but among early Christians who had been profoundly impressed by Jesus, then we are to understand that his character and life, before they had been glorified by legend and when therefore, according to this theory, they were simply human and imperfect and of course destitute of all miraculous power,—that then this character and life so transformed, enlarged, and perfected ritualistic and bigoted Jews that they were able to supplement this character and round it out to full-orbed perfection ! But how would it be possible for Jesus to inspire in men conceptions of truth larger, loftier, and more beautiful than he had ever himself conceived or exemplified ?

---

[1] Hist. of Literature, p. 47.

Here is this character in the Gospels—an effect for which, if we propose to account for it, we must find an adequate cause. Were effects produced by the lesser and imperfect Jesus (assumed by this theory) sufficient as causes to produce the larger, perfected Christ which we find in the Gospels? To ask such a question is to answer it.

Moreover, even if we suppose the loftiest of the utterances and traits ascribed to Jesus in the Gospels were of legendary or mythical origin, we must still account for the *unity* of the character before us. It is perfectly rounded and balanced, and absolutely self-consistent. It strikes no one as patchwork. Diverse characteristics meet in Christ without discord and together constitute a complete and symmetrical whole. Because men differ their ideals differ. If then the incidents and sayings of the Gospel were the ideals of the people, crystallized in legends, how are we to account for the fact that when collected they constitute a harmonious and glorious whole? As well might we expect each one of a multitude to bring a sentence and then by gathering them together produce the noblest and most perfect poem of all literature.

But these are not the only objections to this theory. Time is necessary for the production of myths. They are the outgrowth of generations. In the first edition of his "Life of Jesus," Strauss maintained that his myths were formed in the post-apostolic age; but during the twenty-nine years intervening between that edition and the last, the critics of the Tübingen school conceded that the first three Gospels belong to the apostolic age. Accordingly in his last edition Strauss said: "In this new work I have, chiefly in consequence of Baur's investigations, used the supposition of *conscious and intentional invention* far more freely than before." Hostile critics now assign Matthew and Mark to a place somewhere between A.D. 80 and 90, and sober-minded critics place Mark still earlier. That is, it is now conceded that these two Gospels, at least, were written

during the lifetime of many who had seen and heard
Jesus.

But this is not all. Even the most hostile critics concede the genuineness of Paul's letters to the Romans,
the Corinthians, and the Galatians; and these were
written during the years 57 and 58, that is, within
twenty-five years of the death of Christ. These letters
refer incidentally, and hence the more convincingly, to
several of the most prominent facts in the life of Jesus;
they show that at that early date the Lord's Supper had
been instituted and churches organized; that men believed in Christ's resurrection and supernatural power,
his sinlessness and pre-existence, that they were bap-
tized in his name, trusted in him as the Saviour of men,
and expected him to judge the earth. Throughout
these epistles we find precisely such a character assumed as that depicted in the four Gospels.[1] This does

---

[1] Christ is said to have been "of the seed of David" (Rom. i. 3), and the
"Son of God" (Rom. i. 4); to have died for sinners (Rom. v. 6, 8; 1 Cor. xv.
3); to have been crucified (stated in all four epistles, Rom. vi. 6; 1 Cor. i. 17,
18, 23; 2 Cor. xiii. 4; Gala. ii. 20); to have risen from the dead (Rom. i. 4, iv.
24, 25, vi. 4. 9, viii. 11, 34, xiv. 9; 1 Cor. xv. 4, 13. 16, 20; 2 Cor. iv. 14); to have
been seen after his resurrection "of above five hundred brethren at once;
of whom the greater part remain until this present" (1 Cor. xv. 6), also by
Paul himself (1 Cor. xv. 8).

Christ is spoken of as meek and gentle (2 Cor. x. 1); not pleasing himself
(Rom. xv. 3), yet exalted "over all" (Rom. ix. 5); as pre-existent (1 Cor. x.
4, 9; 2 Cor. viii. 9); as sinless (2 Cor. v. 21); as possessing supernatural power,
"by whom are all things, and we by him" (1 Cor. viii. 6). In all four of
these epistles his name is coupled with that of God the Father in a benediction (Rom. i. 7: 1 Cor. i. 3; 2 Cor. xiii. 14; Gala. i. 3). He was worshipped,
"all that in every place call on the name of Jesus Christ our Lord" (1 Cor.
i. 2); was believed to be the final Judge of all men (2 Cor. v. 10; Rom. ii. 16).
His "gospel" is repeatedly mentioned (Rom. i. 16, xv. 19, 20, 29; 1 Cor. ix. 12,
14, 16, 18; 2 Cor. iv. 4, x. 14; Gala. i. 6, 7, 8, 9); already recognized as "the
power of God unto salvation" (Rom. i. 16). Christ is represented as our "re-
deemer" (Rom. iii. 24; Gala. iii. 13); our "propitiation" (Rom. iii. 25); our
"justification" (Rom. iv. 25, v. 9; Gala. ii. 16, 17); the only foundation (1 Cor.
iii. 11). A wonderful love existed between Christ and his followers, from
which nothing could separate (Rom. viii. 35–39). His followers were "bap-
tized into" him (Rom. vi. 3).

Paul speaks of "the twelve" (1 Cor. xv. 5); refers to the Lord's Supper (1
Cor. x. 16, 17, 21, xi. 23–29); and shows that many churches had already been

THE NEW ERA.

not allow time for the development of myths, and therefore undermines the theory of unconscious additions to
the truth and compels those who do not accept the genuineness of the life and character of Christ presented
in the Gospels to resort to the theory of *invention with
the intention to deceive.* Supposing then a sufficient
motive (which really involves absurdities), we shall find
that the task proposed was an impossible one.

II. The theory of invention is simplified by supposing
that the character before us is the product of one man's
skill rather than the result of collusion on the part of
several. If, as we have seen, the people were not capable of forming such high ideals, let us suppose that the
most gifted man in the nation undertook the invention
of the most exalted and wonderful part of the character
and life of Jesus.

When a man intends to deceive, his fabrication will
be fashioned with reference to those for whom it is intended. It must be made credible in order to success.
He is not only limited by his own inventive powers and
the resources at hand, but also by the intelligence, the
prejudices, the credulity of those for whom he fabri-
cates. We must remember that the supposed inventor
was producing a character, not for the nineteenth century, but for the first; not for Anglo-Saxons or Germans
or Frenchmen, but for Jews.

Why, then, should this inventor have done violence to
the Jewish conception of the Messiah? Why represent
their national Messiah as the Saviour of the world, receiving Jews, Greeks, and Romans on equal terms?
Why represent him as persistently claiming to be a
king,[1] and yet absolutely refusing to be crowned[2] or to
employ the weapons and methods of kings? Such an
invention could never have originated in the brain of a

---

organized (Rom. xvi. 4, 16; 1 Cor. vii. 17, xi. 16, xiv. 33, xvi. 1, 19; 2 Cor.
viii. 1, 19, 23, xi. 8, 28, xii. 13; Gala. i. 22).

How is all this *within twenty-five years of the death of Christ* to be ac
counted for on the mythical theory ?

[1] Matt. xxi. 5, xxv. 34; John xviii. 36, 37.   [2] John vi. 15.

Jew who all his life had been taught that the Messiah was to establish a temporal kingdom and was to "break the nations with a rod of iron and dash them in pieces like a potter's vessel." [1] Nor could a Jew have believed that such an invention would be accepted by his countrymen. To them the claims and conduct of Jesus were contradictory. *We* see that his course was consistent, but this inventor was not fabricating for us.

Why scandalize the Jews by representing their Messiah as associating with publicans and sinners? A publican was deemed even more contemptible than a Gentile. What inventor of the life and character of a reformer or saviour of society would ever think of representing him as inviting into his organization, and at the very outset, extortioners and harlots? Surely it would occur to no such inventor to begin the reformation of society by means of its outcasts.

Why shock the Jews by representing their Messiah to them as a Sabbath-breaker? Why bring him into open conflict with the scribes and Pharisees? We so despise Pharisaism and rabbinism that it is difficult for us to appreciate the veneration in which these men were held by the nation. "Each scribe outweighed all the common people." [2] He was worthy of all honor. He was honored by God himself, and his praises proclaimed by the angels. He would hold the same rank in heaven as on earth. Such was the respect paid to his sayings that "they were to be absolutely believed, even if they were to declare that to be at the right hand which was at the left, or *vice versa.*" [3] The legal determinations of the scribes were even more binding than Scripture itself. Christ repeatedly called these men "hypocrites" and "vipers." Would a Jew ever think of making the national Messiah apply such epithets to these almost sacred representatives of the national wisdom? There was a popular saying that if only two men entered heaven, the one would be a scribe and the

---

[1] Ps. ii. 9.   [2] Edersheim's Life and Times of Jesus, Vol. I. p. 94.   [3] Ibid.

other a Pharisee. Would a Jew ever think of putting into the mouth of the Messiah such words as these : "Except your righteousness shall exceed the righteousness of the scribes and Pharisees, ye shall in no case enter into the kingdom of heaven"[1]?

The profound reverence of the Jews for authority is illustrated by the fact that the great Hillel was wont to mispronounce a word because his teacher before him had done so.[2] Would any one think of making their Messiah, who was to be the crown and completion of all their past, repeatedly begin his teachings thus: "Ye have heard that it was said by them of old time"[3] thus and thus, "But *I* say unto you" differently?

The central truth, made manifest both by Christ's words and deeds, is that of the cross—self-giving for others. And this is made the condition of discipleship for Jew and Gentile, Pharisee and publican, all alike.[4] It is inconceivable that the supposed inventor would or could have formed any such conception. Among all peoples and in all ages human nature has paid tribute to the nobility of self-sacrifice. Examples of self-devotion for others, even unto death, are not wanting among heathen peoples, but they are looked on as almost or quite divine. Their lustre shines down from a height, deemed unattainable by ordinary men. It is inconceivable that any one inventing a character and life as an example to all classes and conditions of men would make self-abnegation for others the law of common life. No one before Christ ever conceived of common humanity as capable of such exalted heroism; no one ever supposed that the weak and the vile, the degraded and the brutish, could ever reach such moral sublimity. And surely no *impostor* would ever dream of making such a transformation the condition of discipleship. It could never have occurred to human wisdom in planning a religion as broad as

---

[1] Matt. v. 20.
[2] Edersheim, Vol. I. p. 98,
[3] Matt. v. ‑
[4] Ibid. xvi. 24, 25,

the world to make the gate of entrance so exceeding strait. Being a Hebrew of the Hebrews would avail nothing. They of the circumcision must pass through the same experience as the despised Gentiles. Could a Jew imagine Israel's Messiah teaching such a doctrine?

The Jews of that generation rejected the conception of the Messiah which is found in the New Testament, and their descendants for nineteen hundred years have continued to reject it. Surely any one having such a profound knowledge of human nature with such consummate wisdom and insight as to be able to invent this character would have had sufficient knowledge of his own countrymen to foresee that rejection. Are we to infer, then, that he did foresee it and intend it; that he planned to make Christianity a world-religion; that he expected the cross, which was a stumbling-block to the Jew and foolishness to the Greek, would prove to be God's power for conquering the world? This is to ascribe a superhuman wisdom to the inventor which the theory denies to Christ.

But we must examine more closely the exact nature of the task which this supposed inventor undertook. According to the synoptic Gospels (I will not appeal to the fourth Gospel in this connection) Jesus makes some astonishing claims, viz.:

That he possesses superhuman power; that indeed all power is his.[1]

That he had power to forgive sins.[2]

That he is king of a heavenly kingdom.[3]

That he is worthy of the supreme love of the race, demanding a love stronger than the love of father, mother, wife, or child.[4]

That he will finally judge all nations.[5]

Certainly only a superhuman character could sustain such claims; and as a matter of fact the most enlightened peoples have, for nineteen centuries, considered

---

[1] Matt. xxviii. 18. [2] Mark ii. 10. [3] Matt. xxv. 34.
[4] Matt. x. 37. [5] Matt. xxv. 31-46.

these claims sustained, and have accepted this character as divine and at the same time human. The problem, then, was, *first*, to invent such a character —one that would be accepted as God's idea of man and man's idea of God; and, *secondly*, to invent a life worthy of such a character—words and acts befitting God, yet human ; words and acts befitting man, yet divine.

1. The invention of a divine human character. Christ gave to the world a new conception of God. He not only made much more real the divine love and fatherhood which the prophets had taught, but he revealed a monotheism of which the Jews seem never to have conceived. They were monotheists, but only in the sense that they believed Jehovah to be the one living and true God. They did not deem him the God of the Gentiles. He could become their God only as they became Jews. Where did this Jew, going about to invent a god, get this vastly higher conception of Deity ?

As nations grow morally and spiritually their conceptions of Deity change. The Zeus of Socrates was very different from the Zeus of Homer. The God worshipped in the middle ages was very different from the God worshipped to-day. We find now that our progress toward a nobler apprehension of Deity has been due to removing the misconceptions with which the God revealed in Christ has been overlaid. We find that our enlarging conceptions are simply fuller and clearer apprehensions of the revelation made nineteen hundred years ago. Are we to believe that this revelation was an invention made by a man nineteen hundred years in advance of his age ?

Again, Christ is accepted as a perfect man. The more one knows of great and good men the more is he impressed with the fact that the greatest and best have their weaknesses and limitations. And the more virile a man is the more positive are his defects; the stronger he is the greater his weaknesses. The human Colossus is never symmetrical. Every man is a fraction of a man, and the larger the scale on which he is built the more obvious are his lacks. Behold now a marvel! Here is a being whose diameter no one has yet measured. The greater a man is the more clearly does he perceive his own littleness beside this character. And yet, notwithstanding the vastness of Christ's nature, no defect appears. His character is so nicely balanced, so completely rounded, that by common consent he is deemed the one perfect example of the race.

And his character is not simply that of a perfect individual, it is generic; uniting the virtues not only of his own race, but of all other races; exemplifying the moral excellences not only of his own generation, but of all subsequent generations. How was it possible for the supposed inventor to combine in one fair flower the beauties of the whole moral flora?

Our conception of human nature is now far broader and more adequate than was possible to any one in the first century. For eighteen hundred years the civilized world has had before its eyes a generic character, a complete man. All men seem to most of the world foreigners, but Christ seems a foreigner to no one. In him every race sees its noblest traits idealized and its deficiencies supplemented. We see in him the common bond which makes possible a brotherhood of mankind. We have learned to talk of the " solidarity of the race " and of a " world-consciousness." Race antipathy is now comparatively slight. Men of one blood can sympathize sufficiently with those of another to understand and appreciate them. Travel and reading have familiarized us with all peoples. We can now make a comparative study of character. We know national types. We can discriminate between that which is common to human nature everywhere and always and that which is merely racial, national, or individual. To sketch a cosmopolitan character is now easy to the literary artist; indeed, he has only to copy from life, for such characters are not uncommon in this generation.

We need to remind ourselves how entirely different

was the situation in the first century. No such conditions for the study and knowledge of mankind existed. There was then comparatively little intercommunication. The attrition of travel had not to any appreciable extent worn off race characteristics. The Jew was intensely Jewish, the Greek intensely Grecian. True, Roman conquest had brought the world under Roman rule, but conquered peoples were not assimilated. The Jew was no less a Jew because forced to wear the Roman yoke. His hatred of the conqueror rather intensified his narrowness. That narrowness had not only been inculcated as a part of his religious training, but it had run in the blood of threescore generations. It was simply impossible for such a race in such an age to invent a world-character as broad as mankind and as comprehensive as the ages. A Jew attempting to picture an ideal man would have drawn simply a typical Israelite.

It may be suggested that a Jew might have found in the Messianic prophecies materials for a true conception of the character of Christ. Certainly, some aspects of his character are there presented, but only a few. These prophecies describe very minutely many of the circumstances of his birth and death, but do not set before us the many and varied elements of his character.

No mind was broad enough or had sufficiently wide knowledge, in that age, to conceive of a generic man. And even if all the elements of perfect manhood could have been found scattered among the nations, no human skill could have united them into the living character before us. The chemist may tell us what are the several elements of the human body and in what proportions they enter into it, but he cannot combine these same elements in these exact proportions so as to produce a living result.

Some of the excellences of which human nature is capable rarely, if ever, coexist in the same character. Like gentleness and zeal they belong to opposite tem-

peraments, and had they not once been united in the
character of Christ, would seem incongruous.

Seldom in nature, art, or character do we find great
strength and rare beauty combined. An exceptional
degree of the one is usually achieved only at the expense of the other. What artist would attempt to
combine in a single face and form womanly grace and
manly strength, the flowing lines of the female form
and the muscular development of the athlete? Yet
Christ is stronger than the strongest character, of history or fiction, in which beauty is wholly sacrificed to
strength, and more beautiful than any character in
which strength is wholly sacrificed to beauty.

Even if the supposed inventor could have found
ready at his hand all the materials which enter into the
character of Christ, it is incredible that he could have
united these heterogeneous excellences of various tem-
peraments so as to produce a homogeneous whole; incredible that he could have blended the many colors of
diverse and beautiful types of character into the white
light of Christ's radiant perfection.

2. But supposing he could have produced in his own
mind the picture which we find in the Gospels, or supposing he might have found all of its elements in the
Messianic prophecies, perhaps the most difficult part of
his task would yet remain, viz., the inventing of a life
which would accurately and adequately express his
perfect conception.

That conception once formed, it would be an easy
matter to describe it. But the Gospels nowhere describe Christ's character. They nowhere tell us that he
was dignified under insult, calm before opposition, sub-
missive under suffering, indignant at the sight of hy-
pocrisy, sympathetic with sorrow. These characteristics
are manifested by him, but never affirmed of him. They
appear only in his words and acts. The writers of the
first three Gospels make no attempt at delineation;
they are apparently quite unconscious that they are
giving to the world a portrait; they make Christ speak

and act before us, and we form our judgment of his character independently, as if we had seen and heard him ourselves. Whatever feelings may spring from reading the Gospels, they are never the result of sympathy with the writers. One could not be sure, judging simply from their style, that the synoptic evangelists were not indifferent spectators of what they recorded. There is no writing for effect, no exhibition of their own opinions, but an unadorned narrative which simply recounts the words and works of Christ. From *these* we get a distinct conception of this divine-human character.

In order better to appreciate the task which the supposed inventor undertook, let the reader propose it to himself. You must originate sayings fit for infinite wisdom to utter, conceptions of truth, wholly new and priceless, which for ages to come men will study and ponder more than all other human words. Moreover you must give to the world not simply truth uttered, but truth applied to life and in action; not simply the laws of life promulgated, but those laws exemplified. You must invent a life fit for God to live in the flesh, one in keeping with the astonishing claims already noticed, and yet it must be a human life, lived amid human relationships and imitable.

Your *simple record of his words and acts* must present a character possessed of the most diverse excellences, each in perfection, yet all in harmony; a character at the same time tolerant and zealous, meek and majestic, charitable and rigorous, lowly and commanding, mild and strict, just and merciful, bold and cautious, artless and profound, gentle as the dawn yet, like the morning light, awaking a world to activity. *What he says and does* must show him capable of intense feeling and yet of entire self-possession, of melting tenderness and yet of withering rebuke; possessed of a colorless judgment and yet of the most delicate feeling, of massive strength and matchless beauty. These diverse qualities, so often mutually exclusive, must unite and blend so as to form a character which, like the garment of Jesus, shall be without a seam.

He must show no sign of repentance, must never confess the slightest fault or error, must indeed claim to be without sin, yet arouse no suspicion of Pharisaism.

Let him associate the name of the Father and the Holy Ghost with his own in some formula; let him declare that all power is his; let him assume to forgive sins, and instead of standing before the bar of human judgment, convicted of the most shocking blasphemy, let him impress men with his absolute holiness.

You must not be content to represent your hero as exemplifying the highest moral standard of the times. He must do vastly more than that. He must originate a purer system of ethics than the world has yet known, and he must announce spiritual truths which are many centuries beyond the acceptance or even the comprehension of the most civilized peoples of this age. He must not teach as other men do, citing authorities, elaborating his teachings from elementary principles by logical inference, showing reasons for his conclusions and commands. He must teach as one having authority, with a simple "*I* say unto you," and yet your readers must never suspect that he is domineering over their understanding.

He must boldly declare that he is greater than Solomon, that he is able to bring all men into subjection to himself, that he is "*the* light of the world," yet he must not seem in the least degree conceited. On the contrary, he must appear meek and lowly and even be able to publish his own meekness without sacrificing his modesty.

He must aspire to a dominion more extended, more absolute than the most insane ambition ever dreamed of, yet he must never be suspected of ambition.

You must invent a character and life whose influence shall flow through the ages with always augmenting power, and whose mystery shall ever attract and forever baffle human study.

Your art must be so consummate as wholly to conceal itself, deceiving even the literary elect, and convincing the world that your work is not an invention, but a faithful record of fact. The character must be so life-like as to inspire the faith of millions and become the basis of the most widely extended and vital organization in the world's history. And more marvellous than all, this invented character must possess a strange, unprecedented power of exciting love—a love stronger than the love of life, stronger than the love of parent or wife or child. You must invent such a character that many centuries hence millions would die for the love they bear it.

To expose the utter absurdity of this theory it remains only to show what is implied by power to invent such a character and life.

The story of Solomon's judgment between the two mothers contending for the living child, if it were a fiction, would show that the author of the fiction himself would have been capable of rendering such a judgment had he been the arbiter.

Any story-writer might have produced the plot of Lalla Rookh, and stated that young Feramorz was a charming poet who by his songs won the fair princess. But in order to sustain the plot by *showing* the youth to be a poet instead of declaring him to be one, in order to introduce a bard whose songs may impress the reader with his poetic genius, the author of the fiction must himself be a poet. That is, if the character presented in the Gospels were a fiction, its marvel and mystery would be transferred to the character of its inventor. Theodore Parker said: "It would have taken a Jesus to forge a Jesus."

The discourses of Christ contain a perfect system of ethics. If, then, this character is not genuine, its inventor of course possessed this unequalled moral insight, and produced this most perfect system of ethics the world has ever known in the interest of the most gigantic fraud the world has ever known!

Christ was often placed in circumstances which, humanly speaking, were most difficult and perplexing, yet in applying truth to life he discovered a power of distinguishing between the faintest shades of right and wrong, wisdom and unwisdom, which was absolutely perfect. If now this is a fictitious character, its inventor possessed a wisdom which was infallible, and a moral sense unimpaired by sin. A deliberate falsifier with an unimpaired moral sense !

It is not the intellect, however profound, which apprehends spiritual truth; such truth is not reasoned out, neither can it be acquired through the senses. It is reflected upon the pure heart from the great source of all truth. The pure in heart see God. The profound spiritual truths uttered by Christ could have been reflected only on an unsullied soul. If we refuse to accept the genuineness of Christ's character, then we must believe that an unscrupulous liar had an unsullied soul !

Christ's apprehension of God was so sublime, so spiritual, that it has satisfied the most exalted conceptions, the deepest spiritual longings of the race for all these ages. Such exceptional knowledge of God could come only through exceptional likeness to him. Is it any more difficult to accept the character of Christ as historic than to believe that of all men the most cunning deceiver of the race was likest God? Surely, if the character of Christ were invented, then, as Rousseau says, "the inventor would be a more astonishing character than the hero"—more astonishing because self-contradictory. We have seen that the supposition of such invention forces us into repeated absurdities.

The two theories, one of which must be accepted if the genuineness of Christ's character is rejected, have both been found untenable. If it is incredible that the lofty spiritual conceptions in the Gospels could have been the unconscious product of a people rigid in the spiritual death of formalism, it is inconceivable that such conceptions could have originated in the interest of fraud. The conclusion of John Stuart Mill touching

both of these theories is as just as it is unbiassed. He
says [1]: "And whatever else may be taken away from
us by rational criticism, Christ is still left: a unique
figure, not more unlike all his predecessors than all his
followers, even those who had the direct benefit of his
personal teaching. It is no use to say that Christ as
exhibited in the Gospels is not historical, and that we
know not how much of what is admirable has been
superadded by the traditions of his followers. . . .
Who among his disciples or among their proselytes
was capable of inventing the sayings ascribed to Jesus
or of imagining the life and character revealed in the
Gospels ?"

One of the greatest masters of all literature ought to
be a judge whether the character in the Gospels is a
likeness reflected from life or the product of consummate art, and Goethe says [2]: "I consider the Gospels
decidedly genuine, for they are penetrated by the re-
flection of a majesty which proceeded from *the person
of Christ;* and this is divine, if ever divinity appeared
upon the earth."

The character and teachings of Jesus are effects for
which no adequate cause can be found in his generation
or nation. He never studied in a rabbinical school.
It is safe to say he never talked with a Platonist or a
Stoic philosopher, quite safe to say he never read a
Greek or Latin book; he very likely never saw a book
of any sort except a few copies of the "Law and Prophets." He probably never saw a map of the world and,
except in his infancy, never travelled outside of a little
country smaller than some of our counties. He spent
his life among the narrowest and most exclusive of all
races; and yet without the broadening influences of
reading or travel or educated companionship he presents a character, a spirit, a sympathy, a doctrine as
broad as mankind and as profound as human need.

[1] Essays on Religion. p. 253.
[2] Gespraeche mit Eckermann, III. page 371.   Quoted by Christlieb.

Other men are the product of their nation and their times; he evidently was not. We can account for Socrates and Aristotle, for Shakespeare and Goethe, for Cromwell and Lincoln, but I find myself wholly unable to account for Jesus on any natural basis. The only way to account for him is to accept him at his own estimate of himself. If Christ's character was genuine, then was it superhuman and supernatural. To imagine an inventor of his character does not relieve the difficulty; it simply transfers the supernatural element from a known to an unknown person, besides involving many absurdities. Nor is there any relief in granting the genuineness of Christ's character and supposing that his life is largely an invention. It is from the story of his life that we gain a large part of our knowledge of his character; the two are inseparably interwoven. Moreover, Jesus is himself the greatest miracle in the Gospels; and after being forced by reason to accept the miracle of his character it is illogical to reject the miracles of his life.

Beyond a peradventure the character presented in the Gospels is a verity. Amid the world's sin a perfect life has been lived; unto the world's doubt an authoritative voice has spoken; upon the world's darkness a heavenly light has shone.

This is apparently to be the universally accepted verdict. Never have the character of Christ and his every utterance been so microscopically studied as during the past half-century, and never before was his influence so wide, so pervasive, so profound as to-day. This influence is vastly broader than the church. Many who misunderstand and even hate the church respect the name and teachings of Christ. Says Keshub Chunder Sen,[1] the founder of the "Brahmo Somaj of India": "Christ exists throughout Christendom like an all-pervading leaven, mysteriously and imperceptibly leavening the bias of millions of men and women."

---

[1] Mozoomdar's Oriental Christ, p. 29.

And this influence already pervades a large part of heathendom as well as Christendom.   Keshub again says [1]: "Christ, not the British Government, rules India. We breathe, think, feel, and move in a Christian atmosphere."   Both in Christian and heathen lands Christ is profoundly influencing many lives outside the Church. Mozoomdar, a disciple of Keshub, and perhaps the greatest living Brahman, bears this remarkable testimony [2]: "In the midst of these crumbling systems of Hindu error and superstition, in the midst of this self-righteous dogmatism and acrimonious controversy, in the midst of these cold, spectral shadows of transition, secularism, and agnostic doubt, to me Christ has been like the meat and drink of my soul.   His influences have woven round me for the last twenty years or more, and, outside the fold of Christianity as I am, have formed a new fold, wherein I find many besides myself."

Many who reject all systems of theology believe that Christ spoke of spiritual things with authority; and many are beginning to see that his teachings are equally applicable to things temporal, that he came to save society as well as the individual, that his words contain the solution of the great problems of our times, and that to disregard them is bad political economy and poor statesmanship.   He is the accepted teacher of an ever-increasing number, with whom his words are authoritative.   And even those who are in doubt whether he is divine or human are, many of them, ready to follow him as their leader.

> "If Jesus Christ is a man,
>   And only a man, I say
>   That of all mankind I will cleave to him,
>   And to him will cleave alway.
>
> "If Jesus Christ is a God,
>   And the only God, I swear
>   I will follow Him through heaven and hell,
>   The earth, the sea, and the air!"
>
> RICHARD WATSON GILDER.

[1] *Missionary Review*, May, 1890, p. 398.   [2] The Oriental Christ, p. 13.

Strauss really rendered an invaluable service to Christianity by his attack on its central citadel. It re sulted in concentrating study on Jesus, which has produced a whole library of Lives of Christ; it has turned religious thought from other teachers to the Great Teacher; it has led to a fresh study of the Master's words, which has thrown new light on every page of the Gospel, and, as Principal Fairbairn says, has made this generation better acquainted with the historical Christ than any generation between him and us. There has been, indeed, a new resurrection of the Christ; and while we of this generation have communed and reasoned together concerning him, verily Jesus himself has drawn near and is opening up anew to us the Scriptures; and do not our hearts burn within us with a new fire of enthusiasm to bring all men and all human institutions and activities under his saving power?

And as he said to the troubled and terrified disciples when he appeared to them at Jerusalem, so now, standing in the midst of modern society, he is saying to our social unrest, to the conflict of classes, to the fears of many, " Peace be unto you."

This nearer and clearer vision of the Christ, this return to the study of his teachings, this discovery that he is the Saviour of *man* as well as of *men*, that he laid down the fundamental laws of social relations on which the perfect society of the future is to be organized,—all this is the timing of Providence that the new era of the near future may indeed be the fuller coming of the Kingdom.

CHAPTER VI.

THE TWO FUNDAMENTAL LAWS.

HUMAN nature has a Godward and a manward side. As a person man sustains relations to God; as a social being he sustains relations to his fellow men.

We are told that no two ultimate particles of matter can touch each other. In like manner every human being has an individuality which cannot be surrendered, a personality which cannot be lost in society as a drop of water is lost in the sea. There are experiences through which every soul must pass as wholly alone as if no other human being existed.

As the poet Keble wrote:

> " Not even the tenderest heart, and next our own,
> Knows half the reasons why we smile or sigh.

> " Each in his hidden sphere of joy or woe
> Our hermit spirits dwell, and range apart." [1]

Moral character is something individual and involves personal accountability. No man can live out of relations to God; and the character of these relations indicates the character of the man.

But if two ultimate particles of matter cannot touch each other, neither can they exist out of relations with each other. It is equally true that men cannot live out of relations with their fellow-men; and the character of these relations determines the character of society. Humanity being what it is, every man must " bear his own burden," and we must also " bear one another's burdens."

---

[1] The Christian Year. Twenty-fourth Sunday after Trinity.

114

These two facts of human nature are fundamental, and found recognition in the beginning when God said to the first man, "Where art thou?" and to the first brother, "Where is thy brother?" These facts being fundamental, it has been no accident that the progress of civilization from the beginning has been along the two lines already pointed out, viz., the development of the individual and the organization of society. And the world's progress in the future must necessarily be along these same lines.

But although these two sides of human nature are fundamental and quite obvious, there has been a constant tendency to overlook the rights and duties which belong to the one or the other—a tendency to sacrifice the development of the individual to the organization of society, or to subordinate the organization of society to individualism. We have seen that the more or less complete triumph of the one over the other marks the fundamental difference between European and Asiatic civilizations. We have seen also that these two principles are not conflicting, but co-ordinate, and that they are alike necessary to the perfecting of the race.

The kingdom of heaven, which cannot fully come on earth until mankind is perfected, must exhibit the complete development and the perfect co-ordination of these two principles. The Great Teacher, if indeed "the Light of the world," must show how this could be accomplished. As founder of the kingdom and its King, he should lay down laws which recognize man's individuality and allow scope for its full development and which at the same time recognize the necessity of society and provide for its perfect organization. And this is precisely what Christ did.

There could be no organization of society without law, and there could be no moral character without freedom. How could the individual be free and yet under law? This great problem of the ages, with which heathen philosophers and all heathen civilizations have struggled in vain, Christ solved with one word.

He did not attempt, like the founders of ethnic religions, to control the life of the individual or of society by means of rules. Lazy human nature would like a pope to be conscience and judgment for it. All heathen religions and corrupted forms of Christianity respond to this desire with a multiplicity of rules by which they aim to shape life from without. But no system of rules could meet the necessities of different nations and ages, of changing social conditions and of new relations. And even were it possible to fashion rules of universal application, they would make children of all who lived by them.

Christ inculcated principles. And as his kingdom is to be universal and eternal, the great principle on which he founded it is as broad as the moral universe and as eternal as God. That principle is LOVE.

Love is to the moral universe what gravitation is to the physical. The attraction of matter to matter is gravitation; the attraction of soul to soul is love. The heavenly bodies are individuals arranged, so to speak, in families, communities, states, and nations—systems within systems—having many centres, yet all, so far as we can judge, circling around one common and ultimate centre. These complex relations and intricate movements are all perfectly harmonious, because gravitation binds each body to every other and brings all under the control of the central sun. Now love is the attracting power and harmonizing principle of the moral universe which makes possible a unity in the midst of endless diversity. This principle Christ applied to man in his twofold relations by means of the two fundamental laws :

" *Thou shalt love the Lord thy God with all thy heart, and with all thy soul, and with all thy mind*," and

" *Thou shalt love thy neighbor as thyself.*" [1]

I. Supreme love to God, enjoined by "The First and Great Commandment," brings a man into right rela-

---

[1] Matt. xxii. 37, 39.

tions with God and establishes that spiritual health
which we call salvation.

Human nature is selfish, and there is no salvation
either for the individual or for society which does not
save from selfishness. A man may observe with scrupu-
lous exactness the rites of the most elaborate ceremonial
and yet remain supremely selfish—the Judaic failure of
ritualism. He may devote his life to the cultivation of
art and yet be ready to sacrifice others to himself—the
Grecian failure of culture. He may conform his outward life to all the requirements of law, may even
make his relations to his fellow-men unimpeachable
under any moral code, and yet remain wholly self-
centred—the Roman failure of legalism. His selfishness will be refined and polished, but none the less
selfish.

Love is the natural opposite of selfishness and its
divine antidote. It reverses the inward movement and
transforms the whirlpool into a fountain. When selfishness has been overcome, it is because

"Love took up the harp of Life, and smote on all the chords with might,
Smote the chord of Self, that, trembling, pass'd in music out of sight." [1]

Ritualism, culture, and legalism have no power to
eradicate selfishness, and therefore no saving power,
because they are impotent to inspire love for God and
fellow-men. Christ not only taught the duty of loving
God and man, but revealed a Godhead and a manhood
that are lovable. He does not ask us to love abstract
holiness, beauty, or law. Abstractions have little power
to kindle the holy passion. As Emerson says, "*Persons*
are love's world." In his own person Christ presents
a character capable of inspiring an overmastering love,
one which is found to be a love both for God and man.
If Christ lacked this love-inspiring power, he could save
neither the individual nor society; possessing it, he can
save both.

This is called the First and Great Commandment be-

---

[1] Tennyson's Locksley Hall.

cause our relations to God are more fundamental, far
more imperative and determinative, than our relations
with our fellow-men. Obedience or disobedience to this
command determines the character of the individual,
who is the social unit. Society cannot be saved until
its units are saved—a truth which the "saviours of
society" commonly forget. It has been thought that
another system of taxation, or a reorganization of industry, or a different method of teaching, or an equal
distribution of property, or the organization of business
on a co-operative instead of the competitive basis—
that, in short, another way of doing things would set
society right and usher in the millennium *per saltum.*
Hamlet said:

> "The time is out of joint: O cursed spite!
> That ever I was born to set it right!"

Many who see that society is out of joint and believe
with Hamlet that they were born to set it right do not
seem to share his sense of burden. They toss off a new
plan for the regeneration of the world before breakfast.
But all quick and easy processes for regenerating society
without regenerating the individuals who compose it
are delusions.

The social problem has two great factors, man himself
and his environment. Socialistic and all other efforts
which practically ignore the more important of these
two factors must fail to find the solution. Personality
is more fundamental than relations. Man's relations
cannot be right while man himself is wrong. Human
systems fail because they deal with relations, environment, and leave character untouched. A right environment is deemed sufficient to rectify human nature.
Depravity passes for nothing or is only incidental—the
effect of a wrong environment. Such is the teaching of
the author of "Looking Backward" in his parable of
the rose-tree in the bog.

But if man is naturally unselfish, how are we to account for the fact that in all lands and in all ages he

has lived precisely as if he were naturally selfish ? If human nature is essentially angelic, how is it that men have spent some thousands of years in cutting one another's throats ? We are told that the social system has rendered them selfish and depraved. But there was not a selfish and depraved social system prepared and waiting for the advent of the race, to which innocent and angelic man fell a victim. Men created their own social system. How could unselfish men produce a selfish system and continue to live under it unreformed for hundreds of generations ?

Without doubt, circumstances have a profound influence on character. Selfishness is aggravated by struggle with selfish competitors; but manifestly society did not produce human nature, it was human nature that produced society, though their influence is reciprocal. Evidently both factors of the problem must needs be reckoned with; and it will be found that man needs a new heart quite as much as he needs a new environment.

Again, obedience to the first great command of Christ not only eradicates selfishness, as we have seen, but makes a man free under law.

There could of course be no virtue, no moral dignity, no moral character, good or bad, without freedom. On the other hand, there could not be a universe without universal law, and there could be no order or harmony without obedience to law. Obedience against inclination is bondage, but where inclination perfectly coincides with the law there is neither restraint nor constraint, but as much freedom as if the law did not exist. " I will walk at liberty, for I seek thy precepts." [1] Laws against murder and arson in no degree restrict the freedom of the good citizen. So far, then, as we love the laws of the universe we are free under them, and so far as we love God intelligently we love his will and his laws which are an expression of his will. Love is the

---

[1] Psalm cxix. 45.

fulfilling of law, not because it is accepted as a *substitute* for obedience, as some seem to think, but because it leads to obedience. "He that hath my commandments and *keepeth* them, he it is that loveth me." "If a man love me, he will keep my words."[1] If men loved God perfectly, they would love all of his laws perfectly and, therefore, be perfectly free under them.

Again, perfect love to God, which is intelligent, would lead to a full development of the entire man, which would be a true and perfect individualism.

Nature is full of variety. Of the millions of leaves in an oak forest no two are exactly alike. God never repeats himself even in his humblest creations, and the higher the rank in nature the greater the individuality. Nature sees to it that children of the same parents and subject to the same outward influences are very different. I take it that God deems every human being of sufficient importance to give him characteristics which when developed will distinguish him from all mankind. False education and conventionalities suppress these differences, but perfect obedience to all the laws which God has implanted in the individual will secure his perfect development, and nothing else can. When we remember that all the laws of our being are expressions of the divine will, and that perfect love to God leads to perfect obedience, it becomes apparent that a true and perfect individualism is to be achieved through obedience to the first great law of Christ. Such an individualism would of course be wholly unselfish.

It may be remarked in passing that exactly here do we see the perfect harmony between religion and culture. When it is supposed that the laws of the spiritual nature are radically different in origin and obligation from those which govern the intellectual and physical life, and when religion is confined to the former and culture to the latter, and the advocates of

---

[1] John xiv. 21, 23.

each depreciate the other, it is not strange that there should seem to be an irreconcilable conflict between them. But what is religion, if not obedience to the will of God? And what is culture, if not the development of man's nature according to its laws? Now when we see that the laws of our entire nature are expressions of the divine will, we perceive that religion and culture are coextensive, that each is concerned with the entire man, and that each is necessary to the perfection of the other.

II. Turn now to the second fundamental law.

Organized society is asking the question to-day, "What must I do to be saved?" And the answer comes from the Great Teacher, "Love thy neighbor as thyself." The individual can be saved only as he accepts the first command; society can be saved only as it accepts the second. This second law was certainly intended to govern men in their relations with each other precisely as the first law was intended to govern men in their relations with God. The one follows naturally from the other. Men could not come into perfect harmony with God without coming into perfect harmony with each other. If God is to be loved as a father, men must be loved as brothers. We cannot suppose that one command was intended for an earthly and the other for a heavenly society, that the one is practical and the other ideal and impracticable. Christ declares that the second is "like unto" the first, and that on "these *two*" hang all the law and the prophets. These two commands rest on precisely the same authority, they are an application of one and the same principle to man in his twofold relations. Evidently the love of our neighbor, inculcated by Christ, was intended to be not simply a kindly sentiment which should mitigate somewhat the results of human selfishness, nor a beautiful ideal to be realized only in a heavenly existence, but *a practical working principle, intended to control the organization of human society.*

This is the verdict of the most distinguished authority

in social science. Mr. Herbert Spencer, as we have
already seen in the preceding chapter, studying social
relations and seeking in human experience for a rule of
life, arrives by a scientific method at the very law laid
down by Christ nearly two thousand years before the
birth of social science. This "royal law," as St. James
calls it, if universally obeyed, would certainly harmonize all human relationships. We should hear no
more of pauperism and crime, of wrong, oppression, and
strife, of strikes and lockouts, of caste and color-line,
of pride and selfishness. Each member of society with
his special gifts developed according to the laws of his
nature, or, in a word, each one *individualized* by intelligent obedience to the first great law, would render the
service for which he was best fitted, thus making possible a closer and higher organization of society. In
such a society there would be perfect organization
without tyranny and perfect individualism without
selfishness—perfect law and perfect liberty, perfect
unity in the midst of complete diversity. Thus we see
that obedience to Christ's two laws would effect the
complete co-ordination of the two great principles on
which depends the progress of civilization.

But Christ says : " A new commandment I give unto
you, That ye love one another *as I have loved you*." [1]
Now Christ sacrificed himself for us, loved us *more*
than he loved himself. This new commandment, therefore, requires us to love our neighbor more than we
love ourselves. Here is a seeming discrepancy. "As
thyself" is a different standard from Christ's self-
giving love. The one is the measure of justice, the
other that of sacrifice. Is not this the explanation ?
Love measured by justice is the law of a *normal*
society, while love measured by sacrifice is *remedial*
and necessary to restore the disordered and abnormal
society of the world to a normal condition. Selfishness
loves itself better than others; its cure is to love others

---

[1] John xiii. 34.

better than self. Selfishness would sacrifice others to itself; its remedy is the sacrifice of self for others.

The church recognizes the remedial law of sacrifice, and in all her saving work exemplifies it; but the law, "Thou shalt love thy neighbor *as thyself*," which is the organic law of a normal society, she has not definitely aimed to make the basis of social organization, because she has not expected to see on the earth a normal and perfect society. Her aim has been to save men out of the world rather than to save the world itself; to fit men for a perfect society in another world rather than to perfect society in this world. Of course bringing many individuals into right relations with God has done much to rectify men's relations with each other, but these good social results have been for the most part indirect and incidental, not included in the conscious and direct aim of the church.

Protestant churches especially have thought that true religion consisted in right relations between the individual soul and God. They have emphasized the first great command, but have failed to appreciate the second; have forgotten, as Dr. Parkhurst aptly says, that "God and one man could make any other religion, but it requires God and two men to make Christianity." The church has regarded the second great command as an ideal beyond the attainment of human society, a beautiful sentiment to be admired rather than a practical law to be obeyed in all the relations of life, social, industrial, commercial, and political. So true is this that many will look on a serious attempt to make the law of love to one's neighbor the warp running through all our social fabric as highly quixotic.

This failure of the church to perceive that it is as much her mission to bring society under the second law as to bring individuals under the first has had far-reaching consequences. It has resulted in maiming the Christian life and belittling Christ's conception of it. Instead of including the entire life, religion has been made an adjunct. Life has been divided into the sacred and the secular. "This distinction which has been so constantly and so fatally maintained was unknown to the early church."[1] According to the New Testament conception the entire man—body, soul, and spirit—and the entire life are sacred. But this restricted view, which the church has held since the early Christian centuries, makes two thirds of the man and about six sevenths of the time "secular." To this large proportion of the life Christ's teachings are supposed to be hardly applicable. For all that is "secular" the standard is furnished by the laws of the land, the requirements of business and of accepted morality. So that many Christian men to-day regard the principles of the Gospel as no more applicable to business than to chemistry or mathematics.

From all this has followed naturally a divorce of doctrine and conduct which Christ so scathingly rebuked in the Pharisees, and on which he would pour his hot indignation were he walking among us to-day. Wherever this divorce takes place religion is supposed to consist in assent to the doctrines of the church and in careful observance of religious days and ceremonies. I am glad to believe that with most professing Christians in this country this divorce is only partial; still it has given to the church generally an exaggerated estimate of the importance of doctrine as compared with conduct, and has created an almost universal impression that religion is concerned much more with worship than with every-day life. But St. John when describing a perfected society on the earth, the new Jerusalem coming down from God out of heaven, said, "I saw no temple therein," which unquestionably implies "that the ideal of the primitive church was one not of worship, but of a life pervaded by the Spirit of God; . . . no temple, but a God-inhabited society."[2] Worship is exceedingly important, as is true doctrine concerning the future life; but, as Canon Fremantle says[3]: "To

---

[1] Canon Fremantle's Gospel of the Secular Life, p. 78.
[2] Ibid. pp. 64, 67   [3] Ibid. p. 78.

gather from the Gospels a system which is solely or chiefly a system of public worship, and of instruction concerning the life to come, would be a strange infatuation. All is directed to insure a present life of righteousness and of love, a life lived in the realization of a present God, whose kingdom is here within us."

God forbid that I should belittle eternal values. There is not the slightest danger that the unseen world will be any too real to us. Out of it come the noblest and mightiest motives of life. The unseen realities are not only greater but seem to me more real than any other. However much a man may have to live for, the good man has unspeakably more to die for. Far be it from me to obscure the eternal life in the perception of any. It is chiefly for the sake of that life that we need true views of this. If the church had faithfully inculcated the second law of Christ, she would have brought many more into obedience to the first.

Nor do I depreciate doctrine. So long as there is a radical difference between truth and falsehood, and so long as truth sustains relations to life, it will make a difference whether men believe true or false doctrine. Doctrines are the roots of life. Great lives do not grow out of false beliefs. Yes, doctrine is immensely important, but not all-important. The root does not exist for itself; it is a means to the tree and the fruit as an end. A Christian truth in the heart brings forth Christian acts in the life as naturally as the root pushes its stalk up into the air and the sun. Cut the stalk, fell the tree, and the root dies at length. A faith without works is soon dead. If our doctrines do not flower and fruit in Christian living, they die. Many a man's creed is a field full of stumps. There was life there once, but because the natural expression of that life was prevented it perished. We have not overestimated the importance of *believing* the truth, but we have underestimated the importance of *living* the truth.

Protestant churches have laid none too much stress on the relations of the individual to God. These relations are fundamental and their importance cannot be exaggerated. The mistake of the churches has been, not in emphasizing the first great command, but in neglecting the second. If the pendulum should now swing to the other extreme and the churches should emphasize the second command to the *neglect* of the first, that would be a mistake greater than the other. This mistake has been made by some unevangelical churches. It was the partial view of religion held by the orthodox churches of New England, their neglect of manward obligations, which led to the humanitarian movement of the Unitarians. There seems to have been a disposition among the latter to make humanitarian service a substitute for piety. This is a radical mistake. There can be no substitute for right relations with God. Service to our fellow-men should be made not a *substitute* for piety, but an *expression of it.* Show me thy works without thy faith, or "show me thy faith without thy works, and I will show thee my faith *by* my works."[1]

It is a lamentable blunder to separate religion and philanthropy, a sad comment on the church that a sharp distinction between them ever came into use. Alas! that the love of our fellow-men is something to be distinguished from the religion of Christ. In their last interview thrice does Peter protest his love to his Master, and thrice Christ bids him show his love by service to his fellow-men. Christ identifies himself with the hungry, the naked, the sick, and the imprisoned, and says: "Inasmuch as ye have done it unto one of the least of these my brethren, ye have done it unto me."[2] Obviously in Christ's conception, to serve men is to serve him. But this is not the common conception; we talk of "divine service" as if it meant only prayer and praise and the hearing of sermons. Visiting the fatherless and widows in their affliction we call philanthropy, and keeping one's self unspotted from the world

---

[1] James ii. 18.   [2] Matt. xxv. 40.

we would probably call morality; but St. James says
that these things are *religion* "pure and undefiled
before God."[1] True religion is philanthropic and true
philanthropy is religious, and to divorce the one from
the other is to libel and cripple both.

The failure of the church to accept and apply the
second fundamental law of Christ, by leading to a false
distinction between the sacred and the secular, and by
divorcing doctrine and conduct, religion and philanthropy, has given to the multitude the impression that
religion is not concerned with real life and has thus
served to separate the masses from the church. This
subject will receive fuller consideration in a later
chapter.

Again, the neglect of the second law has resulted in a
selfish individualism. The emphasis laid on the first
command touching the relations of the individual to
God has developed a sense of his worth and the sacredness of his rights; for if he has duties to God from
which no man can release him, he has rights of which
no man must rob him. But the failure to insist equally
upon the second command has made the individual con-
tracted and self-concerned. He now needs to have
strengthened the sense of duty to society, he needs to
hold in higher esteem the common weal, to gain a
clearer conception of the solidarity of the race, a nobler
conception of its destiny, and a sense of personal responsibility, according to his measure, for its ultimate
perfection.

Again, this failure of the church to perceive that it is
an essential part of her mission to bring society under
the second great law of Christ has naturally resulted in
an organization of society which is not Christian.

Christ's fundamental law of society, as we have seen,
is that of love, fraternity. That this is not the basis of
society even in the so-called Christian countries is too
obvious to require proof.

---

[1] James i. 27.

> " For a' that, and a' that,
> It's coming yet, for a' that;
> That man to man, the world o'er,
> Shall brithers be for a' that."

An evidence that this brotherhood is coming though
not yet come is found in the fact that men are seeking
it. The Masonic order, the Odd Fellows, and the thousand other brotherhoods [1] for insurance, industrial advantage, and the like, are attempts to supply what the
organization of society does not afford. In these, men
are blindly feeling after that which Christ sought to
establish when he laid down his second law, viz., a real
brotherhood of man, based, not as these organizations
are—on self-interest—but on love.

Existing society is organized on a selfish basis; stren-
uous competition is its law, and " Every man for himself " is its motto. Order is preserved by a skilful
balance of conflicting interests, the nice adjustment of
checks and counter-checks, which is the only harmony
practicable to selfishness.

I am not saying that there is no generosity, no disinterestedness in the business or social world. There is
a vast deal of it, but it belongs to individuals, not to the
social *system*.

The existing social system permits, not to say necessitates, practices which are in direct violation of Christian
ethics. Says the author of " Prisoners of Poverty ":
" A business man, born to all good things and owning a
name known as the synonym of the best the Republic

---

[1] For the following significant statistics of lodges as compared with
churches in various cities I am indebted to Dr. Graham Taylor. They were
compiled from city directories.

	Population.	Churches.	Lodges.
Buffalo, 1888–9.	240,000	144	218
New Orleans, 1888–9	216,090	178	270
Washington, 1888–9	203,459	181	316
St. Louis, 1888–9	450,000	220	729
Worcester, 1888–9	85,000	54	88
Boston, 1890	448,477	243	599
Brooklyn, 1890	853,945	355	695
Chicago, 1890	1,099,850	384	1088

offers to-day, states calmly, ' There is no such thing as business without lying,' " which is certainly too sweeping. Another writer says [1]: " It is a common remark that business practices are not what they should be, and that a sensitive conscience must be left at home when its possessor goes to the office or the shop. We helplessly deplore this fact; we lament the forms of business depravity that come to our notice, but attack them with little confidence. We are appalled by the great fact of moral dualism in which we live, and are inclined to resign ourselves to the necessity of a two-fold life."

The widespread and deep discontent of the artisan class is sufficient evidence that our industrial system is not based on Christian principles. That discontent will continue until the great sociological problems of the times are solved; and they will not be solved until the teachings of Christ are applied to them. The old political economy has been called " the applied science of selfishness." We shall have no industrial peace until political economy becomes a department of applied Christianity, or, as some would prefer to say, until Christianity has been substituted for political economy.

We have glanced at some of the disastrous results of accepting and preaching only a half Gospel. Christ gave us no superfluous truths, no truths unrelated to life; and when his teachings are overlooked or undervalued by the church, the neglected truth appears in perverted, caricatured, or fanatical form. The church largely lost sight of Christ's humanity, and Unitarianism was the result. The church has not sufficiently insisted that salvation means salvation from sin, hence the caricature of sanctification taught and illustrated by the modern perfectionists. In like manner the church has neglected Christ's teaching concerning human brotherhood, which is based on the divine

---

[1] The Philosophy of Wealth, by J. B. Clark, p. 157, quoted by H. C. Adams in Relation of the State to Industrial Action.

Fatherhood, and there results the fatherless brotherhood taught by atheistic socialism, which is a caricature
of Christ's teaching.

Until very recent times the church has left the study
of the science of society almost wholly to unbelievers.
It is significant that most of the men who have sought
to reorganize society on a more just and fraternal basis
have been out of sympathy with the church or positively hostile to it, like Saint-Simon, Fourier, Comte,
Proudhon, Marx, Lassalle, and J. S. Mill. True, a generation ago there appeared a small school of Christian
socialists in England, and now an increasing number of
Christian men in the United States call themselves
socialists, but generally socialists have been opposed to
the Christian religion. The socialist Boruttau says:
"No man else is worthy of the name socialist save he
who, himself an atheist, devotes his exertions with all
zeal to the spread of atheism."

The church believes in the divine Fatherhood and is
trying to induce the world to accept it, but conceives of
a human brotherhood only as something theoretical,
and fails to create it. Social reformers have striven
for a human brotherhood, while most of them have
neglected or rejected the divine Fatherhood. The
church is insisting on the first great law, and social
reformers on the second. To this narrowness of aim
may be ascribed the very limited success of both. The
time has come to recognize the fact that these two fundamental laws are alike binding, and that neither can
be perfectly obeyed until perfect obedience is rendered
to both. We must accept both of these hemispheres of
truth and obligation which are alike necessary to produce the new world wherein dwelleth righteousness.

We are now living in the sociological age of the world.
Its problems will not be solved until their solution is
found in the teachings of Christ; and this fact constitutes the great opportunity of the church to retain or
rather regain her hold on the multitude and to mould
the civilization of the future by accepting, preaching,

and practising a full-orbed Gospel. Let us see how true
these propositions are.

Each of the several ages of the Christian era has been
characterized by a germinal idea which has been more
or less central to the thinking of that age. These germinal ideas have followed each other in logical sequence
and have sprung naturally from Christ's revelation of
God. Man's conception of his God and his conception
of himself are closely related; each influences the other.
Without a revelation man's idea of God is little else
than his own image enlarged and projected on the sky.
Give him a new idea of the character of God and there
will follow a new and corresponding idea of human
nature. When, therefore, Christ gave to the world a
new and higher conception of God, there was sure to
result in due time a new and higher conception of man,
from which would be wrought out naturally new conceptions of man's individual life—his personal relations
to God, and new conceptions of his social life—his relations to his fellow-men.

This, then, is the natural order in the development of
human thought and progress to have been expected in
the Christian era; and history shows this to have been
the actual order. First, *theology* proper or the doctrine
of God, then *anthropology* or the doctrine of man, then
soteriology or the doctrine of salvation, which treats of
the relations of God and man, and lastly *sociology* or
the doctrine of society, the relations of man to his fellows.

The discussion of each of these doctrines or each cluster of doctrines occupied several generations, and some
continued through several centuries before they were
authoritatively formulated by the church. Because
these doctrines are logically connected these discussions
naturally overlapped, but they were each of supreme
interest in their respective periods.

The third period closed during the great reformation
of the sixteenth century with the formulation, in the
Protestant symbols, of the doctrine of salvation by

faith, and then began the sociological age, which will continue until its problems are solved by bringing men into right relations with each other.

During the Middle Ages the organization both of the church and of society was such as to suppress the individual. The German Reformation, based as it was on the right of private judgment, gave a powerful stimulus to the development of individualism. A truer conception of the individual, his worth, his rights, his duties, is the great underlying cause of the world's swift progress during the last three hundred and fifty years.

During the Dark Ages, when individuality was suppressed, the most important question concerning every human being was, What are his relations to the church? But as soon as the Roman yoke was broken and individuality asserted itself, men began to seek the proper adjustment of relations between man and man. And precisely here do we find the key of every great social movement or agitation for the past three and a half centuries.

The remarkable progress of democracy means that men have been successfully seeking a better adjustment of their political relations one with another. Woman is assuming her rightful place at the side of man instead of behind him at a respectful distance or at his feet; and woman's changed status means that her social and industrial and marital relations have improved. Slavery has disappeared from Christendom because men have learned that manhood is too sacred a thing to tolerate the relation of master and slave. Labor agitations and reforms mean that men are demanding a readjustment of industrial relations; while socialism avowedly aims to revolutionize the whole social system. That is, all of these great movements are attempts to readjust and rectify the relations of the individual to his fellow-men, showing that this is the sociological age of the world.

Now in each of the preceding ages of the Christian era there were dispute and struggle and unrest through succeeding generations until the majority of Christian thinkers agreed on conclusions which were in harmony or were at least believed to be in harmony with the teachings of Christ. No doctrine of God could stand which was inconsistent with the facts in the life and character of Christ or in conflict with his teachings. No doctrine of man could stand which did not harmonize with the human nature of Christ and the instructions of the Great Teacher. No doctrine of salvation could stand which was not built on him as the only foundation. And if the world's experience for fifteen hundred years is worth anything, no doctrine of the relations of man to his fellows, no social system inconsistent with the great second law of Christ, can endure. The fact that Christ's teachings concerning the nature of God, the nature of man, and the relations of God and man, are accepted as final is ground for assurance that his teaching concerning man's relations to his neighbor will also be accepted as final.

Add to this presumption the sweet reasonableness of the two fundamental laws laid down by the Great Teacher, the fact that they obviously underlie the constitution of man and of normal society, that they recognize the two great principles of individualism and organization on which the world's progress has been so manifestly conditioned, and moreover effect the perfect co-ordination of these two principles which heretofore have seemed conflicting, and who can doubt the final acceptance of Christ's teachings or question that in their application must be found the solution of our sociological problems?

And of course if Christ's teachings are to triumph, whatever is inconsistent with them must give way. If it is true, which I do not believe, that under the present constitution of society "there is no such thing as business without lying," that "a sensitive conscience must be left at home when its possessor goes to the office or the shop," then we may rest assured that the present social system is temporary. Mr. J. B. Clark says:

"When Professor Cairnes demolished the scientific pretensions of *laissez-faire*, he took from us all hope of reconciling the Christian rule of ethics with the prevalent practice of Christian peoples."[1] If this be true, which I do not doubt, then "the prevalent practice of Christian peoples" must cease and will cease. So far as the present social system is selfish it is anti-Christian and, therefore, temporary. The two laws of Christ contemplate a complete and unselfish individualism and at the same time a universal brotherhood; and until these are realized the race cannot be perfected. The present competitive system, though it produces a strong individualism, makes impossible a true brotherhood of all men, and is, therefore, as inconsistent with the highest good of the race and as surely temporary as would be a socialistic system which, though it provided for brotherhood, served to repress the individual.

Our existing social system, then, is destined to undergo great changes before the sociological problems of the age are solved. And as their solution must come through the application of Christ's teachings, this surely is the opportunity of the centuries for the church to mould the civilization of the future by taking to heart and applying to life the teachings of her Lord in all their fulness. "The conversion of the church to Christian theory must precede the conversion of the world to Christian practice."[2]

---

[1] Quoted by H. C. Adams in Relations of the State to Industrial Action, p. 45.

[2] Influence of Greek Ideas and Usages upon the Christian Church, by Edwin Hatch, D.D., p. 170.

CHAPTER VII.

POPULAR DISCONTENT.

THE fact of popular discontent is too obvious to require proof. Its extent may be briefly noticed before we consider its causes and its significance.

It prevails chiefly among artisans and farmers, and shows itself in the numerous organizations among these classes which have sprung into existence in recent years. Among the former the most powerful organization is the American Federation of Labor, which has over 6000 local unions with an aggregate membership of 675,000; while the various Granges, Associations, Leagues, and Alliances of farmers have a combined membership, it is said, of not less than 3,000,000. This discontent has framed the platforms of new political parties, has found many organs in the press, and further utters itself in numerous strikes and serious riots. In this country, from 1881 to 1886 inclusive, 1,323,203 employés were involved in strikes, directly affecting 22,304 establishments.[1] In the summer of 1892, within a few days of each other, the states of New York, Pennsylvania, and Tennessee ordered out their militia, while Idaho called on the United States government for troops to suppress labor riots. In Europe, like discontent finds like expression among the same classes.

First. Let us look at the causes of this discontent.

To some it seems causeless, or at least without excuse, because workingmen are now better fed, better clothed, better housed than ever before; while many working-

---

[1] Report of the Commissioner of Labor, 1887, p. 12.

men believe that their condition is growing constantly worse.

Whether the industrial classes are any happier now than they were a half-century ago may well be doubted, but beyond question their condition is improved. The American economist, Mr. David A. Wells, thinks that, taking into account hours, wages, and prices of food, the average farm-laborer in the United States is twice as well off as he was thirty or forty years ago.[1] "In Mr. Mulhall's 'History of Prices' he shows that 'the condition of the working classes has so much improved that they now consume in all countries twice as much as in 1850.' Textile fabrics are 11 per cent cheaper than they were in 1860, books and newspapers 33 per cent, and the same amount of labor will now buy the workingman of Europe 140 pounds of bread as against 77 pounds in the decade ending 1860. The deductions of this statistician are that '15 shillings will now buy as much manufactures as 20 in the years 1841–50, but in matters of food we should require 22 shillings,' and that, taking increased wages and food-values together, the English workingman is able to purchase 21 per cent more of the necessaries of life in beef, butter, sugar, wheat, and coal than in 1840. Enhanced rent reduces his ability considerably, yet after allowing for this there is still a gain of at least 10 per cent."[2]

Another English statistician, Mr. Giffen, is of the opinion that there has been such a change in the textile, house-building, and engineering trades during the past fifty years that the British workman now gets from fifty to one hundred per cent more money for twenty per cent less work.[3] And for that period the rise of wages has been greater in France than in either England or America.

No doubt the condition of the workingman has im-

[1] D. A. Wells' Economic Changes, p. 409.
[2] The Christian Unity of Capital and Labor, p. 60.
[3] D. A. Wells' Economic Changes, p. 415.

proved, but it by no means follows that he should be any better contented. A savage of the South Sea Islands, being presented with a yard of cloth and a few fish-hooks, may be much more satisfied with his lot than a mechanic who owns his home and has all of the necessaries and many of the comforts of civilized life. We must take into consideration the widely different standards of living. There has been a change for the better in the circumstances of workingmen, but there has been a still greater change in the *men themselves*, which is the secret of increasing popular discontent amid improving conditions. Evidently the problem has two factors both of which must be taken into consideration, viz., the men and their circumstances.

1. In considering how great has been the change in workingmen, mark the increase of popular intelligence during the past century. We have to go back only a few hundred years to find many of the nobility illiterate. It is said that of the twenty-six barons who signed the Magna Charta three wrote their names and twenty-three made their marks. It is less than 350 years since a statute of the English Parliament made provision for the relief of "any the Lord and Lordes of the Parliament, and pere and peres of the Realme, hauyng place and voyce in Parliament, upon his or their request or prayer, claiming the benefit of this acte, *though he cannot reade.*" The average laborer in the United States to-day is more intelligent than many a great noble a few centuries ago. For thousands of years the sun of knowledge was below the world's horizon and only the very top of the social pyramid could catch his beams. The invention of printing was the world's sunrise which drove the black shadows well down the sides of the pyramid, but left the broad lower strata of society still wrapped in the darkness of ignorance. There has occurred in our own times an event, scarcely less important to the world than the invention of printing itself, which has lifted the sun high in the heavens and flooded the very foundations

of society with light. I refer to the successful application of steam to the printing-press. Few appreciate
the tremendous significance of this event. It meant
the enlightenment of the *many*, for the first time in
the world's history.

With the old hand-press two men could make about
250 impressions in an hour. The great Hoe presses now
in use print, fold, and paste a sixteen-page paper at a
speed of 24,000 per hour, or a four-page paper at a speed
of 96,000 ; that is, 384,000 pages in sixty minutes by
steam as compared with 250 pages by hand, or more
than fifteen hundred times as many.

" Forty years ago the post-office [of Great Britain and
Ireland] carried 36,000,000 newspapers annually; now
it carries 250,000,000." [1] The increase of circulation has
been even greater in the United States. Of dailies it is
estimated the number of copies issued in 1850 was 235,-
000,000, or ten to each inhabitant ; in 1880, 1,126,000,000,
or twenty-two to each inhabitant ; and in 1890, 1,981,-
000,000, or thirty-two to every one of the population.
The total number of papers issued in this country in
1890, including dailies, tri-weeklies, semi-weeklies, week-
lies, monthlies, etc., is estimated at 3,368,000,000, or
fifty-four copies for every inhabitant. [2] This indicates
a degree of popular intelligence which would have
been quite impossible without the application of steam
to the printing-press. Before the invention of printing
a written book represented two or three years of labor,
and few indeed could afford such a luxury. The printing-press made books and papers common among the
upper classes, and the application of steam has made
them possible to every one.

Consider how much this means. "The workingman,
this Titan, this monster of the mud-sills," says John
Swinton, "who in other crises has been the bond-slave
of wealth and power, this giant with the basal brain

[1] Mackenzie's History of the Nineteenth Century, p. 194, note.
[2] World Almanac, 1891.

and hairy hands, this Caliban has found his Cadmus; he begins to think; *he has learned how to read.*"[1] We shall not be surprised that reading has operated as an unequalled stimulus upon workingmen when we recall how powerfully it quickened the upper classes in the sixteenth century. This was not the only cause, but it was one of the chief causes of that wonderful outburst of genius and energy which marked the century of Shakespeare and Bacon, of Raphael and Angelo. That stimulus made itself felt in the channels along which the activity of the upper classes was wont to flow, viz., in military and naval adventure and in literature and art. This powerful stimulus, now applied for the first time in history to the popular mind, naturally shows itself in that which is nearest the life of the people—not literature or art, but industry. As the multitude are occupied in getting a living, it is not strange that the results of this new stimulus should appear in labor agitations and organizations.

Second only to the influence of the press on popular intelligence has been that of travel. We know how much the crusades did to give Europe new and enlarged ideas. There is a modern crusade which is unending and which in point of numbers quite belittles the hosts that sought to rescue the holy sepulchre from the grasp of the Mussulman. In 1891 the railways of the United States carried 495,000,000 passengers. Few indeed are the workingmen in this country who did not swell those millions. The educational influence of so vast an amount of travel is beyond computation. Surely we see a fulfilment of the prophecy, "Many shall run to and fro, and knowledge shall be increased."[2]

A few generations ago, workingmen, if they travelled at all, usually went on foot. Their journeys were of necessity few and short. "Each little community sat apart from its fellows, following its own customs, cher-

---

[1] Miss Frances E. Willard's "Glimpses of Fifty Years," p. 528.
[2] Dan. xii. 4.

ishing its own prejudices, feeding on its own traditions,
speaking in a dialect which men from a distance failed
to understand. A stranger was *ipso facto* an enemy.
There were villages in England, at the beginning of the
century, in which the inhabitants incited their dogs to
attack any stranger whose curiosity led him to visit
them." [1]   His native village was then the laborer's
world. Travel and the press have made the modern
workingman a cosmopolitan.

Add to a man's knowledge and you enlarge the
world in which he lives; he sees a wider horizon; his
future contains greater possibilities; he becomes conscious of new wants and higher aspirations, which, if
they cannot be satisfied, naturally breed discontent.
This has been clearly recognized by Count Tolstoï—not
Leo, the great writer, but the Russian Minister of the
Interior—who proposes to stop the growth of Nihilism
by putting an end to the higher education of any members of the poorer classes. In 1887 he issued an order
from which the following is an extract: "The gym-
nasia, high schools, and universities will henceforth
refuse to receive as pupils or students the children of
domestic servants, peasants, tradesmen, petty shop-
keepers, farmers, and others of like condition, whose
progeny should not be raised from the circle to which
they belong, and be thereby led, as long experience has
shown, . . . to become discontented with their lot, and
irritated against the inevitable inequalities of the existing social positions."

Russia may seek to allay popular discontent by such
a reactionary policy, but we cannot. We are bound to
" educate our masters." Popular power makes popular
intelligence a necessity; popular intelligence makes the
multiplication of popular wants inevitable; and the
multiplication of popular wants, if more rapid than the
improvement of the popular condition, necessarily produces popular discontent. It is quite too late for us to

---

[1] Mackenzie's Hist. Nineteenth Century, p. 92.

turn back. The multitude have already tasted of the tree of the knowledge of good and evil and have become aware of their nakedness. The supplies which cover the bare necessities of life are mere fig-leaves. The masses will never be satisfied until their wants are supplied with the fulness of modern civilization.

The average workingman two or three generations ago would no doubt have been well content with the hours, wages, food, lodgings, and clothes of the average workingman to-day, but during the nineteenth century public schools, public libraries, art galleries, museums, expositions, public parks, newspapers, and travel have all become common. Advertising, which is the art of making people want things, appeals to all classes alike. There has been a wonderful levelling up of the "common" people. Once great men were gods, and slaves were less than human. Now all alike are *men*, having much the same wants and quite the same rights. The spread of democracy, the growth of individualism, the equality of all men before the law have suggested the idea of equality of condition and made the masses feel that they are as capable of enjoying the good things of life as the classes. All these have contributed powerfully to increase the intelligence and wants of workingmen, and the resulting elevation of the standard of living has made a home, a table, a coat seem almost intolerable which once would have been deemed comfortable and even luxurious. The workingman of to-day may have, if you please, twice as much as his grandfather had, but he knows, say, ten times as much and wants ten times as much; hence his discontent.

2. We have glanced at the man; let us now look at his circumstances.

The conditions under which he works are radically different from what they were a hundred years ago. Profound economic changes have attended the transition in the world's methods of production and distribution which has taken place during this century and more especially during the past twenty-five or thirty

years. It is to this source we must look for some of the
principal causes of popular discontent which has been
pronounced ever since the commencement of the industrial depression which began in 1873 and affected all
classes, but more especially laboring men.

In the " age of homespun " industry was individual;
it has now become organized. This organization first
extended from the home to the factory. Soon the factory became a part of a larger system, including in its
organization the town, the province or region, then the
whole country; and now we have entered on the last
great stage, viz., that of organizing the industries of
the world.

Each new stage in this development has necessarily
disturbed industry and required a more or less extended readjustment of labor. Every great labor-saving invention has of course thrown thousands out of
employment, though every such mechanical triumph
has ultimately given employment to many for every
one that it has robbed of work. Thus, when Ark-
wright invented his cotton-spinning machinery in 1760,
there were in England some 7,900 persons engaged in
the production of cotton textiles. The introduction of
this machinery threw most of these people out of employment, but twenty-seven years later a Parliament-
ary inquiry showed that the number of persons engaged in this industry had risen to 320,000.[1] In like
manner, the inventions which substituted machinery
for hand labor in the making of stockings created a
great industrial disturbance in England which resulted
in serious riots. But for every one who lost work by
this change doubtless a hundred have found it with
shorter hours and much better wages.[2] Still, we are
told that "from the hunger and misery entailed by
this series of events the larger portion of fifty thousand
English stocking-knitters and their families did not
fully emerge during the next forty years." [3]

---

[1] D. A. Wells' Recent Economic Changes, p. 368.
[2] Ibid. p. 367.   [3] Ibid.

The progress of invention, by causing a continual "dropping" of men, produces among operatives a feeling of insecurity which ministers to discontent. Every one knows he is liable to learn any day that his strength or technical skill has been made useless by a new machine. Moreover, the introduction of machinery and the division of labor have rendered much work irksome by making it mechanical and monotonous.

Thus the various steps which have attended the great revolution in the world's methods of production have occasioned much discontent and not a little distress. The changes which have more recently taken place in the world's methods of distribution have been equally great and equally productive of far-reaching results.

Before the development of modern commercial facilities, each nation was as nearly as it could be a little world of its own, supplying most of its needs from its own resources, aiming to be as independent of all other nations as possible. Indeed, a century ago the sale of food from one country to another was generally prohibited. It is not very many years since England fed herself. Now we are told[1] that eight hundred articles of foreign food are sold in Brighton, and that, not including spirits and wines, England imports food to the value of £185,000,000 per year.

The steam-ship and the railway are making the world one country. "Produce is now carried from Australia to England, a distance of eleven thousand miles, in less time and at less cost than was required a hundred years ago to convey goods from one extremity of the British Islands to the other."[2] The construction of our transcontinental railways soon after the civil war, the projection of great railway systems in Russia and Central Europe (1867–'73), the opening of the Suez Canal (1869), and later the invention of the compound marine engine, within a few years' time, made all civilized peoples

---

[1] *Blackwood's Magazine*, Sept. 1892.
[2] D. A. Wells' Recent Economic Changes, p. 460.

near neighbors. It was impossible thus to bring nations, formerly far separated, into new and close relations without profound industrial disturbances and far-
reaching economic consequences.

One result was that in our great West a territory
larger than that of the thirteen original states was settled in half a dozen years, thus making a vast addition
to the world's agricultural products, and bringing the
cheap lands of the West into damaging competition
not only with New England, but with Old England
and Continental Europe as well. A leading farmer of
Devonshire testified before the British commission in
1886: "I have calculated that the produce of five acres
of wheat can be brought from Chicago to Liverpool
at less than the cost of manuring one acre for wheat
in England." This fact has sent thousands of farm-
laborers into English cities, there to lower wages by
competing for work. "Indian corn has been extensively raised in Italy. But Indian corn grown in the
valley of the Mississippi, a thousand miles from the sea-
board, has been transported in recent years to Italy and
sold in her markets at a lower cost than the corn of
Lombardy and Venetia, where the wages of the agricul-
turist are not one third of the wages paid in the United
States for corresponding labor. And one not surprising
sequel of this is that 77,000 Italian laborers emigrated to
the United States in 1885." [1] This immigration affects
unfavorably the price of labor here and so ministers to
popular discontent in this country. Thus these economic changes consequent upon new methods of distribution act and react all over the civilized world.

We are evidently being forced into something larger
than national life. A *world*-life is becoming apparent,
as yet very imperfect, but distinctly real. The great
movements of commerce and of immigration are a part
of that life. The industrial and economic disturbances
of the past twenty years, which have been well-nigh or

---

[1] D. A. Wells' Recent Economic Changes, p. 91.

quite coextensive with civilization, are appropriately called "growing pains" naturally attendant on the process by which the nations adjust themselves to closer relations and new conditions in the world's progress. And these readjustments, with their accompanying disturbances, will continue to recur until there is at length effected a complete co-ordination of the world's industries, which will enable each people to render to mankind the greatest service of which they are capable, and which will insure to all the largest possible returns for their service.

This co-ordination of industries will be effected slowly, of course, and it will require many years for the nations to gain the full consciousness of a world-life. Popular discontent, therefore, will by no means be temporary ; it will continue as long as these disturbing causes operate.

But let us look more closely at the circumstances of the workingman. He finds himself belonging to a system which, as we saw in the preceding chapter, is essentially unchristian because essentially selfish. He finds his labor rated as a commodity whose price is determined solely by the law of supply and demand. He believes that under the existing system he is the victim of the "iron law" of Ricardo, according to which wages are reduced to the lowest point at which the laborer can sustain life and reproduce his kind.

Oftentimes he is in no position to insist on a fair price for his work. Few are the workingmen who have not been forced at some time to hunt for a job; and those who are getting steady work know that there are many contingencies, any one of which may set them adrift any day. Few except workingmen know how much that means. "I have watched friends of mine," says Mr. H. M. Hyndman,[1] "who have had to go round week after week, month after month, maybe, seeking for a job. Such men do not parade their griefs, never, or

---

[1] Quoted by Pres. E. B. Andrews in *The New World*, June, 1892, p. 207.

very rarely, ask a middle-class man for help, and would utterly scorn to beg. Yet as a highly skilled artisan said to me only a few days ago, 'I would almost as soon go begging bread as begging work: they treat you as if it were a favor you asked.' I have watched such men, I say, skilled and unskilled, too, and the mental effect upon them of these long periods or short periods of worklessness is more depressing than I can describe. Let a man have been never so thrifty, if he has a wife and children, a few weeks of idleness sweep away his savings; then he begins to pawn what little things he has; later he gets behind with his rent. His more fortunate comrades help him,—this is invariable, so far as I have seen, among all classes of laborers; and then, if he is lucky, he gets into work again; if not, his furniture goes and he falls into dire poverty. All the time not only has the man himself been suffering and losing heart, but his wife has been fretting herself to death and the children have been half-fed. In the wintertime, when the uncertainty of getting work becomes, in most of our great industrial cities, the certainty of not getting it for a large percentage of the laboring men and women, things are of course at their worst. After having vainly trudged from workshop to workshop, from factory to factory, from wharf to wharf, after having perhaps fought fiercely but unsuccessfully for a few hours' work at the dock gates, the man returns home, weary, hungry, half dead, and ashamed of his growing raggedness, to see his home without firing or food, perhaps to go to bed in order to try and forget the misery around him." Surely, as Carlyle somewhere says: "A man willing to work and unable to find work is perhaps the saddest sight that fortune's inequality exhibits under the sun." The workingman,

> " Who begs a brother of the earth
> To give him leave to toil,"[1]

would only too gladly accept the primeval sentence,

---

[1] Burns.

" In the sweat of thy face shalt thou eat bread," but he
seeks in vain for some one to bless him with this curse.

Call a man in such a strait "free" to sell his labor in
" open market " ? He is not free; he is the slave of a
dire necessity. He must take what his employer, when
he finds one, is pleased to offer, however unjust the
wage may be. True, competition often forces the employer to pay the lowest possible price for labor; but is
it strange that workingmen who suffer or are liable to
suffer such injustice deem the system which inflicts it
unjust and unchristian ?

Again, the workingman feels that he is not sharing
equitably in the general prosperity.

The spirit of American civilization is eminently progressive. The increase of our population, the springing
up of new cities and the growth of old ones, the extension of our railway and telegraph systems, the increase of our agricultural, manufacturing, and mining
products, the development of our natural resources,
the accumulation of our national wealth,—all these are
simply enormous. Such are the progress of invention
and the increase of knowledge, and such is the rapidity
with which important changes jostle each other, that
years seem like generations.

In the midst of all this progress the workingman
feels that he is practically standing still or worse. He
sees many belonging to other classes waxing rich, while
he is perhaps unable to support his family.[1] If he
could feed and fatten himself and family on the east
wind and lay by all his wages, it would take a lifetime

---

[1] " In Massachusetts, where statistics of labor are the most elaborate published, the average workingman is unable to support the average workingman's family In 1883 the average expenses of workingmen's families, in
that state, were $754.42, while the earnings of workingmen who were heads
of families averaged $558.68. This means that about one third of the sup-
port of the family fell on the wife and children. I am not aware that the
condition of the workingman is at all exceptional in Massachusetts. Of
males engaged in the industries of that state in 1875, only one in one hundred owned a house." See the author's " Our Country," revised edition, pp.
147 and 154.

to save as much as many business and professional men make in a single year.

His wants are increasing with his intelligence, but there is no corresponding increase of his means. We hear it often said and often denied that while the rich are growing richer the poor are growing poorer. The poor are not growing poorer in the sense that their wages will buy less of the necessaries of life or that they are rated lower on the tax list, but it is true in the sense that there is a greater disparity now between the workingman's income and his wants than ever before, and that is the only sense worth considering in this connection.

Authorities do not agree as to the progress, either relative or actual, which has been made in the condition of workingmen. Mr. Wells thinks one cannot resist the conclusion that the very outcasts of England are now better provided for than were multitudes of her common laboring men only forty years ago.[1] And Mr. Giffen claims, as the result of his investigations for Great Britain, that "the average money-wages of the working classes of the community, looking at them in the mass, and comparing the mass of fifty years ago with the mass at the present time, have increased very nearly one hundred per cent;"[2] while Pres. E. B. Andrews is of the opinion that "in many respects the toiling masses are no whit better off to-day than in England four centuries ago," and believes that "the passing of this age of industrial advance and of world-wide land utilization with so slight gain in the ordinary comforts of life on the part of the laboring man goes far to preclude all hope of great improvement for him under present economic conditions."[3] And Prof. R. T. Ely and Pres. Seth Low say[4]: "When we compare the actual amount of wages received by the laboring

[1] Recent Economic Changes, p. 402.
[2] Ibid. p. 406.
[3] *The New World*, June, 1892, pp. 210, 212.
[4] "Present-Day Papers." *The Century*, April, 1890, p. 940.

classes now with their former wages, we find ourselves obliged to abandon that superficial optimism based on an imperfect analysis of industrial conditions. There seems to be an absolute improvement, but can we certainly say that this has been relative ? "

Now here is the point of my contention: the question whether the condition of the workingman has *materially* improved in this century is stoutly debated, *but the question whether there has been most wonderful material progress in general is not debatable;* no one doubts it. Evidently, then, the progress of the workingman is not proportionate to the general material progress. And this fact gives him just ground for complaint.

Mr. Giffen thinks that "the poor have had almost all the benefit of the great material advance of the last fifty years." [1] But it would be quite impossible to convince the workingman of this in the face of many facts with which he is familiar. He knows, for instance, that a car-load of coal can be mined, made ready for market, and loaded in one half the time now that it required ten years ago; but he knows that the miner's wages have not been doubled in ten years. He knows that in cotton factories the operative produces nearly four times as much as he did fifty or sixty years ago, while his wages have been increased only eighty per cent. [2] He knows that in the flouring mill one man now does the work formerly done by four, but he does not receive the wages of four. A woman with a sewing-machine can do probably six times as much work as could a needlewoman fifty years ago; but the seamstress of to-day does not receive six times as much as her mother

---

[1] Quoted by Wells, Recent Economic Changes, p. 358.

[2] " In 1880 the Pacific Mills paid a dividend of twenty-two per cent on a capital of $2,500,000; the Middlesex Mills, twenty per cent. And those very mills which were paying twenty-two per cent dividends were paying the munificent wages of ninety cents a day! The Willimantic Linen Company pay the same liberal wages, and one year declared a dividend of eighty per cent! " See Meriwether, The Tramp at Home, p. 38.

did or work only one sixth as many hours. She works
quite as hard and quite as long, and in many cases for
wages quite as small. In the manufacture of shoes an
operative now does the work formerly done by five or
six or even ten; and in the manufacture of wall-paper
the workman's effectiveness has been increased a hun-
dredfold. A few years ago a skilled workman could
make up three dozen pairs of sleeve-buttons per day.
Now by the aid of the most improved machinery a boy
can make up 9000 pairs, or 250 times as many. The
inventions which make this possible have neither reduced the workman's toil nor increased his wages.
When he set up thirty-six pairs a day, he received two
and a half or three dollars for it. Now the boy who
does as much as 250 men could then receives less than
ninety cents for it. True, improved methods and machinery have both reduced prices and raised wages, but
is it strange if many believe that those who are exploit-
ing labor get the greater share of the benefit ?

No one would pretend that workingmen in the United
States are twenty-five per cent better off now than
they were ten years ago; and yet from 1880 to 1890 the
average wealth of American families rose from four
thousand dollars to five thousand.

In view of the fact just mentioned; in view of our
marvellous mechanical progress, which enables one man
now to do as much as four, six, ten, and in some instances even a hundred men or more, twenty years ago;
and in view of the fact that the intelligence and wants
of workingmen have increased several fold, does it not
seem somewhat puerile to urge that workingmen have
had their share of the general progress because, taking
into account both wages and prices, they have made "a
gain of at least ten per cent in half a century ? "

The real question is not whether the laborer is receiving larger wages than formerly, nor even whether his
increase is proportionate to the general increase of
wealth, but whether he is receiving his *just dues.* It
is often claimed that all wealth really belongs to him

because he has produced it all. This is absurd. Besides the skill, time, and strength of the workman, several other factors enter into the cost of the product, viz., the material, tools, machinery, and perhaps building. Without these the workman can do nothing. If he furnishes all of these as well as the work, then the product is wholly his. If capital furnishes a part, then a part of the product belongs to capital. Precisely how much is the fair share of each is the difficult question. But thus much is clear: capital and labor together produce sufficient wealth every year, in this country, to lift laborer as well as capitalist above want for a year. Over and above all expenditure and all waste, our average annual increase of wealth from 1880 to 1890 was $1,781,700,000. If then the industrious and economical laborer has not been lifted above want, he evidently has not had his due share, and ought not to be satisfied until justice is done him.

Workingmen will not deny that different services have different values. But in view of the fact that capital is as helpless without labor as labor is without capital, that both are alike necessary to society, it is difficult, and becoming increasingly so as workingmen grow more intelligent, to convince them that there is any justice in so wide a disparity as exists between their condition and that of capitalists. The limits of such a work as this permit us to note but few of the many lights and shadows which mark the strong contrasts of the social picture.

Mr. Thomas G. Shearman, in an article[1] which has attracted much attention, but whose force I think has not been materially impaired by criticism, says that "the average annual income of the richest hundred Americans cannot be less than $1,200,000, and probably exceeds $1,500,000."

If 100 workingmen could earn each $1000 a year, they would have to work 1200 or 1500 years to earn as much

---

[1] *The Forum*, Nov. 1889.

152 *THE NEW ERA.*

as the *annual income* of these 100 richest Americans. And if a workingman could earn $1000 a day he would have to work until he was 547 years old, and never take a day off, before he could earn as much as some Americans are worth.

Mr. Shearman, after having given good reasons for the opinion, says: "It may safely be assumed that 200,000 persons control 70 per cent of the national wealth." That is, three tenths of one per cent of the population control 70 per cent of the property. In other words, in the distribution of the national wealth, one man in three hundred receives $70 out of every $100, and 299 men receive $30, which if averaged would give them about ten cents each.

The wealth of Crœsus was estimated at only $8,000,-000, while there are seventy American estates, according to Mr. Shearman, which average $35,000,000 each. The nabobs of the later Roman republic became famous for their immense fortunes, but the entire possessions of the richest were not equal to the annual income of at least one American. In anticipation of the coming "billionaire," Mr. Shearman says:[1] "Several non-speculative estates have increased fivefold in less than forty years. Interest is now very low; but, adding to interest the steady increment of city lands, an addition of at least four per cent per annum, at compound interest, may be counted upon for these great estates. At that rate a present fortune of $200,000,000 would become a billion ($1,000,000,000) in less than forty years. Financial conditions remaining unchanged, the American billionaire might reasonably be looked for within that time, and several billionaires might be expected within sixty years."

Many rich men render services of very exceptional value to society by means of their exceptional executive abilities, which services deserve a high reward: but there is a growing class of idle rich, whose only

[1] *The Forum*, Jan. 1891, p. 548.

business is their own amusement, and who, though "they toil not, neither do they spin," yet rank Solomon himself in luxury.

In sharp and instructive contrast are the many who toil longer and harder than beasts of burden and fare worse. A man sixty years old, once prosperous, but caught in the financial crash of 1873, worked seventeen hours every day on a street railway. He "had a Sunday off eighteen months ago, and hoped he might get another in the course of five or six months more." The *horses* on that road work four hours and rest twenty. The standard of the London cab horse, which General Booth pleads for the English poor, might not be amiss in this country.

It is said the Durham miners sometimes have to "hew coal in seams 1 ft. 10 in. to 2 ft. thick, lying for hours on their side, all but naked, in some inches of water, and under a sort of shower-bath from the roof, picking and shovelling as best they can. That not being the sort of place to take a lunch or dinner in, they work on, taking only a sup of cold tea or a bit of bread and butter, till time to leave the pit." "That men who rise at three o'clock in the morning to do such work are 'queer in the legs' from early manhood, and broken down at fifty, is not strange;" [1] nor is it strange that 80,000 of these miners, in the spring of 1892, should strike against a reduction of 7½ per cent in their scanty wages.

"We read about women who make twelve shirts for seventy-five cents, and furnish their own thread, in Chicago; about women that finish off an elegant cloak for four cents; about children that work twelve hours a day for a dollar a week; about some women who are glad to get the chance that offers six cents for four hours' work." [2] We are assured on what seems to be good authority that the "sweating" system is forcing men and women to work sometimes for thirty-

---

[1] *The Christian Union*, June 11, 1892. [2] Frances E. Willard.

three, and even thirty-six, consecutive hours to avoid
starvation.

> " Alas that gold should be so dear,
> And flesh and blood so cheap!"

The Rev. L. A. Banks has introduced us to the white
slaves of the Boston " sweat-shops." Some of these
women earn sixty cents by sewing sixteen or seventeen hours a day. One woman makes cheap overcoats
at four cents apiece ; another, knee " pants " for boys
at sixteen cents a dozen pairs. Another by working
very late at night earns sometimes as much as fifty-two
cents a day, and thinks it would be " almost a Paradise
if she could make fifty-two cents every day." One
poor girl, who was compelled to make a dozen pairs of
overalls a day, said that when she was in the House
of Correction she had to finish only eight pairs a day,
and had comfortable lodgings and good food besides.
" She had sometimes asked herself whether it would not
be better to commit some crime and be incarcerated
where life would be far more endurable than in the
close and noisome tenement." [1]

In this same city there is a fruit market "which has
existed for thirty years upon the whims of the rich.
Hamburg grapes at ten dollars a pound are regularly in
stock. In winter, strawberries and asparagus sell
easily at three dollars a box or a bunch. When the
first Florida berries come, thirteen in a cup, at four dollars a cup, parties are supplied. One hundred and
twenty-five dollars' worth of fruit to a single order
causes the dealer no surprise." [2]

In New York City, where, according to *The New York
Tribune*, there are 1103 millionaires, "worth from one
to one hundred and fifty millions" each, more than two
thirds of the population live in tenement-houses. Of
course many of these houses afford very comfortable

---

[1] W. P. Adams, *Christian Union*, Aug. 1, 1891.
[2] Elizabeth Stuart Phelps, *Forum*, May, 1889.

quarters, but others would be unfit for stables. Several years ago 2000 of these tenements were reported in the official statistics as "very bad." "Recent certified revelations," says Bishop Huntington, "have laid bare the multiplied horrors and depravities of the tenement population in great cities, where forty-one out of every hundred families live each in a single room, and where the poorest pay more rent than the richest for each cubic foot of space and air." [1]

Sometimes forty-five people sleep in one room. And even these wretched lodgings are insecure to their more wretched occupants. During the winter months of a recent year, in three judicial districts of New York City over 21,000 men, women, and children were evicted because unable to pay their rent; and in the course of the year 23,895 families, not less than 119,000 persons, suffered the loss of their homes in like manner. [2] The story of one of these victims is briefly told in a newspaper item: "Mrs. Clara Kloin was evicted on Saturday; turned out in the cold rain (in February) with a baby only a few weeks old, because she was unable to raise the paltry rent. She walked about all day Saturday seeking a lodging. The baby died on Washington's birthday, and the mother is likely to die." In this same city we read of a ten-thousand-dollar banquet and of 3819 dead who in a single year are thrown into the Potter's field, too poor either to live or die decently. We also read that the other night, while a ball costing $50,000 was in progress at Delmonico's, out on the curbstone there shivered a woman with a babe in her arms. A passer-by saw her crying, and spoke with her. She said the little one was sick. He looked at the child and saw that it had been dead for some hours. It had starved and frozen to death.

In Scotland official figures (1870) show that "one third of the families live in a single room, and more

---

[1] *The Forum*, Oct. 1890.
[2] *The Arena*, April, 1891, p. 634.

than another third in only two rooms,"[1] while the hunting-grounds of an American millionaire extend across the Highlands from sea to sea. The remarkable and most valuable analysis of the population of London made by Mr. Charles Booth[2] shows that there are in that city 938,293 " poor," 316,834 " very poor," and 37,610 of the lowest—a total of 1,292,737, or about thirty per cent of the entire population living in poverty.

Doubtless much poverty is due to drunkenness, and again much drunkenness is due to poverty. It would appear from Mr. Booth's investigations in East London that fifty-five per cent of the very poor and fully sixty-eight per cent of the other poor are so not through any fault of their own, but because they lack employment, while only an insignificant proportion are loafers. It is estimated that the suffering of fifty-three per cent of the needy in New York is for lack of work.[3]

Wealth is often a well-earned reward and poverty is sometimes a well-deserved penalty, but they are becoming more and more in this country a matter of inheritance—a distinction which finds no shadow of justification in the character of those whose circumstances point so strong a contrast.

Our discussion thus far has related more especially to the artisan class; some attention must be given to the complaint of the farmer.

In many parts of the United States there has been a notable decline in the value of agricultural lands. Many farms in New England can be bought for less than the cost of the buildings and walls on them. There is excellent land in the heart of Massachusetts whose market value has depreciated one half in sixty years. Governor Foraker said in 1887 that farm property in Ohio was then from twenty-five to fifty per cent cheaper than it was in 1880. During the same

---

[1] Henry George in " Twilight Club Tracts," p. 37.
[2] Life and Labor of the People.
[3] Pres. E. B. Andrews, *The New World*, June, 1892, p. 207.

interval the value of agricultural land in the ten cotton states declined $459,000,000, or thirty-one per cent.[1]

There were 25,354,714 more acres cultivated in this country in 1888 than in 1880, and the total cereal productions were 491,548,499 bushels greater; but for their increased toil and larger crops in 1888 the farmers received $41,242,306 *less* than in 1880.[2]

There has been a like depression of agriculture in Europe. Though the wealth of Great Britain has more than doubled since 1840, there has been since then a decline of £138,000,000 in the value of lands.[3] In eleven years the amount of land under cultivation decreased considerably more than a million acres. " In France," we are told, " the peasant proprietors have ceased to buy land and are anxious to sell it; and in the department of Aisne, one of the richest in France, one tenth of the land is abandoned, because it is found that, at present prices, the sale of produce does not cover the expenses of cultivation."[4] Germany, Austria, Spain, and Portugal afford no exception to the general rule; while in Russia the army of beggars includes in its ranks tens of thousands of landowners, some 80,000 of whom have surrendered their land, finding the costs of ownership greater than the profits of cultivation.[5]

This general depression of agriculture is due to the radical changes in the methods of production and distribution which have taken place especially during the last third of a century. The disturbances and consequent discontent in the industrial world which resulted from invention appeared much earlier among artisans than among farmers, because machinery was applied to manufactures much earlier than to agriculture. Our

---

[1] Report of a committee of citizens of the ten cotton-growing states " On the Causes of the Depressed Condition of Agriculture, and the Remedies," 1887. Quoted by D. A. Wells.

[2] United States Statistical Abstract No. 13, 1890, p. 320.

[3] D. A. Wells' Recent Economic Changes. p. 423.

[4] Ibid. p. 377.

[5] Correspondence *London Economist*, 1887. Quoted by D. A. Wells.

civil war, which took so many men from the farms,
greatly stimulated the invention and introduction of
agricultural machinery. Then, following close on the
war, came the great changes in the method of distribution—the transcontinental railways, which opened up
a vast territory to settlement and cultivation; and the
compound marine engine, which brought our western
products into most damaging competition with the
agriculture of Europe. And of course the Middle States
and New England farmers also suffered from the same
competition.

One might suppose that with the European and American markets delivered over to them the western
farmers might have flourished beyond all precedent;
but they complain that all profits and in many cases
even their farms have been eaten up by interest, the
railways, and the middlemen.

During the era of rapid settlement after the war, the
farmers borrowed vast sums of money, often at exorbi-
tant rates of interest, to enable them to improve their
land and to buy machinery which had now become a
necessity, while the planters of the cotton states probably became more generally and more deeply involved
than the farmers; the fall in the prices of produce
practically increased their indebtedness; the railways,
at whose mercy the farmers were, charged "all that
the traffic would bear," and a swarm of middlemen
left for the producers but a small fraction of the prices
paid by the consumers. Thus, notwithstanding the
Mississippi valley has become the granary of the world,
its farmers and planters have become painfully embar-
rassed, and many of them through mortgages have
suffered the loss of everything. Investigations of the
last census, made in ten counties in Kansas, showed
that less than twenty-four per cent of the farmers held
their farms unincumbered.[1]

The deep discontent of the farmers will be by no

---

[1] Extra Census Bulletin No. 18.

means temporary, since it has been produced by causes which will continue operative for years to come. The changes in the methods of production are not yet complete. Mr. D. A. Wells says that it is coming to be the opinion of many of the best authorities, both in the United States and Europe, that the only possible future for agriculture is to be found in large farms, worked with ample capital, especially in the form of machinery and with labor organized somewhat after the factory system.[1] Moreover, though most of the public agricultural lands are taken, less than one fifth of our arable land is under actual cultivation. So far as agriculture is concerned, therefore, the greater part of our territory is practically unoccupied. Furthermore, according to Mr. Edward Atkinson, we could double our produce without putting another acre under the plough, "by merely bringing our product up to our average standard of reasonably good agriculture." All of which means that our farm products are capable of being increased some tenfold.

Thus it appears that the causes which have produced the discontent of the farmers—the changed methods of production, the great increase of agricultural products, the existence of mortgages, and the exactions of railways and middlemen—are all likely to continue for some time to come.

No doubt the condition of the farmer and of the workingman will improve in the future, but as improvement of condition has been accompanied by increasing discontent during the past century, we cannot infer that future improvement, under the existing organization of society, will allay discontent.

Second. Having examined the causes of popular discontent, we are now prepared to consider very briefly its significance.

This is not the first age of the world when there has been a widespread discontent, but it means more in

---

[1] Recent Economic Changes, pp. 461, 462.

this age than it ever meant before, because there is greater popular intelligence. An intelligent discontent will not suffer in dumb despair; it has resources, means of expressing itself and of enforcing its demands. It can agitate, and educate public opinion. It knows enough of the progress of the world in the past to hope for the future, and it is easy for hope to purpose and achieve.

Again, popular discontent means more in this age than ever before, because it appeals to more tender sensibilities. There have been greater miseries in other ages, but in this day those who suffer are not paralyzed by despair, and those who witness suffering are not frozen with indifference. Conditions which a few centuries since were taken for granted and caused no comment now excite indignation and horror. Once men were insensible to the sufferings of strangers; now a calamity by fire or flood or pestilence or famine brings quick relief from distant parts of the world. Once gentlefolk found amusement in sights of blood and horror and death ; now cruelty even to animals is a crime. Once human suffering was a matter of course, and the misery of the many was deemed the will of God; to-day all suffering is seen to imply something abnormal, and all agree that if possible its cause must be removed.

Perhaps there is no better illustration of the change in the world's sensibilities than that which is afforded by the punishment of criminals now and a few centuries ago. Once the death penalty was inflicted by slowly immersing the victim in a caldron of boiling oil. Harrison, the regicide, was sentenced to be hanged, then revived, maimed, drawn, and hanged again: and this torture, remember, was *judicial*, inflicted by the highest court of the most Christian nation in the world. Now, public opinion insists that the death penalty, when inflicted, be as nearly painless and instantaneous as possible. As the world's nerves are refined, suffering of every sort becomes more and more intolerable.

Moreover, as society becomes more highly organized and intimate relations are multiplied, it is becoming more and more true that its different classes are members one of another, and when one member suffers all the members suffer with it. One class *cannot* remain indifferent to the wrongs of another.

Again, the discontent of the people is more significant now than ever before, because now the people rule. When they were slaves, crushed under law, custom, institutions, and all the rigid strata of the social structure, their discontent signified little until it gathered the might of an earthquake sufficient to shatter society with its upheaval. Now, numbers possess the power and can exercise it through the established channels of the law. What king or emperor or aristocracy may think or propose is to us of no consequence, but what the masses think or propose is of utmost consequence, for they are to determine the future of civilization. The rich and powerful are naturally conservative. It is of course those who are discontented with their lot who want a change; hence it is that new ideas, whether political or religious, generally gain currency first among the poor. Evidently, popular discontent has profound significance. What *is* that significance?

It is as true of society as of the individual, that self-dissatisfaction is a sign of upward, not downward, movement. Popular contentment marks a stagnant civilization—China; popular restlessness marks a progressive civilization—Japan. New wants are rungs in the ladder of progress; and civilization, reaching up to them, mounts to something higher.

The discontent of the masses means that they feel the pulsations of a new life, born of increased intelligence. As we have seen, to add to a man's knowledge is to enlarge his horizon, to make him conscious of new wants, and to show him new possibilities. The popular ferment of to-day means a struggle to realize the possibilities of a new and larger life.

Twice before in modern times has there been a deep

and widespread discontent among the people—once on the eve of the great Reformation of the sixteenth century and once on the eve of the French Revolution. Certain conditions which appeared just before the former reappeared just before the latter. It is most significant that these same conditions, among the most important of which is popular discontent, have again reappeared.[1]

The first of these great movements was primarily religious, the second was political, the third will be social and economic. The first destroyed spiritual despotism; the second struck the deathblow of political despotism; is it not quite possible that the third will put an end to economic despotism?

It was shown in the first chapter that the great changes of the nineteenth century have been beginnings rather than endings, and that they have prepared the way for still greater probable changes in the twentieth century. We have seen that popular discontent is deep-seated and widespread, that it is not likely to be temporary, that it will be satisfied with nothing less than most important and far-reaching economic and social changes, and that the restless masses are the power which will determine our future.

Does it not look as if there were about to be a new evolution of civilization? If this evolution is to bring the solution of our great sociological problems, it must be along Christian lines. Men are unconsciously seeking to harmonize in modern society the two great principles of individualism and organization, and so to readjust our social and economic relations as to co-ordinate these two seemingly conflicting principles. It was shown in the preceding chapter that this must be done by the application of the teachings of Christ. Surely, if the new era is to mark an advance in the coming of

---

[1] See a valuable article, " A Third Revolution," by Edward P. Cheyney, in *Annals of the American Academy of Political and Social Science*, May, 1892. He points out no less than five conditions which have thus reappeared.

the Kingdom, the multitude that is being quickened with a new life and is to fashion our unfolding civilization must be brought under the power of Christian truth.

Oh that men of God everywhere might discern the signs of the times, and seeing, seize the priceless opportunity of the hour!

> ". . . Suppose
> Mount Athos carved as Persian Xerxes·schemed,
> To some colossal statue of a man.
>
> The peasant, gathering brushwood in the ear,
> Had guessed as little of any human form
> Up there, as would a flock of browsing goats.
>
> . . . 'Tis even thus
> With times we live in, evermore too great
> To be apprehended near." [1]

The Great Teacher pronounced a blessing on the eyes that *see.* [2]

---

[1] Mrs. Browning's "Aurora Leigh." [2] Matt. xiii. 16.

CHAPTER VIII

VAST movements of population are of profound significance both in their causes and effects. While we hear much of the millions of aliens who are flooding our shores and foreignizing our cities, but little is said of a movement hardly less momentous, whose consequences, though not so obvious, are perhaps equally far-reaching. I refer to the tide of population which is setting so strongly from country to city, and which is depleting the one and congesting the other, to the detriment of both.

The following table shows this movement of population for one hundred years:

Census Years.	Population of the United States.	Population of Cities.	Per cent of Urban Population.	Per cent of Rural Population.
1790	3,929,214	131,472	3.35	96.65
1800	5,308,483	210,873	3.97	96.03
1810	7,239,881	356,920	4.93	95.07
1820	9,633,822	475,135	4.93	95.07
1830	12,866,020	867,509	6.72	93.28
1840	17,069,453	1,453,994	8.52	91.48
1850	23,191,876	2,897,586	12.49	87.51
1860	31,443,321	5,070,256	16.13	83.87
1870	38,558,371	8,071,875	20.93	79.07
1880	50,155,783	11,318,547	22.57	77.43
1890	62,622,250	18,235,670	29.12	70.88

Thus it appears that in one century the population in cities of 8000 or more has risen from one thirtieth to nearly one third of the whole, the rate of increase being much greater from 1880 to 1890 than ever before. During these ten years the rural population increased only fourteen per cent, while the urban increased sixty-one.

The limit at which the government draws the line between rural and urban populations must of course be arbitrary, but 8000 would seem to be high. The conditions which make the city attractive and insure its growth exist to a considerable degree in towns of five or six thousand inhabitants. Hon. William M. Springer is of the opinion that "if the classification should embrace cities of 4000 inhabitants and upward, it would undoubtedly appear that the rural population had decreased during the decade."[1] Certain it is that, with the existing high limit, there are seven states whose rural population was smaller in 1890 than it was ten years before. While the cities of Maine, Vermont, Massachusetts, Rhode Island, New York, Maryland, and Illinois gained 2,509,000 inhabitants, the rural districts of these states suffered an actual loss of 200,000; and, excepting the South and the new states of the West, the increase of the rural population was insignificant as compared with that of the urban. For instance, in Connecticut the former was 12,000 and the latter 111,000; in Ohio, the country gained 60,000 and the cities 414,000. Twenty-eight of the counties of that state lost population. These counties are chiefly rural. On the Western Reserve sixty-six townships suffered a loss between 1870 and 1880, and 124 lost population between 1880 and 1890. Often the county-seat grows at the expense of every rural town in the county, and though the county shows a gain, it may be that every town in it save one has been depleted. This movement is closely connected with the depression in agriculture, discussed in the preceding chapter. Not a few farmers, unable to sell or rent their farms, have abandoned them altogether. A few years since, the Commissioner of Agriculture and Immigration of New Hampshire re-

[1] *Forum*, Dec. 1890, p. 474.

ported 1442 vacant or abandoned farms, with tenantable buildings, in that state.

In 1889 the Commissioner of Agriculture and Manufacturing Interests in Vermont issued a circular, stating that in the town of Reading there were 4000 acres of land offered for sale at one or two dollars per acre. One half of these, he says, "are lands which formerly comprised good farms, but with buildings now gone, and fast growing up to timber ; some of this land is used for pasturage, and on other portions the fences are not kept up, leaving old cellar-holes and miles of stone walls to testify to former civilization." In the town of Vershire "there are from thirty-five to forty farms, contiguous or nearly so, abandoned and unoccupied." In the town of Wilmington there were 5000 acres in the same condition.[1]

These abandoned farms are by no means peculiar to the New England States. A correspondent of *The New York Nation,* under date of Nov. 23, 1889, wrote: "In the rural districts in Wayne County (New York) there are no less than 400 empty houses. The town of Sodus alone has over fifty deserted houses, and Huron has thirty or more."

In Michigan there were 7419 fewer farmers in 1890 than in 1880, though the population had meanwhile increased 457,000.[2]

This movement of population from country to city, of which abandoned farms are the sad and silent witnesses in many states, is shown by a comparison of the Eleventh Census with the Tenth to have been remarkably general. Eight of the newer states and territories had not been divided into townships in 1880, and therefore do not afford the necessary data for comparison; but an examination of every township in every other state and territory shows that of 25,746 townships in thirty-nine states and territories 10,063, or 39 per

---

[1] *The Nation*, No. 1266.

[2] Ninth Annual Report of Bureau of Labor Statistics for Michigan, 1892.

cent, lost population during the ten years preceding
1890.

Of the 1502 townships in New England 932, or 62 per
cent, were more or less depleted. In New York 69.5
per cent lost population; in Ohio 58 per cent; in Indiana 49 per cent; in Illinois 54 per cent. The accompanying table shows that the movement was common
to the South and. West as well as to the Middle and
Eastern States, though the rural districts in the region
of large cities naturally felt their attraction most.

	Number of Townships.	Number of Townships which lost Population, 1880-1890.
Alabama	704	244
Arizona	13	4
Arkansas	895	185
California	352	132
Connecticut	153	79
Delaware	32	15
Florida	161	44
Georgia	1,181	414
Illinois	1,441	792
Indiana	998	489
Iowa	1,513	686
Kansas	1,047	268
Kentucky	803	293
Louisiana	402	96
Maine	540	348
Maryland	221	101
Massachusetts	298	154
Michigan	1,088	407
Minnesota	1,297	271
Mississippi	360	79
Missouri	1,115	324
Nebraska	526	58
Nevada	18	13
New Hampshire	241	152
New Jersey	250	117
New York	922	641
North Carolina	863	190
Ohio	1,331	775
Oregon	329	88
Pennsylvania	2,075	918
Rhode Island	26	12
South Carolina	407	81
Tennessee	1,392	571
Texas	572	137
Utah	211	80
Vermont	244	187
Virginia	424	177
West Virginia	324	43
Wisconsin	977	398
Total	25,746	10,063

Let us now observe some of the results of this remarkable movement as they appear in the country.

The general public has little knowledge of the rural
districts. When the public travels, it is usually by rail;
it sees as much of the country as can be seen from the
car-window. The thriving villages and prospective
cities, strung like beads on the lines of travel, give the
impression of general prosperity. We hardly appreciate how large a proportion of the population lives
five, ten, or fifteen miles back from the railroad under
conditions very different. The reporter, ubiquitous
along the lines of telegraph and railway, is wanting
here. It is the life of the city that is reflected in the
press; that of the country is unreported. In view of
these facts, the Evangelical Alliance for the United
States, in the summers of 1889 and 1890, carefully investigated the condition of a large number of rural communities in the State of New York. Five counties were
explored, two in the central part of the state and one in
each of the three lobes,—northern, southern, and western. Excepting the cities, these counties were carefully
canvassed, the people being visited in their homes or
diligently inquired after. A study was made of economic, moral, and religious conditions, and statistics of
population, churches, church membership, and church
attendance were gathered.

From one quarter to one tenth of the population were
found in church on a pleasant Sunday. Somewhat less
than one half of the Protestant population claimed to
be church-goers (and many base such claims on the fact
that they sometimes attend a funeral in a church). In
fifteen villages, containing a population of about
30,000, all in one county, only 23 per cent of the
people were church-goers. One pastor reported that in
his calls, the summer before, he found two hundred
and fifty heads of families not connected with any
church. Many Protestant church buildings were seen
falling into decay, having been abandoned long since to
" bats and brickbats." In one village, with two disused

Protestant churches and one active Roman Catholic church, there were fourteen saloons, all within a distance of a quarter of a mile. There were a few years ago in one town a large Presbyterian church, two Methodist churches, a Baptist church, and a flourishing Baptist seminary. To-day the Presbyterian church is used as a barn, the Baptist church is abandoned, the two Methodist churches are almost extinct, and the Baptist seminary is utilized as a Roman Catholic church. In many villages there were twice as many churches as were needed, all feeble and struggling with each other for life, while along the Erie Canal for eight miles were found scattered hamlets, containing together a considerable population, where there was no religious service of any kind from one year's end to another. Information from other parts of the state indicates that these five counties are fairly representative of the rural districts of New York. A clergyman in another county writes: "We have investigated the condition of the county and find it little less than appalling. Not one half of its children have Sabbath-school privileges, and wide stretches of country are without any religious activities of any kind."

From other investigations made in Ohio, Pennsylvania, and several of the New England States it appears that such conditions are not so exceptional as many might imagine. At an interdenominational meeting held in Waterville, Maine, in November, 1891, a Methodist clergyman of that state, Rev. C. S. Cummings, made the following statements, which were not questioned by any speaker: "There are at least seventy towns in Maine in which no religious service is held.[1] At the same time there are scores of towns in which

---

[1] Rev. A. E. Dunning, D.D., in *The Andover Review* for November, 1890, says: "There are ninety-five towns and plantations in Maine where no religious services of any sort are held, and more villages in Illinois without the gospel than in any other state in the Union. These statements are made on the authority of superintendents and secretaries of missions in the fields named."

two or more little churches are struggling for existence,
calling for missionary help and expending most of their
energies in raising money to pay current expenses.
Moreover, 55,000 families in Maine do not attend
church services.   In Oxford County but 38 per cent
of the people go to church. In Waldo County only
31 per cent attend.   The Maine Bible Society report
19,013 families visited one year, 56 per cent of whom
were non-church-going.   Of children of school age
45,000 do not attend Sunday-school.   There was a time
when to die without the benefit of the clergy was
a penalty of law for public offenders; but now it is a
common   occurrence.   Of seventy-eight funerals at
which I officiated last year forty-one were in non-
church-going families, and thirty-one of them were of
adults who were sick and died without a visit from any
religious person, a prayer, or a word of Christian hope.
I did not know that such people existed until I was
sent for after death."   The speaker proceeded to show
that vice and im   rality were rapidly growing, and
said that society was "honeycombed with gambling
and lottery schemes."

Of course it is not pretended that the above describes
the condition of all country communities; but it is only
a question of time when precisely such conditions will
result from well- stablished tendencies which exist
wherever the population is being depleted.   Investigations justify the following generalizati ns relative to the
results in rural communities of this movement of population from country to city

1. Roads dete orate.   It costs as much to keep roads
in repair for one thousand peopl as for two thousand,
and the burden rests more and more heavily on each
tax-payer as population falls off.   A sparse population
rarely has good roads, especially in hilly or mountainous
regions.   They are generally poor, often execrable,
sometimes impassable.

Roads are an index of civilization, and good roads are
among its most important factors.   They affect not only

economic conditions, but intellectual, moral, and religious as well.

It makes a great difference to the farmer whether he
travels ten miles in one hour or in three, and whether
his team can draw two tons of produce or a half-ton.
The value of his farm is affected by its distance from
market, and a poor road may lengthen five miles into
fifteen.

As the road deteriorates he is practically moved
farther and farther back from the village. The post-
office is now so far away that he very likely drops the
weekly paper, attendance at church becomes more irregular as it grows more difficult, and at length ceases
altogether. Few attend church from a greater distance
than two miles. Investigations in the rural districts of
New York showed that from seventy-five to ninety-five
per cent of the church-goers lived within two miles of
the church.

2. When population decreases and roads deteriorate
property depreciates, mortgages multiply, sheriff's sales
increase, and everything has a downward tendency. Of
course the market value of agricultural land falls as
the demand for it diminishes, and the removal of population affects all of the kinds of business which exist at
the village. It has been announced that during the first
three weeks of 1892 no less than sixteen country stores
in a single New England county stopped business.
Thus business is following to larger centres the little
factories which used to be scattered along the water-
powers of New England. And as this movement of
business is a result of the centralization of population it
also serves to increase that centralization at the expense
of the country.

3. The removal of population very seriously weakens
the churches and impairs the schools. As church
privileges and school advantages become poorer, those
who prize them most highly have increasing reasons for
leaving; so that there is a constant tendency toward
the loss of the best elements, and the churches suffer

more than the community at large. The depleted churches, in their struggle for existence, almost necessarily fall into competition with each other, and the smaller the village the sharper becomes the sectarian rivalry. Instead of making the church a means to save men, men are sought, if at all, as a means to save the church. Thus the churches lose their hold on the population; and as they grow weaker the minister' upport dwindles until he is forced to divide his time with some other feeble church in a neighboring village, or turn aside to farming in order to eke out his scanty living, or leave altogether. In this way the churches are enfeebled until many of them become extinct. During the past thirty years thousands of churches have thus died from exhaustion in the rural districts of the United States.

4. Again, this emigration is often accompanied by an immigration which results not in the depletion of population, but in an exchange of the native for a foreign stock. This is the reason that more states did not show an actual loss of rural population from 1880 to 1890. Says Prof. Rodney Welch:[1] "It may sound strange to eastern readers, but it is nevertheless true, that in the States of Illinois, Wisconsin, and Iowa more farms have been deserted by their owners than in New Hampshire, Vermont, and Massachusetts. In the New England States owners leave their farms because the labor spent in cultivating them is no longer remunerative, but such is not the case in the prairie regions f the West. There the owners of farms leave them for the reason that they can obtain sufficient rent from tenants to enable them to support their families in towns. Cities in several of the Western States contain hundreds of retired farmers, . . . who have divided their farms into small tracts, erected cheap buildings on them, and leased them, generally to persons of foreign birth.[2] The result of this

[1] *The Forum*, Feb. 1891, p. 697.

[2] Extra Census Bulletin No. 18 shows that in ten counties investigated in Kansas 33.25 per cent of the farmers were tenants, in ten counties in Ohio 37.10 per cent were tenants.

is the formation of a distinct peasant class, such as is found in Bavaria and Bohemia. In entire counties in Illinois and Wisconsin the English language is scarcely ever heard outside of the large towns." Thus one result of this migration is the development of an ignorant rural peasantry and a class of absentee landlords.

5. One other result of this movement of population from country to city must be noted as of the utmost importance.

When population decreases and roads deteriorate there is increasing isolation, with which comes a tendency toward degeneration and demoralization. The mountain whites of the South afford an illustration of the results of such a tendency operating through several generations. They come chiefly from good English and Scotch-Irish stock, but living remote from civilization and out of the current of modern progress, they have been swept into eddies which have carried them back toward barbarism. Their heathenish degradation is due not to their antecedents, but primarily to their isolation. Like conditions have produced like results in many parts of the world, and would prove as operative in Massachusetts and New York as in eastern Tennessee and northern Alabama. Indeed, the writer knows of a town in one of the older New England States where such conditions have obtained for several generations and have produced precisely the same results, —the same large families of twelve or fifteen members, the same illiteracy, the same ignorance of the Christian religion, the same vices, the same "marriage" and "divorce" without reference to the laws of God or man, which characterize the mountain whites of the South. These mountain whites of the North came from the old New England stock, and lived in the hill country, where their ancestors settled in isolation from the surrounding community. When we consider the meaning of this depletion of the rural towns, it becomes painfully significant that there are 932 townships in New England where this process of deterioration has already

begun; that there are 641 such townships in New York,
775 in Ohio, 489 in Indiana, 792 in Illinois, 571 in Tennessee, 919 in Pennsylvania, and more than 10,000 in the
United States.

If this migration continues, *and no new preventive
measures are devised,* I see no reason why isolation,
irreligion, ignorance, vice, and degradation should not
increase in the country until we have a rural American
peasantry, illiterate and immoral, possessing the rights
of citizenship, but utterly incapable of performing or
comprehending its duties.

It becomes, then, a question of the utmost interest
whether this movement is temporary or not. Some
hoped that the census of 1890 would show that a reaction toward the country had already set in; but such
hopes could not have been based on a knowledge of the
causes of this movement. It has been thought to result
from conditions naturally attendant on the growth of
a new civilization and the rapid development of the
West. Such causes have had their influence, but there
are others which are at the same time more powerful
and more permanent.

This migration from country to city is by no means
peculiar to the United States. It is a world movement.
From 1851 to 1881 the population of England increased
forty-five per cent. But this increase was entirely in
the cities; the rural population remained stationary.
From 1880 to 1885 the population of Germany increased
about a half million a year, but the rural population
decreased 156,000. During the same period there was
a small increase in the population of France. The cities
gained several hundred thousand, but the rural districts lost 450,000.[1] All this might be attributed to the
vast and sudden expansion of agriculture in the United
States, but this same movement appears in parts of
Asia,—Japan for instance—with whose agriculture we
do not come into competition.

---

[1] *Journal of the Royal Statistical Society,* London, June, 1889, pp. 210, 258

This tendency is not peculiar to our times; it has always existed, and this mighty movement of population has been due to certain causes which in our century have made this tendency exceptionally operative.

Later we will examine these causes, but let us first look for a moment at this tendency; it is as old as human nature. Far back in the beginning it asserted itself, and the record of it is found in the words, Cain "builded a city." Here population gathered, not as in later times, because a few nobles held the land and the many were huddled into a corner called a city; not because men must needs find security from hostile armies behind high walls and strong gates; not at the demands of commerce, for then India and Egypt sent out no caravans to exchange their strange and costly merchandise; nor under the influence of manufactures, did this city rise. The causes to which we usually ascribe the origin of modern cities were absent. Cain's city was an expression of man's social nature which has asserted itself in all lands and in all ages.

A poor Irishwoman was found half starved in the lower part of New York City, and was sent by some benevolent people into the country, where work was provided for her. In the course of a few weeks she was seen back again in her old haunts. "Couldn't you find work enough?" she was asked. "Yis." "Didn't you have enough to eat and to wear, and weren't you comfortable?" "Yis." "Well, then, why did you come back here to starve rather than live there in comfort?" "Paples is more coompany than sthumps," was the answer; and it contained whole chapters of philosophy on the origin and growth of cities.

Aside from powerful commercial and industrial causes for the growth of urban population, man as a social animal has always sought his fellow; and because men would rather live together than apart, the city has always been as large as it could well be, with a constant tendency in former times to outgrow its supplies, which resulted in frequent famines. Many of the sovereigns of England vainly attempted by proclamation to stop the growth of London and turn the human tide back into the country. Even in the century before Christ it was complained that Rome was overcrowded, and Virgil sang, "The plough is no longer honored; the husbandmen have been led away, and the fields are foul with weeds."

In his admirable work,[1] the Rev. Samuel Lane Loomis lays down the law of the growth of cities as follows: "The urban population in every country is always as large as its circumstances allow." The radical changes in the methods of production and distribution which characterize modern civilization have made it possible to feed a city of any size, have added powerfully to the attracting influence of the city and at the same time liberated great numbers from agricultural pursuits. These are the causes which in our century have made this tendency toward the city exceptionally operative.

The invention of agricultural machinery makes it possible for a comparatively small number of men to produce the necessary food. "It is a fact, estimated by careful men thoroughly conversant with the changes that have taken place, that by the improvement in agricultural tools (machinery) the average farmer can, with sufficient horse-power, do with three men the work of fourteen men forty years ago, and do it better."[2] These ten men thrown out of employment in the country seek it in the city. The implements which have supplanted them on the farm are made in the city. These manufactures and a thousand others attract labor, and the railway makes it easy to mass populations and to feed them when massed. Hence this world-wide movement of population from country to city wherever modern civilization has gone, and the reasonableness of the conviction that this movement is no more temporary than the railway, the factory, and agricultural machinery.

---

[1] Modern Cities, p. 35. Baker & Taylor, New York.

[2] Report of Special Agent on Agricultural Implements, *Tenth Census U. S.,* Vol. II. p. 700. Quoted in " Modern Cities."

Modern sanitation and invention are making the city less unsafe and more attractive for residence every year. The agricultural population is necessarily limited to those who find employment in agriculture and cannot be increased beyond a certain limit. The city may grow indefinitely. There is, therefore, every prospect that for generations to come an ever-increasing proportion of our population will be urban.

We must, therefore, expect the steady deterioration of our rural population, *unless effective preventive measures are devised.* How to devise such measures is *the problem of the country.*

We shall not appreciate the full importance of this problem unless we remember that the degeneration of the rural population means the later degeneration of the urban population also, for the latter draws its life from the former. "The city," says Emerson, "is recruited from the country. The city would have died out, rotted and exploded, long ago, but that it was reinforced from the fields. It is only country which came to town day before yesterday that is city and court to-day." [1] "Sociologists tell us that 'only the agricultural class possesses permanent vitality; from its overflow the city population is formed, displaced, renewed.' 'Any city population, if left to itself, would die out in four generations.' 'The city is an inland lake, fed by constant streams, but without an outlet.' As are the fountains, so will be stream and lake. The problem of rural Christianity is the problem of national Christianity stated a few generations in advance." [2]

[1] Prose works, Vol. I. p. 482.
[2] President William De Witt Hyde, "Impending Paganism in New England," *Forum*, June, 1892, p. 528.

CHAPTER IX.

THE PROBLEM OF THE CITY.

A GENERATION ago Professor Francis Lieber, I think it was, said that the city was "the most difficult and perplexing problem of modern times." And more than forty years ago Alexis De Tocqueville, whom Mr. Gladstone calls the Edmund Burke of his generation, wrote: "I look upon the size of certain American cities, and especially upon the nature of their population, as a real danger which threatens the security of the democratic republics of the New World." If the judgment and fears of Lieber and De Tocqueville were well founded, the problem of the city is now much more perplexing and the necessity of its solution far more urgent, for our urban population is to-day six times as large as it was forty years ago, and more than twice as large relatively. In 1850 one eighth of our population lived in cities of 8000 and over; now considerably more than one fourth.

The city means both the place and the population. Each influences the other. In an important sense the place makes the people, and in a more important sense the people make the place. Both the people and the place, then, enter into the problem of the city. That problem, so far as the place is concerned, is to make the city serve in the highest possible degree the physical, intellectual, and moral health of the people. So far as the population is concerned, the problem of the city is to secure the noblest possible manhood and womanhood.

But this may be said to be the great problem of the city and of civilization always and everywhere, while there are certain distinctive problems of the city whose solution is peculiarly difficult in the United States, and, as we shall see, especially urgent at the present time. There are many subordinate problems or factors which enter into the one great problem, but there are two which because of their overshadowing importance will occupy our attention in this discussion, viz., municipal government and city evangelization. These two, which are intimately related, together constitute the distinctive problem of the city, for this generation at least.

So much has been said and written on these two subjects the past few years that it may be presumptuous to attempt to add anything. What I may venture to suggest toward the solution of the problem of the city will be found in a later chapter. My present purpose will be accomplished if I succeed in presenting in a strong light the nature and unappreciated importance of the problem.

I. The government of the city is by a "boss," who is skilful in the manipulation of the "machine," and who holds no political principles "except for revenue only." His sentiments and practice accord perfectly with the brutal and infamous utterance of Senator Ingalls: "The purification of politics is an iridescent dream. Government is force. Politics is a battle for supremacy. Parties are the armies. The Decalogue and the Golden Rule have no place in a political campaign. The object is success. To defeat the antagonist and expel the party in power is the purpose. In war it is lawful to deceive the adversary, to hire Hessians, to purchase mercenaries, to mutilate, to kill, to destroy."

The "boss" is the natural product of a vicious political partisanship, together with a large foreign population which has not sufficient character and intelligence for independent or individual judgment and action. While in the aggregate there are many foreigners to whom this remark does not apply, we still have the "Irish vote," the "German vote," the "Roman Catholic vote," and the like, which by appeals to race or religious prejudice or for "value received" may be cast in great blocks—which of course constitutes the city the demagogue's Paradise. Human nature is no weaker in the city than in the country, no more corrupt in America than in Europe. The existence of great masses of votes which can be easily bought and sold or otherwise controlled is sure to find unscrupulous men who are only too willing by such means to seize power and plunder.

European cities are in population remarkably homogeneous and native; ours are remarkably heterogeneous and foreign. London is deemed a little world, because one may meet there the representatives of almost every race; and yet "out of every one hundred Londoners in 1880, sixty-three were natives of London, ninety-four of England and Wales, and ninety-eight of Great Britain and Ireland. The Emerald Isle furnished but 2.1 per cent of London's population; and all foreign countries put together, only 1.6 per cent."[1] Contrast this with the foreign element of our cities. The Tenth Census showed that of our fifty principal cities 29.8 per cent of the population were foreign-born, while those who were foreign by birth or parentage often constituted three fourths or four fifths of the population.

Most of these foreigners have little understanding of our political issues and less of our institutions. They see nothing to be gained by independent action at the polls and much to be gained by concerted action. They accordingly follow their leaders, and are led into whatever camp bids highest in patronage or plunder. Doubtless in every city the good citizens who want honest government are in a majority, but with fatal folly they divide on political questions which have no more to do with municipal government than with the moon; and this division enables the "bosses" to hold the balance of power and dictate their terms. The perfectly natural result is a debauched city government.

---

[1] *Census of England and Wales*, 1881, Vol. IV. p. 59. Quoted by S. L. Loomis in "Modern Cities."

The officials of European cities are often eminent men, the fittest possible for the place, who honor their office and are honored by it. But such is the corruption of municipal politics here that only now and then will a man of high character accept office. Many of the more intelligent are so disgusted that they will not even go to the polls. Others stay away because, as they say, "It's no use;" while others are "too busy" to vote. A few years ago there was an important election in New York, the result of which would determine whether criminals were to be vigorously prosecuted. And though there was more than usual interest in the election three miles of brownstone fronts on Fifth Avenue furnished but twenty-eight votes! It is quite possible that Cherry Street and "The Bend" furnished more votes than they had voters. Some one has said with as much truth as wit: "The mediæval sovereign hired a fellow to be his fool; but the 'popular sovereign' often hires the fellow to be his master, and is his own fool."

To how great an extent he is his own fool who absents himself from the polls or who respects party lines in municipal elections, does not appear until he reckons up how much it *costs* to hire the fellow to be his master.

It costs a heavy burden of debt and taxation. Ten of our larger cities, whose aggregate population is 6,466,000, have a total indebtedness of over $351,000,000, or fifty-four dollars per caput for each inhabitant. Mr. Bryce gives the following table of the increase of population, valuation, taxation, and debt in fifteen of the largest cities of the United States, from 1860 to 1875.[1]

Increase in population	70.5 per cent.			
"	" taxable valuation	156.9	"	"
"	" debt	270.9	"	"
"	" taxation	363.2	"	"

The increase of the municipal debt of New York in a single generation was from $10,000,000 in 1840 to

---

[1] The American Commonwealth, Vol. I. p. 607.

$113,000,000 in 1876. The Rt. Hon. Joseph Chamberlain in a comparison of Birmingham and Boston shows that of these two cities, having about the same population in 1890, the latter expends more than six times as much as the former for the same objects. After examining the management of a hundred of our cities, great and small, he says: "Americans pay for less efficient service in their large towns nearly five times as much as is paid in the case of a well-managed English municipality."[1]

If the objects for which these great expenditures are made were really secured, the waste would be less lamentable; but they are not. The streets are generally ill-paved and filthy, sanitary provisions are neglected, the public health is involved, and public works are rarely creditable. An extremely able commission, of which Hon. W. M. Evarts was chairman, referring to the debt of New York City, said: "The magnitude and rapid increase of this debt are not less remarkable than the poverty of the results exhibited as the return for so prodigious an expenditure. . . . In truth, the larger part of the city debt represents a vast aggregate of moneys wasted, embezzled, or misapplied."[2] A memorial presented to the Pennsylvania legislature in 1883 by a number of the leading citizens of Philadelphia contained the following: "Philadelphia is now recognized as the worst-paved and worst-cleaned city in the civilized world. The effort to clean the streets was abandoned for months, and no attempt was made to that end until some public-spirited citizens, at their own expense, cleaned a number of the principal thoroughfares. The system of sewerage and the physical condition of the sewers is notoriously bad—so much so as to be dangerous to the health and most offensive to the comfort of our people. Public work has been done so badly that structures have had to be renewed

[1] "Municipal Institutions in America and England," *The Forum*, November, 1892.
[2] Quoted in "The American Commonwealth," Vol. I. p. 609.

almost as soon as finished. Others have been in part
constructed at enormous expense, and then permitted
to fall to decay without completion. Inefficiency,
waste, badly-paved and filthy streets, unwholesome
and offensive water, and slovenly and costly management, have been the rule for years past throughout the
city government."[1] One might naturally ask, If we
must have dangerous pavements and foul streets, unsanitary sewers and pestilential tenements, wouldn't it
be possible to secure them for less than four or five
times as much as the English pay for good service?

Another part of the cost of hiring "the fellow" to
be our master is the "giving away" of valuable fran-
chises which ought to bring the city many hundreds of
thousands of dollars.

But the cost in money is a small matter compared with
the sacrifice of health, physical, intellectual, and moral.

The public health has been intrusted to "sanitary
inspectors," who not only lacked all special training
and fitness, but also common intelligence—rumsellers
and low pothouse politicians. A few years ago some
of these "health-wardens" in New York testified before an investigating committee of the state that there
were cases of "hyjinnicks" (hygienics) in their wards.
Some of these guardians of the public health thought
the people "had the hyjinnicks pretty bad," while
others were of the opinion that the patients "got over"
them quite easily.[2]

In different wards of the same city different sanitary
conditions sometimes cause a variation in the death-
rate of ten or more in a thousand. A rise of *two* in a
thousand for the entire city of New York would mean
over 3000 additional deaths. In our large cities doubtless thousands of lives are sacrificed to *politics* every
year, not to mention the sickness and suffering which
do not cost life.

[1] Quoted in "The American Commonwealth," Vol. I. pp. 606, 607.
[2] "The Government of American Cities," by Andrew D. White, *The Forum*, December, 1890.

Our public schools are often sacrificed in like manner. The school board is made a political prize; and men take charge of the education of the city who, in some instances, I am assured, are unable to read or write. Many thousands of children in our cities are forced to grow up in ignorance for lack of school accommodations. It was stated not long since that a recent investigation in Chicago revealed the fact that in one ward there were 4500 more children than there were school sittings.[1]

But the most serious part of the cost of such government is the price which is paid in moral character. Criminal houses flourish so openly that it is impossible not to infer official complicity with vice. Strange that officers whose business it is to ferret out crime are unable to discover moral slaughter-houses which respectable citizens cannot help knowing! Instead of making vice difficult and dangerous, every facility is afforded for corrupting the youth.

All this it costs in debt and taxation, in discomfort and disgrace, in life, health, and character, to introduce politics into municipal elections; that is, for good citizens to divide on issues which are absolutely irrelevant to the business of city government, thus permitting unscrupulous demagogues to hold the balance of power and ride into office.

This unspeakable folly is all but universal. Occasionally outraged citizens become sufficiently indignant to rebel against party leaders and, in a moment of sanity, set up an independent candidate. But usually a partisan press succeeds in whipping enough good men back into line to defeat the reform movement. Returns from 127 cities show only *one* independent or non-political mayor. Politics is thoroughly rooted in our system of municipal government, and has so vitiated that system that its failure has become notorious. "There is no denying," says Mr. Bryce, "that the government

---

[1] *The Christian Union*, June 11, 1892.

of cities is the one conspicuous failure of the United States." [1] Mr. Andrew D. White, who has enjoyed exceptional opportunities of observation, says : " Without the slightest exaggeration we may assert that, with very few exceptions, the city governments of the United States are the worst in Christendom—the most expensive, the most inefficient, and the most corrupt." [2]

Let us consider now the significance of this fact. It means that the social structure is weakest at the precise point where it ought to be strongest, viz., where it suffers the severest strain. Because the city is the microcosm of the civilization which has produced it, it gathers into itself representatives of all classes of society; and because it is the point of most intense activity, every maladjustment of society produces the greatest friction and soreness there. It is there that riots occur; it is there chiefly that the unnatural duel between capital and labor is fought; it is there that social extremes are found in sharpest contrast and the deepest jealousies are felt; it is there that haters of society gather, men who are the implacable enemies of all order, which Schiller calls

> " The keystone of the world's wide arch ;
> The one sustaining and sustained by all,
> Which, if it fall, brings all in ruin down."

There are some thousands of such men in our large cities who pour contempt on all authority and openly advocate anarchy. Of course they constitute a small proportion of our city populations, and well-to-do men are only disgusted with their ravings; but they are an evil leaven, which under favorable circumstances might leaven a large lump. In the city is found extreme misery, which easily becomes desperate; to the city human wreckage floats and there serves to wreck other lives; it is in the city where saloons and gambling hells and brothels abound, and it is there where such forces

---

[1] The American Commonwealth, Vol. I. p. 608.
[2] " The Government of American Cities," *The Forum*, December, 1890.

of evil increase their strength by organization. It is there that criminals resort, and crimes multiply. Col. H. M. Boies, member of the Pennsylvania State Board of Charities, says that Philadelphia County furnishes about seven and a half times and Allegheny County nearly nine times as many criminals to the population as the average of the rural counties.[1] That is, there is more lawlessness in the city than anywhere else, and there where the dangerous classes congregate the government is the most inefficient and corrupt.

Of course there can be no government without law. The less popular respect for it there is, the more centralized must the government be to prevent anarchy. Such a government may control lawless people, but how shall lawless people control themselves? The fact is that here in the United States those classes which most need to be controlled are themselves very generally in control of the city.

And this fact has far more than local significance. Our political fabric rests on two fundamental principles, that of local self-government and that of federation. The latter was at stake during our civil war; and South and North are now alike agreed that this principle is settled for all time. *The former principle is to-day at stake in the government of the city.* This principle is as vitally essential as the other; its subversion would involve national destruction as surely as the dismemberment of the Union.

The experiment of self-government has proved successful in the rural districts and the towns, and it is upon these that our states have relied for safety. Mr. Theodore Roosevelt, speaking on "The Menaces of Civilization" before the Congregational Club of New York City, said: "In any attempt to reform them by law, would we not find nine tenths of the city members in the legislature hostile? The only hope of reform lies

---

[1] A series of papers on Prisoners and Paupers. See *The Scranton Tribune,* January 16, 1892.

in the action of the country members. The average
grade of our city politicians is a serious menace to
good government. Four fifths of the representatives at
Albany from New York and Brooklyn can be depended
upon to vote on the wrong side of every question."
"This," said a leading New York editor, "from an
observation of twenty years, we believe to be true." [1]   .

Our cities are now dependent on their respective state
legislatures for the measure of autonomy which they
are permitted to enjoy. The cities have abused their
power to such an extent that the states do not entrust
them with full liberty. It has been judicially held that
municipal government is a subordinate branch of state
government and subject to the state legislature. We
have not dared to apply to the cities one of the two
fundamental principles of the republic. But whether
or not they will prove safe guardians of it, the time is
soon coming when the cities will take this principle into
their own hands. This is the sure prophecy of the dis-
proportionate growth of the city, which was discussed
in the preceding chapter.

When the population of the city exceeds that of the
country, it will be able to dominate both the state and
the nation. And if our municipal government is a
failure *then*, the governments of state and nation, controlled by the city, will also be failures, and our free
institutions will fail. Was not this day of domination
by the city what Wendell Phillips had in mind when
he said that our great municipalities would yet strain
our institutions as slavery never did ?

We may not flatter ourselves that this movement of
population from country to city is temporary and local.
It is neither. It is not incident to a new civilization.
London is gaining 125,000 a year, Paris 50,000, and Berlin
is growing faster than New York. Calcutta, Madras,
Bombay, Shanghai, and Tokio, and even the cities of

---

[1] Quoted by Rev. Daniel Dorchester, D.D., in an address before the Washington Conference of the Evangelical Alliance, 1887,

Africa as well as those of Asia and Europe, have felt the mighty impulse. The unprecedented growth of cities in recent years is a world-phenomenon. And as the causes of this growth, which were pointed out in the preceding chapter, will continue, we have every reason to expect this growth will continue. There is a natural limit to the growth of agricultural population, but none to that of the city. The great bulk of the vast population which the United States is capable of sustaining will some day live in cities. And if the rate of growth and movement of population from 1880 to 1890 continues until 1920, *the city will then contain upwards of ten millions more than the country.*

The relative growth of city and country during recent years may not be maintained during the next quarter of a century, but if the dominance of the city is somewhat delayed, it will surely come, and the intervening period of national probation will be none too long in which to regenerate municipal government and make the city a safe factor in our national life. The sooner we undertake the cleansing of these Augean stables, the less herculean will be our task. For, as a rule, the larger the city the more powerful is the ring which rules it, the more debauched and debilitated is public sentiment, and the more difficult is it to execute righteous laws. Take prohibitory liquor laws, for instance: the larger the city, the more difficult is it to enforce them. If the American people propose to root out the saloon, they would better do it before the city dominates the land; for if the saloon continues to govern the city, what will happen when the city governs the state and the nation?

The peril to the republic through the threatened failure of one of our two fundamental principles is as real as when the government was shaken by the shock of civil strife. And perhaps the peril is all the greater because the crisis is less imminent and to many gives no warning. Men are not apt to sleep when the drum beats the nation to battle. A generation ago men were awake to the peril of the hour, their patriotism was aroused, and no sacrifice of blood or treasure was too precious to lay on the altar of country when the principle of federation was endangered. But the peril which now threatens the no less fundamental principle of local self-government is insidious. It beats no drum, it fires no cannon, it does not solidify a public sentiment against itself, it kindles no patriotism, and inspires no sacrifice in its opposition; but it is slowly, secretly, and surely undermining one of the two foundations on which rests the arch of our free institutions.

Touching municipal government, the problem of the city is to make it capable of governing itself; and this problem must be solved speedily before it assumes national proportions, before the city dominates the country, for if it remains unsolved, it will then involve our republican institutions in national ruin.

II. Turn now to the problem of city evangelization. Not only must the city be made a safe factor in our civilization; it must be saved.

1. One of the most important factors of this problem is the *composition* of the city, which is thoroughly heterogeneous. It is an interesting fact, and not without significance, that the names of the nine largest cities in the United States represent no less than seven languages—New York, Boston, and Baltimore the English, Brooklyn (formerly Breuckelen) the Walloon, Philadelphia the Greek, Cincinnati the Latin, Chicago the Indian, St. Louis the French, and San Francisco the Spanish. Their population is still more polyglot. The Tenth Census shows that New York, Philadelphia, Chicago, and San Francisco each has residents from Africa (not specified), Asia (not specified), Atlantic islands, Australia, Austria, Belgium, Bohemia, Canada, New Brunswick, Newfoundland, Nova Scotia, Prince Edward Island, British America (not specified), Central America, China, Cuba, Denmark, Europe (not specified), France, Baden, Bavaria, Brunswick, Hamburg, Hanover, Hessen, Lübeck, Mecklenburg, Nassau, Olden-

burg, Prussia (not specified), Saxony, Weimar, Würtemberg, Germany (not specified), Gibraltar, England, Ireland, Scotland, Wales, Greece, Greenland, Holland, Hungary, India, Italy, Japan, Luxemburg, Malta, Mexico, Norway, Pacific islands, Poland, Portugal, Russia, Sandwich Islands, South America, Spain, Sweden, Switzerland, Turkey, and the West Indies. All of these continents, countries, and provinces save one are represented in Brooklyn, Boston, and Baltimore; all save three are represented in St. Louis and New Orleans; and all save four in Cincinnati. What mosaics of living stones our city populations are, representing all colors, shades, and climes! In New York one would scarcely look in vain for a representative of any people. Employed in one factory there are thirty men from Haran, the home of Abraham, where Terah died. There may be heard a babel of all tongues. It is said that seventeen languages were spoken there before the Revolution, when the population was less than 22,000.

Though only about one third of the population of the United States is foreign by birth or parentage, this element rarely constitutes less than two thirds of our larger cities, and often more than three fourths. When any question is submitted to a popular vote this element easily controls. It is stated that at an election in Cincinnati the guardians of the ballot-box were a German, a Scandinavian, and an Irishman, and they refused to let a native American vote because he could produce no naturalization papers.

Our cities which have foreigners in sufficient numbers for the several nationalities to segregate themselves contain a little Germany here, a little Italy there, a little Ireland yonder, and the like, which constitute socially a sort of crazy-quilt patchwork, only the different pieces are not stitched together. And it becomes very difficult, if not impossible, for influences which would otherwise be generally pervasive to reach and mould these strange and varied elements.

If the foreigners were scattered among the native population, our language would be a necessity to them, and they would soon become acquainted and assimilated; but segregated they simply live the old country life on our soil. They are like unmasticated food. Mastication is a process of *separating*, without which digestion is a slow and painful process.

Not only different languages but also different ideas and habits of life combine to make the evangelization of these peoples more difficult. Their presence has very noticeably and lamentably lowered the standard of Sabbath observance and impaired habits of sobriety in the cities.

I bring no sweeping accusation against foreigners. Many of those who come to us—perhaps more than we commonly suppose—are Christian in fact as well as in name, while not a few have rendered eminent service to religion, morals, literature, and political reform. Still we are compelled to recognize facts, and the facts are that a majority of immigrants believe either in a perverted and superstitious form of Christianity or in none at all. A great majority were peasants, whose lives, in many instances, have been subjected to spoliation and wrong, and who have learned, therefore, to associate law with tyranny, and conceive of freedom as freedom from law, or, in one word, license. We must not wonder, therefore, that the foreign element produces far more than its due proportion of criminals, and heterogeneous as is the city in the nationality of its people, it is of course no less so in their character. It gathers the good and the bad, and contains that which is fairest and foulest in our civilization.

2. Another most important factor in the problem is *environment*, which in the slums is such as to discourage everything except a divine faith and love.

The crowded tenement is the hot-house of physical and moral disease. As the compression of matter develops heat, so the compacting of populations produces a sort of fever heat which manifests itself in morbid passions and appetites. In a single square there are crowded together two, three, and even four thousand souls, as many as in the country might be found occupying twenty-five or fifty square miles. Mrs. Ballington Booth finds seven families huddled together in one room. In a room not more than ten by twelve feet, Dr. A. T. Pierson finds eighteen people, men, women, and children, black and white, eating, sleeping, living. Sometimes as many as forty-five people sleep in a single room. Speaking of one tenement, Helen Campbell says: "The sun never enters thirty-two of these rooms —darkness means the devil's deeds—and they never get a breath except from the rooms into which they open. You sleep in one once and there's a band around your head when you wake and a sinking and craving at your stomach; you don't want to eat. There's nothing answers it but whiskey. And in the basement of the building you may find a smiling fiend in immaculate white apron, ready to pour the bubbling glass full, and usher you into the anteroom of hell."

We read of fifty-eight babies in one tenement. Think of the thousands born of drunkenness and lust, whose welcome into the world is a curse, whose lullabies are blasphemies, whose admonitions are kicks, whose examples are vice and crime! Bishop South says: "A child has a right to be born, and not damned into the world." How many children of the slums by an awful heritage from both father and mother are indeed "damned into the world," receive their life and live it under conditions that make disease of body and soul as certain as natural law! What a mistake many children make in being born humans instead of wild beasts! A writer in *The Christian Union*[1] says that in two foul alleys of New York the death-rate of children under five years had reached the enormous figure of seventy-three per cent. *Happy children that died!* But many children of the slums are condemned to live.

---

[1] July 9, 1892.

" Is it well that while we range with Science, glorying the Time,
City children soak and blacken soul and sense in city slime ?

" There among the glooming alleys Progress halts on palsied feet,
Crime and hunger cast our maidens by the thousand on the street.

" There the master scrimps his haggard sempstress of her daily bread,
There a single sordid attic holds the living and the dead.

" There the smould'ring fire of fever creeps across the rotted floor
And the crowded couch of incest in the warrens of the poor." [1]

No wonder that General Booth exclaims: "Talk
about Dante's Hell, and all the horrors and cruelties of
the torture-chamber of the lost ! The man who walks
with open eyes and with bleeding heart through the
shambles of our civilization needs no such fantastic
images of the poet to teach him horror." [2] When one
thinks of the commingled mass of venomous filth and
seething sin, of lust and drunkenness, of pauperism and
crime of every sort, which characterize the slums, he is
reminded of the witches' caldron in Macbeth:

" Double, double toil and trouble;
Fire burn, and caldron bubble."

Professor Huxley, who once lived as a medical officer
in the east of London, spoke out of his personal knowledge when he declared that the surroundings of the
savages of New Guinea were much more conducive to
the leading of a decent human existence than those in
which many of the "East Enders" live. [3]

The city cannot be saved while such conditions exist.
The people cannot be elevated while their environment
remains unchanged. A much more robust virtue than
exists in the slums would yield to the conditions which
there prevail. On the other hand, we cannot very
materially change the environment while the people
remain unchanged. Both must be transformed together; while moral and spiritual influences are
brought to bear on the people, the physical causes of
their degradation must be removed. The sending of

---

[1] Tennyson's Locksley Hall Sixty Years After.
[2] In Darkest England, p. 13.
[3] Ibid. p. 158.

an occasional missionary with a gospel message is like
trying to bail out the Atlantic with a thimble; and the
preaching of a half gospel in elegant up-town churches
does not have the remotest tendency to transform the
slums—to save that part of the city which most needs
saving. An occasional rescue mission, like the devoted
city missionary, may do much good by the saving of
individuals and families, but the awful supply of ruined
men and women is not reduced. A missionary may
reasonably hope to elevate a tribe of savages in a generation of time, because every one brought under his
influence reinforces that influence and becomes a
helper. Not so in the slums. When a man or a family
are reclaimed they move out, and their places are
quickly taken by others equally needing reclamation.

We shall continue to have the slums until the causes
which produce them are removed.

3. Another factor of the dark problem before us is the
isolation of the city, which is no less real than that of
the country.

Where men are most crowded together they are
farthest apart. In the village or out in the country
everybody knows everybody else, and personal acquaintance makes personal interest and influence easy.
Misfortune becomes quickly known and brings with it
helpful sympathy. Moreover, the fact that a man is
known and that something is expected of him helps
wonderfully to keep him up to the mark. We know to
what an extent reputation is dependent on character,
but do we appreciate to how great an extent character
depends on reputation? Every man has some sort of
standing where he is known, and until he has lost all
self-respect desires to sustain whatever good reputation
he possesses. Let him go among strangers, and this
external restraint is lost.

This suggests one of the reasons, and possibly the
principal one, why there is so much more of pauperism
and crime in a city of 500,000 than among an equal
number of people scattered in small towns and villages.

In the city there is little or no sense of neighborhood. You may be separated from your next neighbor by only a few inches, and yet for years never see his face or learn his name. Mere proximity does not imply social touch. Association is determined by wealth, occupation, intelligence, taste, nationality, church connection, and a dozen other conditions. Society is, therefore, divided into classes, which are again subdivided into groups; and between these there is no intercourse unless it be of a business character.

And classes are not only separated socially but also geographically, which is an added obstacle to city evangelization. Water communication has been a very important factor in the development of American cities. Nearly all of our large cities have an ocean, lake, or river front, which limits their expansion in one or more directions. Wealthy residences and churches retire before advancing business, while the poorer classes must remain near their work; so that there come to be an "up-town" and "down-town," an "east side" and "west side," which are far separated geographically, and vastly farther socially.

There are still other causes of isolation, which are peculiarly operative in American cities. The three great natural bonds which bind men together into nationalities and social organizations are identity of race, of language, and of religion. In England, however widely classes may be separated socially, they are generally bound together by these three bonds. The lord and the peasant boast the same national history, speak the same tongue, and presumably they are both Protestants. But the great heterogeneous masses of our cities are separated by differences of blood, of language, and of religion. Only slowly can they evolve the conditions which make it possible for them to enter into a common national life, to say nothing of closer social relations.

Thus many different lines of cleavage run through our cities, dividing them into isolated fragments, making it very difficult, if not quite impossible, for influences which would otherwise be generally perva sive to reach and mould these varied elements and greatly complicating the problem of evangelization.

4. Still another factor of the problem is the *lack of homes.* The home is one of the two great conservative institutions of society, and is peculiarly needed in the city.

A very large proportion of our country population live in homes of their own, but of our urban population only a very small proportion. Real estate in the city is beyond the reach of the many; and as population increases and land values rise, the proportion of those who are able to own a home in the city will become constantly less. Investigation would probably show that, as a rule, the larger the city the smaller would be the proportion of homes in it. In 1890 New York had over 37,000 tenement-houses, in which more than two thirds of the population of the city lived. Sixty-six and three fourths per cent of the people lived over twenty to a dwelling, while eighty-three and a half per cent lived ten persons or more to a dwelling. Dr. Lyman Abbott says that there are wards in our great cities where "there are actually more men, women, and children to the square foot of land than there are of bodies in any cemetery in the country." Homes cannot exist under such conditions.

Many evil influences and results attend a life of renting or boarding, one of which is that a very large proportion of our city population moves every year or oftener; thus social and church relations, if any exist, are broken up; and not being looked after, many who had begun to attend church and even many who are church members fall back into the non-church-going class.

Furthermore, the city is depleted of homes by the removal of business men to the suburbs. These men are usually of the better class; and the elevating influences of their homes, their votes, their church membership, their contributions to church support, and their Christian work all constitute a great loss to the city.

In the " City " of London, that is, within the limits of
the old walls, the day population is more than five times
the night population.[1] There is a similar exodus from
our great cities every day at the close of business hours.
The salt is heaped round about the city instead of being
scattered through it, and what remains in the city is,
for the most part, massed in localities.

5. The principal remaining factor of the problem is
the *rapid growth* of the city. In 1880 the number of our
cities having a population of 8000 or more was 286; in
ten years the number had leaped up to 443. A hundred
years ago we had but six. Between 1870 and 1890 the
number of cities having a population of 100,000 or more
doubled, rising from fourteen to twenty-eight. In a
number of states nearly all the increase of population
from 1880 to 1890 was in the cities. Of the total increase
in Maryland, the one city of Baltimore furnished fully
nineteen twentieths. The following table gives a score
of cities among the many which made a very remarkable growth:

Cities and Towns.	Population.		Increase.	
	1880.	1890.	Number.	Per cent.
Anniston, Ala	942	9,876	8,934	948
Birmingham, Ala	3,086	26,178	23,092	748
Chicago, Ill.	503,185	1,099,850	596,665	118
Dallas, Tex.	10,358	38,067	27,709	267
Denver, Colo.	35,629	106,713	71,084	199
Duluth, Minn.	3,483	33,115	29,632	850
El Paso, Tex.	736	10,338	9,602	1,304
Findlay, Ohio	4,633	18,553	13,920	300
Fresno, Cal.	1,112	10,818	9,706	872
Kansas City, Kan	3,200	38,316	35,116	1,097
Kansas City, Mo.	55,785	132,716	76,931	137
Lincoln, Neb	13,003	55,154	42,151	324
Los Angeles, Cal.	11,183	50,395	39,212	350
Minneapolis, Minn	46,887	164,738	117,851	251
Omaha, Neb	30,518	140,452	109,934	360
Pueblo, Colo	3,217	24,558	21,341	663
St. Paul, Minn	41,473	133,156	91,683	221
Seattle, Wash	3,533	42,837	39,304	1,112
Sioux City, Iowa.	7,366	37,806	30,440	413
Spokane Falls, Wash.	350	19,922	19,572	5,592
Tacoma, Wash	1,098	36,006	34,908	3,179
Wichita, Kans	4,911	23,853	18,942	385

[1] The Statesman's Year Book, 1890, p. 18.

Thus it appears that a number of cities of considerable size in 1880 increased three or four fold in ten years, while Chicago more than doubled her population of half a million. Our cities taken together increased 61 per cent, making a total addition to our urban population of nearly seven millions.

Without doubt the city is soon to control the nation by the dominance of numbers. It is now, as it has always been, the centre of civilization, and the source of moulding influences. As civilization grows less martial and more industrial, wealth becomes an increasingly important factor, and wealth is being massed more and more in the city. With the increase of popular intelligence, the press is exerting an ever-widening influence. And this tree of the knowledge of good and evil, whose leaves are not altogether for the *healing* of the nations, grows in the city. The city is already, and is to become increasingly, the source of determinative influences, bad as well as good. It becomes, then, a question of vital importance whether the growth of the Christian church in the city is keeping pace with the rapid strides of population.

The accompanying table, giving the relative increase in the number of churches and the population, would seem to indicate that the growth of the city has generally been far in excess of church provision. If all our large cities had been included in the investigation, there is no reason to think the result would have been substantially different.

NUMBER OF PROTESTANT CHURCHES TO POPULATION.

	Boston.	Brooklyn.	Buffalo.	Chicago.
1840........	1 to 1,228 souls	1 to 1,294 souls	1 to 1,069 souls	In 1836 1 to 1.042 souls
1850..... ..	" 1,200 "	" 2,105 "	" 1,509 "	In 1851 1 to 1,577 souls
1860.	" 1,368 "	" 2,051 "	" 1,690 "	" 1,820 "
1870.........	" 1,898 "	" 2,052 "	" 2,402 "	" 2,433 "
1880.	" 2,311 "	" 2,442 "	" 2,216 "	" 3,062 "
1890.........	" 2,581 "	" 2,890 "	" 2,650 "	" 3,601 "

	Cincinnati.	New York.	St. Louis.
1840..	1 to 1,449 souls	1 to 1,992 souls	In 1842 1 to 2,500 souls
1850..........................	" 1,581 "	" 2,026 "	In 1848 1 to 2,100 souls
1860..........................	" 2,064 "	" 3,294 "	" 2,870 "
1870..	" 2,533 "	" 3,510 "	" 4,144 "
1880	" 1,932 "	" 4,021 "	" 3,130 "
1890..........................	" 2,195 "	" 4,361 " *	" 2,913 "

* According to the census taken by the city authorities, there was one Protestant church to every 4,930 inhabitants.

We must remember, however, that church buildings and church memberships are larger now than formerly, so that a relative decrease in the number of churches is not conclusive of the point in question. Let us inquire, therefore, as to the relative increase or decrease in the number of church members in our cities. As the statistics of many denominations do not afford the requisite data, our inquiries will be necessarily limited to six important denominations.[1] Their increase as compared with that of the population in fifty of our largest cities is shown in the following table:

In 1840, 12.67 inhabitants to one communicant.
" 1850, 15.30 " " "
" 1860, 17.33 " " "
" 1870, 19.05 " " "
" 1880, 18.81 " " ."
" 1890, 20.14 " ' "

That is, in fifty of our largest cities these six denominations taken together have grown only 63 per cent as rapidly as the population during the past half-century. Or in other words, relative to the growth of the cities these churches have fallen behind about 37 per cent.

---

[1] The Presbyterians, Old and New School, when separated; the Southern Presbyterian General Assembly, the Methodist Episcopal, the Methodist Episcopal Church South, the Congregationalists, and the Dutch Reformed.

For this valuable table (except only the figures for 1890), the preparation of which no doubt involved weeks of investigation, I am indebted to an ad dress by Dr. Daniel Dorchester at the Washington Conference of the Evan gelical Alliance, 1887.

It is quite possible that if the facts concerning all the Protestant denominations could be ascertained, the showing would be somewhat improved. Still it would seem sufficiently clear that the cities are outgrowing the churches.

And these statistics are the more significant when we consider that while the membership of these churches fell from one in 15.30 of the population of these fifty cities in 1850 to one in 20.14 in 1890, the Protestant church membership of the whole country rose from one in 6.54 of the population in 1850 to one in 4.65 in 1890.

The proportion of churches to population is from one half to one quarter as large in the city as in the country, and the proportion of church members is generally from one half to one fifth as large. Nor is this all.

Those parts of the city which need the most churches have the fewest. Archdeacon Mackay-Smith stated in 1890 that there was a district in New York containing a larger population than Detroit, in which there were substantially no Protestant churches, but only a few chapels and three Roman Catholic churches. In some wards there are one or two hundred times as many saloons as churches. In the Thirteenth Ward of Boston with upwards of 22,000 souls there is not a single Protestant church; while in the Eleventh—the Back Bay—with a smaller population, there are thirty. Ten of the wealthiest wards of Cleveland, having a population of about 53,000, contain one half of all the Protestant church members of the city; while the other half is scattered through thirty wards, having a population of about 215,000. The worst portions of our cities are fearfully destitute of churches, and generally growing more so. It was stated by Dr. A. F. Schauffler in 1888 that during the twenty years preceding nearly 200,000 people had moved in below Fourteenth Street, New York, and seventeen Protestant churches had moved out. One Jewish synagogue and two Roman Catholic churches had been added. So that, counting churches of every kind, there were fourteen less than there were twenty years before, when there were nearly 200,000 fewer people. This is an illustration of the "up-town" movement which is taking place in all our large cities.

Thus we have seen that while our civilization is suffering a greater strain in the city than elsewhere, the two great conservative institutions of society, the church and the home, are weaker in the city than anywhere else. And as the city grows larger and the strain becomes more severe, the home and the church are growing relatively weaker.

We see then the existing situation and tendencies— a mottled population, containing the worst elements of society, far removed from saving Christian influences and peculiarly difficult to reach with them, growing rapidly in numbers, political influence, and commercial importance, while church provision is steadily becoming more inadequate.

What is to be the outcome? One of three things. Present tendencies will continue until our cities are literally heathenized, or their arrested growth will enable the churches to regain lost ground, or the churches will awake to their duty and their opportunity. To accept the first alternative is to despair of our country and of the Kingdom: to entertain the thought for a moment would be disloyalty to Christ. Any hope of escape by the second alternative must be based on ignorance of the causes of this great world movement toward the cities. It has already been pointed out that as these causes are permanent this movement will also be. The third alternative, then, is the only one that can be accepted. The first must not be, the second cannot be, the third, therefore, shall be. *The churches will awake.*

There is no occasion for panic, there is not even room for doubt as to the issue. The city is to be saved; it *must* be saved before the Kingdom can fully come; it, therefore, *can* be saved. "Ability and necessity dwell near each other," says Pythagorean wisdom; "I can do all things through Jesus Christ, which strengtheneth me," exclaims Christian faith.

The first city was built by the first murderer, and crime and wretchedness have dwelt in the city ever since, but the city is to be redeemed. Every generation might have said with the Psalmist, "for I have seen violence and strife in the city; mischief also and sorrow are in the midst of it;"[1] but when John in apocalyptic vision sees a perfected society, a heaven on earth, it is a *holy city* which inspires his prophecy. "And there shall in no wise enter into it anything that defileth, neither whatsoever worketh abomination, or maketh a lie;"[2] and in it there shall be "neither sorrow nor crying, neither shall there be any more pain, for the former things are passed away."[3]

---

[1] Ps. lv. 9, 10.   [2] Rev. xxi. 27.   [3] Ibid. xxi. 4.

CHAPTER X.

"How to reach the masses" has been a standing chal lenge to the wisdom of religious conventions for several years. The fact of a separation between the masses and the church has thus been generally assumed. It has, however, been questioned by a few on the ground that church membership is increasing more rapidly than the population. It is true that according to the best available statistics the Evangelical communicants in the United States in 1800 were 7 per cent of the population. In 1880 they had risen to 20.07 per cent; and in 1890 to 21.42.

Thus, the proportion of Evangelical church members to the population was three times as large in 1890 as in 1800. It does not follow, however, that the proportion of the population attending church has increased in like ratio, nor indeed that it has not decreased.

The proportion of attendants who are non-communicants has been greatly reduced, until now it is a very narrow margin. The great body of church attendants to-day are communicants or the children of communicants, most of whom in due time will become members of the church. The gospel has brought nearly all to acknowledge its claims who have come statedly within the sphere of the pulpit's influence.

Thus, it has been quite possible for the church to grow more rapidly than the population while at the same time it was losing its hold on the multitude. We have been known as a church-going people. De Tocqueville was greatly impressed by our Sabbath observance

and church attendance. Few appreciate to what extent
we have now become a non-church-going people. Mr.
Moody said a few years ago: "The gulf between the
church and the masses is growing deeper, wider, and
darker every hour." The reality of such a gulf is not a
matter of opinion. Careful investigations have been
made in city and country which give us definite knowledge. From these investigations, made in some hundreds of towns in several different states, it appears
that somewhat less than one half of the people profess
to attend church; and it should be remembered that
many claim to be attendants who are shown by a little
cross-questioning not to have been inside a church for
years.

In Vermont, a few years ago, forty-four towns, believed to be above the average of the state in church
attendance, were carefully canvassed. All were counted
attendants who professed to be, and all children and
invalids in church-going families were reckoned attendants; and yet only 49 per cent of the people found, or
44 per cent of the population called themselves church-
goers. Of those living two miles or more from church
probably not more than 30 per cent ever attend.

Fifteen counties were canvassed in Maine, and of
133,445 families, 67,842 reported themselves as not
attending any church.

Five representative counties in New York were canvassed, and the proportion of those who reported themselves non-attendants was about the same as in Vermont. An intelligent and careful man who canvassed
two of these counties said that he did not believe more
than 25 per cent of the people were regular attendants
upon church. The actual attendance at the Protestant
churches of these two counties, on a pleasant day,
was found to be 23 per cent of the Protestant population.

---

[1] Address of Rev. Henry Fairbanks, Ph.D., at Boston **Conference** of
Evangelical Alliance, 1889

A gentleman who had canvassed many thousands of families in the South told me that he found about the same proportion of non-church-goers there as exists in the North. Doubtless the proportion is much larger among the scattered populations of the West.

When city congregations are counted on a pleasant Sabbath morning, usually about one fifth of the population are found in church. In an Ohio city, which has church accommodations for about one half its inhabitants, a count on a beautiful winter morning showed only 35 per cent of the sittings occupied, or considerably less than one fifth of the population in church. In a Pennsylvania town, where there is a church membership of some 1300, a delightful summer Sabbath found only 600 people in church, all told.

If the many towns and cities which have been investigated in various states are fairly representative of the whole country, we may infer that less than 30 per cent of our population are regular attendants upon church, that perhaps 20 per cent are irregular attendants, while fully one half of the people of the United States, or more than 32,000,000, never attend any church service, Protestant or Roman Catholic.

Take another line of reasoning, which enables us to form an intelligent judgment where no canvass has been made. Of course not all church attendants are present at any one service. If we knew what proportion of the whole are found in the average congregation, by counting the latter we could of course estimate the former.

In a large number of towns we have learned by house-to-house inquiry how many persons profess to be church attendants, and the actual attendance has been taken by count. In New York state it was found that the average attendance fell a trifle below one half the number who professed to be church-goers. In Vermont the average attendance was found to be 61 per cent of the number who profess to attend. If we suppose that the church-going population is twice as large as the average church attendance, it would probably be a generous supposition.

Now, observe, the average congregation is hardly as large as the church membership. It should be remembered that pastors *count* the names on the church roll, but usually *estimate* church attendance, and almost invariably overestimate it. An actual count will show that in the average church the average congregation is smaller than the church membership. The membership of the Evangelical churches in the United States is 21 per cent of the entire population, and the average attendance on these churches is somewhat less. We may, therefore, infer that the whole number of professed attendants upon these churches is not far from 40 per cent of the population. If we should count all Roman Catholic communicants as church attendants, this would raise the number of church-goers to only a little more than one half of all the people. But a large number of Roman Catholics fall away from their church in the United States and attend nowhere; so that by this process of reasoning we arrive at our former conclusion that fully one half of the population of this country are non-church-goers.

We must not forget that many children come under religious influence in the Sunday-school who do not attend church; but Sunday-school attendance should not be deemed an equivalent of church attendance. So far as the Sunday-school is made a substitute for the church its influence is mischievous instead of beneficial. Usually, the habit of attending church is formed in childhood, if at all. Multitudes of youth "graduate" from the Sunday-school every year, and most of them who have not already established the habit of church attendance drop into the great non-church-going class. That class contains comparatively few who attended church regularly in childhood, but many who were once Sunday-school scholars.

Our estimate that 50 per cent of the population are church-goers includes all who are only occasional attendants, and the many who profess to attend, but never do. Probably the latter are quite as numerous as the number of Sunday-school scholars who are not church attendants; so that all the facts within our knowledge indicate that about one half of our population are quite estranged from the church.

Consider now that, generally speaking, it is the workingmen and the farmers on whom the church has lost its hold. We have already seen that somewhat more than one half of our rural population are non-church-goers. A large proportion of those who do attend live in the villages, while probably 70 per cent of those who live two miles from church (which of course means farmers) do not attend. As two thirds of our entire population live in the country it is evident that farmers constitute a large proportion of the non-church-going class. Most of the remainder are the workingmen of the cities. Says Mr. Loomis on this subject: "It will not be difficult to convince those who are acquainted with the life of our cities that the Protestant churches, as a rule, have no following among the workingmen. Everybody knows it. Go into an ordinary church on Sunday morning and you see lawyers, physicians, merchants, and business men with their families; you see teachers, salesmen, and clerks, and a certain proportion of educated mechanics; but the workingman and his household are not there. It is doubtful if one in twenty of the average congregation in English-speaking, Protestant city churches fairly belongs to this class; but granting the proportion to be so great as one in ten or one in five, even then you would have two thirds of the people furnishing only one tenth or one fifth of the congregation." [1]

A few years ago I was in conversation with four Brooklyn clergymen, and the rector of one of the largest Episcopal churches in the city said: "Gentlemen, I would like to know if my church is exceptional.

---

[1] Rev. S. L. Loomis, "Modern Cities," p. 82.

We have not a single workingman in our membership."
The pastor of a Dutch Reformed church said: "That is
true of mine." The pastor of a large Congregational
church said: "We have one carpenter in our church,
but we haven't a single serving-man or a serving-
woman." The pastor of one of the leading Presbyterian
churches of the city said: "We have some master-
workmen in our church, who employ labor, but of what
would be called workingmen we haven't one in our
church or congregation." These four churches had at
that time an aggregate membership of some twenty-two
hundred. I cannot think that these churches are fairly
representative of city churches in general; but they do
represent many, and show that a condition of things is
common which ought to be impossible.

A minister told me that he found in one shop sixty
men (none of them Roman Catholics), only six of whom
ever went to church at all. In another shop, out of
about one hundred and ten Protestants he found that
only seven attended any church. According to the
careful estimate of a clergyman in one of the largest
New England factory cities, not more than one in fifteen
of the Protestant operatives in that city ever attends
church.[1]

A few years ago, Rev. A. H. Bradford, D.D., made
investigations touching church attendance among the
poorer classes in a large number of typical manufacturing towns, such as Elizabeth, Newark, Paterson, and
Jersey City, in New Jersey; New York, Brooklyn,
Albany, and Buffalo, in New York; Waterbury, Norwich,
and New Britain, in Connecticut; Lowell, North Abing-
ton, Lynn, and Fall River, in Massachusetts. His inquiries elicited the fact, "which came almost without
qualification, that church neglect among the poorer
classes is rapidly increasing."[2] Dr. Washington Gladden said in 1885: "In my own congregation, which wor-

---

[1] *The Christian Union*, April 24, 1890.
[2] Discussions of Inter-Denominational Congress in the Interest of City
Evangelization. Cranston & Stowe, Cincinnati, 1886.

ships in a very plain church, the seats of which are free, in a neighborhood easily accessible to the working-classes, and which has been known always as an extremely democratic congregation, I find only about one tenth of the families on my list belonging to this class. . . . This is the result of repeated special efforts made in the interest of the working-classes, with several courses of lectures on Sunday evenings for their benefit." [1]

In this connection Dr. Gladden added: "How is it with the other extreme of society? In this same city I asked one of the best-informed citizens to make me out a list of fifty of the leaders of business. He did not know my reason for wishing such a list, but after it was put into my hands, I found that 55 per cent of these men were communicants in the churches, and that 77 per cent of them were regular attendants upon the churches. A large proportion of the capitalists are more or less closely identified with the churches, while of the laborers only a small share are thus identified, and the number tends to decrease rather than increase." A similar inquiry in an eastern city of about 40.000 inhabitants showed that three fifths of the leading citizens were church members, while four fifths were regular church attendants.

Of course, in the aggregate there are many wealthy people and many intelligent people who do not attend church, and many of the laboring classes who do; but, speaking broadly, it is the well-to-do classes which constitute the church-goers and the poorer classes, the "masses," which constitute the non-church-goers.

The situation in England seems to be the same. Canon Farrar, speaking of the Church of England, says: "Not 3 per cent of the working-classes, who represent the great mass of the people, are regular or even occasional communicants." [2] And at an anniversary of the

---

[1] Discussions of Inter-Denominational Congress in the Interest of City Evangelization. Cranston & Stowe, Cincinnati, 1886.

[2] "The Salvation Army," *Harper's Magazine*, May, 1891.

Open-air Mission in Islington, Shaftesbury said that not more than 2 per cent of the English workingmen attend any place of worship, Papal or Protestant.

When we ask after the causes of this separation between the church and the masses, we find at once that they are many and complex.

(1) Ideas of duty are not so strict now as formerly, and men, therefore, more readily yield to inclination. The present generation of young people have had a training very different from that which their grandparents or even their parents received. In most families the rod, like Aaron's rod, has budded and brought forth almonds and sugar-plums of all sorts. Children are hired and coaxed instead of being commanded and required, and accordingly grow up to consult inclination rather than obligation. Attending church is not now commonly considered a sacred duty. People go, if they feel like it; and for a great variety of reasons most people do not feel like it.

(2) Prevalence of the Continental ideas of the Sabbath, which have come to us with immigration, have helped to reduce church attendance.

(3) The rush which characterizes modern, and especially American, living brings a Sunday lassitude which affords an excuse quite sufficient to placate many an easy conscience for neglecting the sanctuary.

(4) The pulpit once afforded the people most of their intellectual, as well as spiritual, stimulus. Now it must compete with books, magazines, and papers, and especially with the Sunday-morning newspaper.

(5) The Sunday-school, notwithstanding all the good it has done and is doing, by being considered "the children's church," has interfered with the formation of church-going habits on the part of many children, and so has eventually contributed not a few to the non-church-going class.

(6) Our almost nomadic habits of life break up church relationships, which often are not renewed among strangers.

(7) A wrong conception of the Christian life has led laymen to hire the minister to do their Christian work for them. In the cities, where churches are more apt to be large, the minister is fully occupied with his duties to his congregation, so that the non-church-goers are not looked after at all, except as this duty is occasionally laid on a lonesome city-missionary.

(8) Private ownership in church pews has an influence, though it is probably more of an excuse than a reason.

(9) Church dress also is a deterrent to workingmen and their families, when Sunday best, if they are fortunate enough to have any, is such as to make them conspicuous for their plain appearance.

(10) But more important than any of these causes is an indifference which too often rises into a positive class antipathy—an indifference on the part both of church-goers and of non-church-goers.

There are in every church choice men and women, just the material to make a heaven of, who believe that Jesus Christ died for every man, and who see in every man, however degraded or besotted in sin and ignorance, the possibility of glorious likeness to Christ; men and women who long and labor to see this possible likeness become actual. But I fear that a very large proportion are indifferent or worse than indifferent in regard to reaching the masses with Christian influence, under the impression that the church is a kind of religious coterie or "steepled club," existing expressly for "our sort of folks." They are under the impression that "our sort of folks" would pretty nearly exhaust the list of the elect; they are willing that the masses should be saved, but not in their church or by their instrumentality.

In the weekly prayer-meeting of a wealthy and influential New England church a gentleman arose and said: "I went recently to call on that man who, at the fire the other day, so heroically saved the lives of eight or ten persons by risking his own life. I found that he and his family are poor and that they attend no church. I invited him to our church; and now I hope, brethren, when they come, if they do come, you will give them a cordial welcome, and make room for them in your pews." When he took his seat the wealthiest and most influential man in the church arose and said: "I don't want any such man or family in my pew; I don't want them near my pew; I don't want them in this church." The pastor of that church was angry and sinned not, and when he arose to rebuke that spirit he said: "I will not cease my efforts until yonder door swings in to the lightest touch of the poorest man in this city." But that pastor, though a man of great ability and of national reputation, was presently unseated.

In another prayer-meeting a member said: "I want your prayers for a man who has been a slave to drink. . . . Pray for him; he's a gentleman; he's no 'bum.' He's worth $200,000, and he's a gentleman; he's worth saving!" Preference for the "man with a gold ring, in goodly apparel" is not always so frankly expressed, but this speaker represents a large class who "have the faith of our Lord Jesus Christ with respect of persons."

There is a church in the Mississippi valley which is "rich and increased with goods and hath need of nothing"—nothing except some Christianity—whose pastor, it is said, when some working girls presented themselves for membership, discouraged them, not on the ground that the evidence of their Christian experience was unsatisfactory, but because there would be no "affinity," no "congeniality," between them and his flock. It was that same church of which the story is told that when a reformed drunkard presented himself for membership, he was informed by one of the officers that he believed there were no "vacancies" in the membership of the church just at that time! "I was a stranger, and ye took me not in. . . . Inasmuch as ye did it not to one of the least of these, ye did it not to me."

A clergyman of New York told me that some years

ago, when he was a lay member of a down-town church, he started out with a friend, in obedience to the command to "go out into the highways," to gather up the *gamins* and recruit their Sunday-school. Their efforts were successful, but as the school began to grow, members of the church began to be frightened. The parents said: "Why, we don't want that kind of children in our Sunday-school. If you are going to bring in such children, we will take ours and go home;" and that Christly work had to stop. I am very glad to be able to state that to-day that church is dead. It was *dead* at that time, but it is buried now. And the death by which it glorified God was a natural one. For a church is like a tree. The tree thrusts its roots down into the soil and lives and grows because it assimilates that soil, because it transforms dead, unorganized matter into living fibre, thus lifting it up and glorifying it. The church, in its membership, thrusts its roots out into the community and lives by assimilating the humanity in which it is planted; it grows by transforming men, dead in sin, into the living likeness of Jesus Christ, thus lifting them up and glorifying them. And when church or tree ceases thus to assimilate, ceases thus to transform death into life, it naturally begins to die—it must die unless it is transplanted.

Precisely this is the reason why so many churches are moving up-town in our great cities, not because there are no perishing men all around them, but because the class for which they exist has moved up-town; showing unmistakably that they are class churches.

On the other hand, workingmen are generally indifferent to the church when they are not positively hostile to it, and believe that the church is indifferent or hostile to them. In the investigation made by Dr. Bradford some years ago and referred to above, every letter received from a workingman indicated that men of his class feel that they are not wanted in the churches, and almost every letter from workers among the poor recognized that the poor do not think they are welcome.

The Committee on the Work of the Churches of the Massachusetts Congregational Association made inquiries as to the attitude of the workingmen of Massachusetts toward the churches. Circulars were sent to some two hundred state and local labor leaders. The many failures to reply, together with the tone of curt refusals to answer or the return of blank circulars, indicated anything but a kindly feeling toward the churches. Most of the replies sent expressed the opinion that laboring men have been alienated from the churches. "The causes given of alienation are all modifications of the charge that churches and preachers are allied with and subservient to the 'oppressing class.'" "Seldom is the church just enough even to be neutral. It is a 'mammonized' institution; it belongs to the plutocrats," [1] etc.

Like charges are common at labor meetings. At such a meeting in Union Square, New York City, one of the foremost representatives of organized labor in the United States, a man of national reputation, occupied some twenty minutes in pouring out a lava stream of vituperation against the church and its ministers, both Protestant and Roman Catholic. The Young Men's Christian Association was called "that scab institution." "Cooper's Institute did more good in a week than all the New York churches in a year," and a certain New York daily paper "represented the spirit of true brotherhood more in a single issue than the Christian ministers, the parasites of society, could do in an age of their hired mouthings." And these utterances were lustily cheered by the large audience of workingmen.

In their struggles, workingmen have little expectation of sympathy or help from the churches. They do not appreciate the fact that, apart from their own class,

[1] Rev. John P. Coyle, "The Churches and Labor Unions," *The Forum,* Aug. 1892.

most of those who are seeking to secure the rights of
labor are Christian men, and a large proportion of them
clergymen. Still it is not strange that the attitude of a
majority of churches and ministers should be supposed
to represent the whole. Prof. R. T. Ely writes:[1] "The
secretary of the Journeymen Baker's National Union
sent out appeals to the clergy of New York and
Brooklyn to preach against Sunday labor and help
them to abolish it. Five hundred circulars were sent
out, but little response was met with. In a reply to a
query as to their success, the disgusted secretary sent
this answer to the writer of the present paper: 'Out of
the five hundred circulars sent to the clergy of New
York and Brooklyn half a dozen answered. You will
have a hard time, Professor, to convince the toilers of
this country that the clergy will ever do anything for
them.' "

(11) There is another short and easy explanation of
the alienation of the multitude from the church, viz.,
their total depravity. It is quite true that the natural
man loveth not the things of God, but the workingman
is not any more "natural" than his employer. Depravity is supposed to belong naturally to all classes
alike. If separation from the churches characterized
all classes in like degree we might then resort to the
total depravity theory to account for it; but we are
trying to find out why this is true of one class rather
than another. And we cannot apply this theory to
explain the estrangement of the masses unless we
assume, as Dr. Gladden says, that their depravity is
"considerably more than total."

In like manner the first seven causes which have
been enumerated may serve to explain a general loosening of the church-going habit, but they are no more
applicable to workingmen than to professional men.
They do not explain why the church has lost its hold on
one class rather than another. The next three causes
mentioned show why class churches cannot reach men

---

[1] "A Programme for Labor Reform," *The Century*, April, 1890.

of another class, but do not explain why this other class
is not found in churches of its own.

Jesus Christ was a workingman. The common people
heard him gladly. As one of the evidences that he was
indeed the Messiah he pointed to the fact that he
preached the gospel to the poor; and in all ages and in
all lands the poor far more than the rich have flocked
to his following. But now it is the well-to-do who have
the gospel preached to them and who hear it gladly,
and it is the humbler classes, with whose life Christ's
lot was cast, and who for eighteen centuries have been
most easily attracted to him, who now are estranged
from his church. Once, not many wise men, not many
mighty, not many noble were called; now, not many
ignorant, not many poor, not many humble. Surely,
here is a modern marvel not usually reckoned among
the wonders of the nineteenth century—and one which
demands explanation.

When seeking an explanation it is more important to
find *the cause* than the causes. We have noted some of
the causes of the separation of the multitude from the
church, but evidently we have not yet laid our scalpel
on *the cause.*

When those classes which in all Christian history
have been the most susceptible to the gospel become the
least susceptible to it, there is something wrong, something abnormal. Has human nature changed? Has
the gospel changed? Is it not worth while to ask
whether indifference or antipathy to the church is
identical with indifference or antipathy to the gospel?
And when that question has been answered it will be in
order to inquire whether the gospel we preach is really
Christ's gospel.

Recent investigators have stated that the "German
Social Democrats, though hostile to official Christianity,
are ready to avow themselves followers of Jesus."
This led the committee of the Massachusetts Congregational Association, when making the inquiries already
referred to, to ask whether the workingmen who disbe

lieve in the churches also disbelieve in Jesus. "With
few exceptions the answers are that belief in Jesus is
common; and this testimony is borne in many cases,
with much warmth. . . . It is commonly said that if the
churches and ministers would be faithful to Jesus, no
alienation would exist." [1] It has been repeatedly said by
workingmen that they do not disbelieve in Christianity
but in "*Churchianity.*" The distinction was made clear
and marked by that great audience in New York which
applauded the name of Christ and hissed a mention of
the church.

We need not stop to inquire in what sense men who
disbelieve in the church "believe in Jesus." This distinction, on which they insist, forbids the assumption
that the masses are indifferent or hostile to the gospel
because they are indifferent or hostile to the church;
and forces upon us the question whether the church
really teaches and exemplifies the gospel of Christ.

The church teaches the gospel of personal salvation;
but as we have already seen (Chapter VI), this is only
one half of Christ's gospel. He preached the gospel of
the *Kingdom*, which is the gospel of social regeneration.
He taught the gospel of human brotherhood as well as
that of divine Fatherhood, and laid down the law of
both; and the second fundamental law of Christ, which
is the organic law of a normal society, the church has
neglected. If she had accepted and inculcated and exemplified this teaching of Christ as the practical law of
every-day life, it is quite safe to say she would never
have lost her hold on the masses.

But it may be said, This is no new neglect on the part
of the church. If it is indeed the cause of the alienation of the masses, why is this effect so modern, why
did it not appear many centuries ago? For the reason
that in its progress the world did not reach the sociological age until modern times. Christ's second law was
intended to solve the problems which rise out of social

---

[1] Rev. John P. Coyle, ' The Churches and Labor Unions," *The Forum*,
Aug. 1892.

relations. Not until those problems began to attract general attention did men generally begin to see and appreciate the fact that Christ's teachings had not been applied to social organization, and that the church had failed to teach and exemplify Christ's social law.

The workingman, even though he never goes to church, knows that Christ taught the duty of loving our neighbor as we love ourselves. He does not see this duty exemplified by the church, and perhaps makes a sweeping charge of insincerity or at least of inconsistency against its members. He misjudges the church because he does not know it. Almost the only contact between the artisan class and well-to-do church members is contact in business, and business which is intensely competitive, i.e., selfish. How could men whose knowledge of Christians is gained by such contact avoid wrong impressions of the church? They do not know how much of genuine Christian love there is in it. To be sure, if there were all there ought to be, no one could help knowing it. But as a matter of fact there is a great deal which finds but little *personal* expression. The average Christian to-day is hiring his Christian work done by proxy—by societies, institutions, the minister, the city missionary. He is so very busy that he would rather give his money than his time. His interest in his fellow-men, therefore, is expressed through various organizations which make a business of philanthropy. Thus our Christian work has become largely *institutional* instead of *personal*, and, therefore, largely mechanical instead of vital.

There is an enormous amount of good done by Christian organizations and institutions, and a great deal of Christian self-denial exercised in their support, but they appeal very little to the average non-church-goer. The dissatisfied classes, who believe that they are not receiving their just dues, that they are wronged by the capitalist class, look on charitable institutions not as an expression of Christian love, but as a mere sop to Cerberus.

The one conclusive proof of love is sacrifice; and of
this the world sees in the church a "plentiful lack."
It is only *self*-giving which can carry conviction to the
doubter; and this proof of love is rarely seen across the
chasm which separates the masses from the church.
When the church goes to the masses with proof that the
brotherhood of man is not simply a fine phrase, but a
living reality, both taught and exemplified by the
church, the alienation of the masses will cease. In the
thrilling address made by Dr. Parkhurst at the Chicker-
ing Hall Conference he said: " You know how the Gulf
Stream works. The waters of the Atlantic are heated
in the Gulf by some power which we do not understand,
but which is a divine power. That heat thrown off,
wonderfully modifies the climate of all the northern
portion of Europe, and there is wrought the recurrence
of the cold polar waters, which return to the Gulf and
are there heated. So, if we have started a current of
Christian life that works out from the church in the
same way that the heated waters work out from the
Gulf of Mexico, we will have the cold waters returning,
coming into the church, and in their turn getting
warmed. We have no circulation now. We have great
coagulated masses of piety in our churches, that show
no blood-beat. Once start the circulation, let the world
see that the church has a heart that throws the warm
blood out, and then there will be no difficulty about
getting the cold blood in. . . . We have occasions for
money; but we make money subserve the purposes that
only love can subserve. When the poor leper came to
the Lord to be healed, you might have expected that
the Lord would say to Peter, . . . 'Peter, you go touch
that fellow, and I'll pay you for it.' Now that is the
way we run a good deal of our mission work. We say,
'I don't quite feel like going down there, but I will
draw my check, and I will pay somebody else for doing
it.' And the more money there is given in that way,
the more the dirty, sin-sick, loathsome recipients of
your bounty will hate the church and all that pertains

to it. . . . We have got to give, not our old clothes, not our prayers. Those are cheap. You can kneel down on a carpet and pray, where it is warm and comfortable. Not our soup—that is sometimes very cheap; not our money—a stingy man will give money when he refuses to give himself. Just so soon as a man feels that you sit down alongside of him in loving sympathy with him, notwithstanding his poor, his sick, and his debased estate, just so soon you begin to worm your way into the very warmest, most determinative spot in his life."

Our modern church habits and methods have signally failed to manifest a personal love for non-church-goers, and it is not strange that they disbelieve the existence of any such love. Here, then, is the great cause of the alienation of the multitude, viz., the fact that the church has failed to teach and to exemplify the gospel of human brotherhood.

The fact of the separation of the masses from the church has been shown, together with its cause. Permit a word on the significance of that fact.

It has a spiritual significance which is familiar to every Christian, but which is appreciated by none. It is not, however, to this that I desire especially to call attention. There is a great discontented class; there is a great non-church-going class. Let us now weigh the fact that *these two classes are substantially one and the same.* It is the masses who are discontented; it is the masses who rule and who will determine our future; it is the masses who constitute the non-church-goers.

Let us again remind ourselves that in this country the masses are the sources of power, the arbiters of destiny, the supreme judicature. We are concerned not with aristocracies or kings, but with the people. And when we say that the people rule, that means that mere numbers rule, that the complex and difficult questions of government and statesmanship, questions on whose answers may depend the rights and well-being of millions and even the future of civilization—that such questions are settled ultimately not by the intelligence and conscience of the wisest and best, but by *mere majorities.*

Not only do we find industrious, intelligent and law-abiding workingmen and farmers among the non-church-goers, but also the criminal classes, the army of tramps and vagrants and a larger army of saloon keepers, the illiterate, the venders of votes and the anarchists, who at the last presidential election cast twice as many votes in New York City as did the prohibitionists. The dangerous elements in general are found in the non-church-going multitude.

Evidently, if the church is to purify society, if she is to solve the great problems of the times, if she is to mould the civilization of the future, if she is to accomplish her mission by ushering in the full coming of Christ's kingdom, then the great body of her work, yet to be done, is to be found in the non-church-going class, and she is separated from her greatest and most urgent work by a deep and wide chasm.

She is spending her energies on the *best* elements of society, her time is given to teaching the most *intelligent,* she is medicating the *healthiest,* she is salting the *salt,* while the determinating masses, which include the most ignorant and vicious, the poorest and most degraded, are alike beyond her influence and her effort.

CHAPTER XI.

THE MISSION OF THE CHURCH.

WE have inherited from the Latin fathers a vicious dualism which runs throughout life a line of cleavage, separating it into the sacred and the secular.

In mediæval times the common was profane. That alone was sacred which was especially set apart to religious uses. The church was sacred, the state secular. The occupation of the clergy was holy, and they were under obligations to lead holy lives; the occupations of the laity, the common activities of the world, were profane, and the people were expected to live lives more or less worldly. They were, to be sure, under obligations to give a part of their time and substance to religion, but the remainder was their own, to be applied to secular uses.

Nature was profane. Instead of being a manifestation of the Creator, the natural was so incompatible with the divine that God could reveal himself in nature only by setting aside or overriding nature's laws.

Soul and body were in conflict. Manicheism, which attributed the visible world to the devil, and looked on the body with contempt and hatred, continued to exert a wide influence for many centuries after it had been declared heretical by the church. Natural appetites were unholy, and the body must be depleted in order to cultivate the spiritual life.

This tendency to separate the sacred from the secular culminated in monasticism, which was an attempt to overcome the world by running away from it.

Luther saw clearly that all of these distinctions were false, and, according to Bunsen, all of the reformers of the sixteenth century agreed with Luther that there was no difference between religious and secular acts.[1] But the Reformation failed to free the church entirely from these misconceptions, and we still talk of sacred and profane history, of religious and secular duties, of sacred and secular callings. The church is content to accept as her province only a small part of the life of men. She claims the "sacred" as her sphere. The "secular" life must of course be lived under the restrictions of the moral law; but such a life is not supposed to be religious, and is held to be quite foreign to the sphere of the church.

This meagre conception of her sphere, and hence of her mission, has at the same time belittled and perverted the life and influence of the church. Next to a mighty spiritual quickening, which is of supreme importance to the church in every age, her greatest need to-day is a broader, truer conception of her mission. To gain this broader, truer view let her go back to her Master and study his example and teaching.

He did not begin to preach until he was thirty. Would any venture to say that only the three years of Christ's public ministry were sacred and that thirty years of his life were secular? Was he any less divine, any less beautiful in the eyes of the Father, any less consecrated to his great mission, while at the carpenter's bench than when preaching in the synagogue or on the mount? It was eighteen years before he entered on his public ministry that he said, "Wist ye not that I must be about my Father's business?"

Now Christ was a revelation not only of God to man, but of man to himself. As a man, he was a revelation of what man was intended to be, ought to be, may be, will be when perfected. The thoroughly Christianized man, whatever his occupation, will *always* be about his

---

[1] Allen's Continuity of Christian Thought, p. 274.

Father's business ; will live in constant obedience to the command, "Whether therefore ye eat, or drink, or whatsoever ye do, do all to the glory of God," [1]—words which are absolutely all-inclusive, which embrace the entire circle of human activities, and which, therefore, leave no room for the secular.

After Christ entered on his public ministry, he did not confine himself to preaching the gospel; he ministered to bodies as well as to souls. The blind received their sight, the lame walked, the lepers were cleansed, the deaf heard, the dead were raised up. He went about "healing every sickness and every disease among the people" as well as "teaching in their synagogues, and preaching the gospel of the kingdom." [2] He had compassion on the multitude, not only because they were spiritually without a shepherd,[3] but also because they had *nothing to eat*.[4] When after his resurrection he appeared to his disciples on the shore of Galilee, his first word was, "Children, have ye any meat ?" And this inquiry was not with reference to his own wants, but theirs. He told them where to cast their net that their night's labors might not prove fruitless, and when they landed, tired and hungry, as fishermen are apt to be, they found a fire and a prepared meal awaiting them.[5] Some struggling men think that if Christ were walking among us in the flesh to-day, it would be just like him to ask the toilers, as of old, "Have ye any meat ?" Why should he not show the same interest in men's physical well-being now that he did then ? "Jesus Christ, *the same* yesterday, to-day, and for ever." [6]

His representation of the last judgment is for the instruction of all generations, and indicates the one ground of judgment for all. Christ represents that in the person of his fellow-men he was hungry, thirsty, a stranger, naked, sick, and in prison. And in their

---

[1] 1 Cor. x. 31.   [2] Matt. ix. 35.   [3] Ibid 36.
[4] Matt. xv. 32.   [5] John xxi. 5-13.   [6] Heb. xiii. 8.

person his bodily wants had been ministered to or neglected. Strange as it may seem to us, this is the one ground he names on which all the nations are to be approved or condemned.[1]

Evidently Christ was interested in the physical as well as the spiritual, and both by teaching and example emphasized the importance of caring for the body. Either the common idea that "Religion concerns the relation in which the soul stands to God"[2] is very inadequate, or much of Christ's life and teaching was not religious, and the final judgment will not be a religious court. One thing is certain: we must either consent to drop the old distinction between the sacred and the secular, or admit that the perfect life was most of it secular.

Christ fed the multitude and healed their diseases because he loved men, and that in most cases was the natural and most convincing way to show his love. Men must be reached on the plane on which they live. The lives of the multitude are chiefly physical. Though spiritual needs are the deepest they rise into conscious wants only occasionally, while physical needs make themselves felt daily and hourly. Hunger and cold and pain are far more real to the many than the sense of sin or high spiritual aspirations. If, then, Christ was to convince men of his love, he must do it by meeting needs which they actually felt.

And Christ's example is a good one for his church to follow. If she is to reach the masses, she must do it on the plane where the masses live. If she would convince them of her love (of which they sorely need to be convinced), she must do it in ways that appeal to them, she must deal with things which *they* regard as real. And having laid hold of men on the physical plane, she can then lead them up to the spiritual.

While the old distinction of "sacred" and "secular"

---

[1] Matt. xxv. 31–46.
[2] Rev. M. J. Savage, in *The Arena* for April, 1890, p. 510.

is thoroughly false and mischievous, it is not altogether a distinction without a difference. There is a difference which is misinterpreted and misnamed. The root differs from its fruit, but that difference does not warrant our saying that the one belongs to the husbandman and the other does not, that the one serves him and the other does not, that the one has much value and the other little or none. They are alike his and they alike serve, only the one serves more *directly* than the other. The root is valuable because it ministers to the fruit which ministers to man; and man is serving himself as truly when cultivating the root as when plucking and eating the fruit.

Now the difference between the physical and the spiritual is real, but this fact of difference does not justify the distinction of secular and sacred. The physical exists for the spiritual and from it derives its dignity and worth, but this does not warrant our saying that one belongs to God or serves him any more truly than the other. Some things minister more directly than others to spiritual results, some uses are higher and some lower, but every lawful thing is a step somewhere in the great stairway up to God. Whatever has no place in that stairway is not "secular," but unholy, and has no right to be.

The old conception that the sphere of the church is the sacred and that she is to deal only with the soul may be accepted, provided we broaden our view enough to see that all of God's creations are sacred, and that all pertain to. the soul. Walt Whitman's poems have a "marked physiological stamp," and yet he writes:

"I will not make a poem, nor the least part of a poem, but has reference to the soul.
  Because, having looked at the objects of the universe, I find there is no one, nor any particle of one, but has reference to the soul."

When the church sees this truth she will enlarge her conception of her mission.

Because the creation is a *universe*, which word means one system or whole, all created things are marvellously and mysteriously interrelated. I suspect that the whole of any one truth is all truth. This was recognized by Tennyson when he sang:

> " Flower in the crannied wall,
> I pluck you out of the crannies :—
> Hold you here, root and all in my hand,
> Little flower—but if I could understand
> What you are, root and all, and all in all,
> I should know what God and man is."

If the view taken in Chapter II is correct, the divine purpose, in the fulfilment of which all nature and history are at length to find their interpretation and unity, is the final and triumphant coming of the kingdom of God. Now this kingdom is not a divided realm (" every kingdom divided against itself is brought to desolation " [1]); no portion of it is beyond God's authority, outside his plan. It would be unworthy of infinite wisdom not to have a plan which included all the resources of the universe. The "plan of salvation" is vastly more comprehensive than some have supposed. It is a plan for perfecting the race, and includes not only spiritual facts and forces, but all of nature's resources, laws, and processes. "His kingdom ruleth over all." [2] Coal-fields and climates, latitude and longitude, mountain ranges and coast lines, the Gulf Stream and the equinox, as *really* enter into that plan as do the birth and death of Christ.

And all nature is obedient to the laws of the kingdom; only man is rebellious. When all mankind by perfect love to God are brought into perfect harmony with his will and, therefore, into perfect harmony with his laws, which are an expression of his will, the race will then be perfected, and " all things " will " work together for good " to all—which will be the Kingdom fully come.

This does not mean that the kingdom of God is simply a materialistic paradise. It is " not meat and drink," that is, does not *consist* in these things; " but righteous-

---

[1] Matt. xii. 25.   [2] Psa. ciii. 19.

ness, and peace, and joy in the Holy Ghost." [1] It is the spiritual which has essential and absolute value; all else is relative. Still the Creator certainly places a high estimate on the importance of the physical, for he spent unmeasured time and exercised infinite skill in perfecting the physical conditions of spiritual life; and surely the church will not err in placing a like estimate on the importance of those conditions. If for no other reason, the physical must be respected and studied and perfected because of the subtle and powerful influence both for good and evil which it exerts over the spiritual. We may no longer despise the body or look upon it as the enemy of the soul instead of its servant and helper, its medium and instrument. Science has revealed the interdependence of the two. We now know that, other things being equal, the more nearly normal the physical life is, the more nearly normal will be the intellectual and spiritual life. We now know that the race cannot be perfected without the perfecting of the body. Society cannot be entirely saved until man has been saved physically.

And as the body was made subservient to the soul, so the material world, which is the bodily life of our civilization, was intended to serve the spiritual. The two are not enemies, but allies. Few men appreciate to what extent intellectual and moral progress depend on material conditions. But students of civilization are beginning to see that the natural order of growth in society as well as in the individual is first the physical or material and afterward the intellectual and spiritual. Says Mr. William G. Sumner of Yale University: " The notion that progress proceeds in the first instance from intellectual or moral stimuli, or that progress is really something in the world of thought, and not of sense, has led to the most disappointing and abortive efforts to teach and ' elevate' inferior races or neglected classes. The ancestors of the present civilized races did not win

[1] Rom. xiv. 17.

their civilization by any such path. They built it up
through centuries of toil from a foundation of surplus
material means, which they won through improvements
in the industrial arts and in the economic organization." [1]

In the scale of being, the nobler the rank the later
and more slowly does it mature, so that the higher
naturally rests on the lower and is necessarily conditioned by it. This being true, an *intelligent* interest in
the moral or intellectual progress of the race necessitates interest in men's material progress. If the church
is to labor intelligently for the elevation of the spiritual
life, she must be interested in all that pertains to the
physical life. To be concerned for the former and indifferent as to the latter is like being anxious for a
crop but indifferent as to the soil in which it is to grow,
—careful of effects, but careless of causes.

We shall not gain a true view of the meaning and
value, the dignity and beauty, of the physical, nor shall
we intelligently cultivate the spiritual until we understand how intimately the two are related in the kingdom of Christ. Indeed, as President John Bascom has
said: "The true synthesis of the universe of God,
physical and spiritual, is the kingdom of heaven." [2]
The Master taught us to pray: "Thy kingdom come.
Thy will be done, as in heaven, so in earth." [3] When
the latter petition is fully answered, then the Kingdom
will have fully come. If we look more closely at this
second petition and perceive the largeness of its meaning, we shall better understand the place of the physical
in the kingdom of God.

What we call natural laws are expressions of the will
of nature's Creator. All of the laws given to guide us
in our complex relations to nature and to our fellow-
men, whether revealed by science or by the progress of
civilization, whether pertaining to matter, or to our

[1] *The Independent*, Jan. 15, 1891.
[2] Sociology, p. 264. [3] Luke xi. 2.

social, political, industrial, or commercial relations, all
are *God's* laws, as truly as if written on tables of stone
and delivered to us by a second Moses. And all of
God's laws, physical as well as spiritual, from the
highest to the lowest, are laws of the Kingdom, and
were undoubtedly intended to minister to the perfection
and blessedness of its citizens. What God desires for
the race, the end of all his patient discipline, is that men
live in perfect harmony with all the laws of their being.
These laws are an expression of his infinite love guided
by his infinite wisdom. They require only what our
highest good requires; they forbid only what our highest good forbids. They are the best possible paths to
the highest possible blessedness. As Burke said: "Law
is beneficence acting by rule." All the ills of life,
bodily, mental, moral, social, political, industrial, financial, and every other possible sort, are the thorns which
God has set along these paths to turn us back when we
wander from them. These ills of life are the penalties
of violated law—penalties appointed by God's far-seeing
love as truly as were the paths of law which these
penalties were set to guard. Just so far as men walk in
these God-appointed paths, the ills of life disappear.

God's laws are laid upon all created existence, from
the ultimate particle of matter up to the highest intelligence; and the higher the form of existence, the greater
is the number of laws to which it is subject. More
laws lay hold of the flower than of the "crannied wall"
from which it is plucked, and more lay hold of the
brute than of the flower, and more lay hold of the man
than of the brute; and the more highly man is developed, the greater will be the number of laws to
which he is subject. His progress depends on his
obedience to law. Every law discovered and obeyed
lifts him higher. What is the progress of science but
the discovery of God's laws? And what is wisdom but
their application to life? What we call our conquest of
nature is only obedience to nature's laws. Here is a
paradox: disobey nature's laws, and you are her slave;

obey, and you are her master; and the more laws we obey, the freer and more masterful do we become. If you would do me good, if you would save me from some impending evil or bless me with increased power, a larger liberty, a richer happiness, show me another divine law that I may obey. Unknown laws are blessings in reserve; steps in the upward path of the race not yet taken. All true progress of civilization is nothing more or less than the discovery of God's laws and their application to life.

We see, then, how comprehensive is the kingdom of God. It is of course as far-reaching as the laws of the King, though it is actually established only where those laws are obeyed, and in the Lord's prayer, "Thy kingdom come: thy will be done in earth as it is in heaven," we are taught to pray (and therefore to labor) for the complete establishment of that kingdom in all the earth, through perfect obedience to God's will as expressed in his laws.

This conception of the Kingdom is not altogether familiar. Some need to be reminded that by the kingdom of heaven or the kingdom of God, of which Christ speaks so often, he does not mean the abode of the blessed dead, but a kingdom of righteousness which he came to establish on the earth, of which he is the king, and whose fundamental law is that of love.

We talk a great deal of heaven and a great deal of the church, and think that the mission of the latter is to prepare souls for the former, but we say little concerning the kingdom of God. Now Christ had very little to say of heaven and only twice does he refer to the church,[1] but his teachings were full of the Kingdom. Before his birth that kingdom was made the subject of prophecy, "Of his kingdom there shall be no end."[2] When he was about ready to enter on his public ministry, John proclaimed, "The kingdom of heaven is at hand."[3] And when Christ began his ministry, this was the first note of his preaching.[4] He declared that for

---

[1] Matt. xvi. 18, xviii. 17. [2] Luke i. 33. [3] Matt. iii. 2. [4] Matt. iv. 17.

this he was sent, to "preach the kingdom of God;"[1] and for this same purpose he sent out the twelve.[2] The gospel that he preached was "the gospel of the *kingdom;*"[3] the mysteries which he explained to his disciples were "mysteries of the *kingdom.*"[4] He began his sermon on the mount by pronouncing a blessing on those to whom "the kingdom of heaven" belonged.[5] He stated the conditions of entrance into that kingdom,[6] and told who would be great and who would be least in it.[7] In a single discourse to the multitude and later to his disciples, he presented the Kingdom in a half-dozen different aspects by as many different parables.[8] In the prayer which he taught his followers, a prayer which comprehends the daily needs and what should be the deepest, daily longings of every Christian, the second petition is for the coming of the Kingdom, and the third repeats the second in a different form.[9] He taught that this kingdom was to be the first object of endeavor.[10] And when he showed himself to his followers after his resurrection, he spoke of "the things pertaining to the kingdom."[11]

Reference has been made to only a small proportion of the passages in which Christ spoke of the Kingdom, but these suffice to show that it was his great mission to inaugurate the kingdom of God on the earth, and ours to extend it.

We must not infer that Christ regarded the life here as more important than the life hereafter. I infer rather that he believed the best way to fit men for doing God's will in heaven was by teaching them to do God's will on earth; that the best way, in fact the only way, to get men into heaven was to get heaven into men.

We are now prepared to get a closer and clearer view of the mission of the church. We are taught explicitly and repeatedly that the church is the body of which

---

[1] Luke iv. 43.   [2] Luke ix. 1, 2.   [3] Matt. iv. 23.   [4] Matt. xiii. 11.   [5] Matt. v. 3.
[6] Matt. v. 20, vi. 21, xviii. 3; John iii. 5.   [7] Matt. v. 19.
[8] Matt. xiii.   [9] Matt. vi. 10.   [10] Matt. vi. 33.   [11] Acts i. 3.

Christ is the head.[1] It is the office of the body in all its members to serve the head and execute its purposes. It is, therefore, the mission of the church to accomplish the purposes of Christ, to complete the work which he began. It was Christ's mission to inaugurate the kingdom of God on the earth. It is, then, the mission of the church to extend it until the kingdoms of this world are become the kingdoms of our Lord,[2] and the prophetic prayer of Christ that God's will might be done on earth as in heaven has found its fulfilling answer.

These views harmonize perfectly with the conclusions of a previous chapter (VI), viz., that Christ laid down the fundamental law which was to govern men in their relations to each other as well as that which was to govern them in their relations to God, and that it was as much the duty of the church to inculcate and exemplify the one law as the other.

Inasmuch then as perfect obedience to the will of God involves obedience to all the laws of life, in all our being, all our activities, and all our relations; and since the Kingdom cannot fully come until perfect obedience is rendered to God on earth even as it is in heaven; and since it is the mission of the church to hasten to its consummation the glorious coming of the Kingdom— evidently the church is vitally concerned with man's entire being and all that affects his welfare. As man is to be perfected in character and condition when the Kingdom is fully come, the church is commissioned to work out his perfection, and is interested, or ought to be, in everything on earth that touches for good or ill man's physical, mental, or spiritual health and well-being.

But it is asked, "How can the church be thus interested in all human concerns, touch and influence life at all points, without exercising or trying to exercise a correspondingly wide authority, thus trenching on the province of the state?"

---

[1] Col. i. 18.   [2] Rev. xi. 15.

The function of the church and that of the state are quite distinct, and should ever be kept so. No principle of our free institutions is more characteristic and none is more thoroughly established than that of the entire separation of the two. But precisely what is meant by the separation of church and state is not commonly or, indeed, often understood. There does not seem to have been made a clear distinction between *function* and *sphere*, for lack of which there has been much confusion, and most people have gained a radically wrong idea of the sphere of the church. Sphere is the *extent* or *field* of activity, while function is the *kind* or *nature* of that activity. The sphere of an organ is *where* it operates, its function is *what it does.* Thus, in the animal organism tissue and blood have almost exactly the same sphere, but the functions of the two are entirely different.

The higher the organization, the more are its several organs with their separate functions specialized. As society becomes more highly organized it becomes more important to keep the function of church and state separate; but it is as great a mistake to limit the sphere of the church as it is not to limit its functions. The sphere of the church includes that of the state and much more. It is as broad as the sphere of conscience, which is as far-reaching as all human activity.

One of the greatest blunders and sins, productive of endless evil, is the limitation of the sphere of conscience, excluding it from politics, business, and what are called "secular" occupations. A notable instance, already referred to, was afforded by the United States Senator who outraged the moral sense of the nation and at the same time pronounced his own political death-sentence by declaring that politics had nothing to do with the Ten Commandments or the Sermon on the Mount.

It is wrong and dangerous to exclude conscience from any sphere of human activity; and if this is true, it is wrong and dangerous to exclude the church from any, for it is the duty of the church to educate the individual conscience and itself to be the conscience of the social organism. Christ has laid down the fundamental law of this organism, and it is a function of the church to say to men in all their relations to one another, "You *ought* to obey this law."

The distinction in function between the church and the state is happily made by Mr. W. T. Stead as follows: "The state and municipality differ from the church in this, that whereas the church says 'You ought,' the municipality says 'You must.'"[1] Of course the church has and ought to have authority in the administration of her internal affairs, but she should have no authority whatever over the public or over any individual outside her own institutions. Beyond her own walls let the church have unbounded influence, but not one iota of authority. She has much influence now and ought to have infinitely more. That influence ought to extend to everything that concerns the kingdom of her Lord—and what does not? To executives, to legislative bodies, to corporations, to trades-unions, to classes, to society as a whole and to individuals—to all these the church has a right to say "You ought;" and she should be able to say it with such cogency of reason and such obvious purity of motive as to carry public opinion with her, and thus mould the entire life of the community.

Under the influence of the old and vicious distinction between the sacred and the secular, even the conscientious man brought only a fraction of his life to the touchstone of conscience. But when he learns that all the laws of life, that all "natural" laws, are God's laws, that all his activities sustain relations to the coming kingdom, then he is able to stretch the sceptre of conscience over his entire life. In like manner, when the church has learned to call nothing common or unclean except that which is unholy, when she has learned

---

[1] *The Review of Reviews*, February, 1892.

that politics and trade and education and all other
things which are building the kingdom of God among
men are not "secular" but sacred, then she will see
that she sustains relations to them all, that all belong
to her sphere, and that as the conscience of organized
society she should exert a determinative moral influence over its entire life.

Of course there are many questions on which this
conscience of society cannot declare itself, because it is
not as yet sufficiently educated—the churches are not
yet agreed touching these questions; precisely as the
conscience of the individual is silent concerning a given
question so long as he is wholly uneducated with regard to it or while he is in doubt as to the right and
wrong of it; but when these become clear, conscience
makes itself heard. There are many questions on
which the churches differ, and on which, therefore, they
cannot say "You ought;" but there are others on
which they are agreed, and there are many others on
which increasing light will enable them to agree. On
all such questions this social conscience should utter
itself.

This broader conception of the mission of the church,
while it has been held by individuals, has never been
grasped by the church herself. She has deemed the
world a hopeless wreck, and herself commissioned to
save out of it as many as possible, whom she is to land
on the heavenly shore. It has not yet dawned on her
that she is to save the wreck itself. She has sought to
fit men to do God's perfect will in heaven instead of
consciously aiming to hasten the answer to her Lord's
prayer, "Thy will be done *in earth* as it is in heaven."
She does not seem to have perceived that God had the
world in his heart and plan. "God so loved the *world*"[1]
that he gave his Son for its redemption. Christ came
into the world, not to condemn it, "but that the *world*
through him might be saved."[2] "Behold the Lamb of

---

[1] John iii. 16.   [2] Ibid. 17.

God, which taketh away the sin of the *world.*"[1] And the last words of our ascending Lord were: "All authority hath been given unto me in heaven *and on earth.* Go ye, therefore, and make disciples of *all the nations,* . . . teaching them to observe all things whatsoever I commanded you."[2] Paul saw that in the fulness of time all things would be gathered together in Christ, "both which are in heaven *and which are on earth.*"[3] And John saw the redeemed earth in the vision of the New Jerusalem, which, says Canon Fremantle, "is the world under the dominion of Christ. Like the visions of the older prophets, it has its realization, not in a heavenly state beyond this world, but in a progressively righteous state in this world."[4]

If the church had grasped her Lord's idea of the kingdom and recognized her relations to it, her history and the world's history would have been differently written. The narrowness of her conception and of her life has lost to the church much of her influence and sadly limited her usefulness. I have not one pulse of sympathy with the hostile critics who regard the church as a failure. If she has not yet saved society, she has at least kept it from rotting; and her saving work is vast and precious—so vast, indeed, that when we remember how small a fraction of her possible force she has made actual, in how narrow a sphere her influence has been exerted, what inadequate and oftentimes mistaken methods she has employed, there is kindled in us a great hope that when she sees the largeness of her mission, avails herself of latent force and employs the methods demanded by modern conditions, she will mightily hasten the millennium, and become what she ought always to have been, the promoter of all good, the enemy of all evil.

The church ought always to have been the first to recognize and relieve human needs and to right human

---

[1] John i. 29.   [2] Matt. xxviii. 18–20.   [3] Eph. i. 10.
[4] The World as the Subject of Redemption, p. 135.

wrongs. But with a narrow conception of her mission she has sat with folded hands while a thousand organizations have sprung up at her side to do her proper work. No benevolent work or reform inspired by a Christian spirit should ever have been forced to go outside the Christian church for organization. The Young Men': Christian Association, the Woman's Christian Temperance Union, the Charity Organization Societies, the Red Cross, the White Cross, and scores of similar organizations are all doing the proper work of the church. I rejoice greatly in the manifold fruits of their work. I do not see how the dreariest pessimist could acquaint himself with them and not be converted to a good hope for humanity. I rejoice that when these organizations became necessary they appeared; but if the church had fully recognized her relations to society, if she had appreciated the largeness of her mission, they would never have been needed.

All of these organizations draw their life, their inspiration, and most of their members from the church; but their success is not her success, their influence and their honors are not hers, and some of them contribute little or nothing to her upbuilding. There is a law in nature that the tree's fruit shall contain the seed which reproduces the tree. There are a thousand beautiful charities and blessed reforms which are the fruit of Christianity, but which contain no seed for the reproduction and increase of the church because they were not produced by the church.

One or two illustrations where an indefinite number might be given. The Charity Organization Societies, which are doing so much good in our great cities, are an immense advance on the slip-shod, unscientific methods, or rather lack of method, which they are displacing. They are eminently Christian in spirit; they should be avowedly so. Like Peter and John, when the impotent man asks an alms, instead of giving silver or gold, they take him by the hand and set him on his feet, making him capable of earning his own silver and gold;

but unlike the apostles they do not do this "in the name of Jesus Christ of Nazareth." Their admirable philanthropic work ought to be distinctly religious also, and would be more successful if it were; but cannot be, it is said, because Jews and skeptics as well as the churches contribute to their funds. Exactly so; which fact being interpreted means that the churches, *as such*, ought to do this work. They have no right to delegate it to an organization which cannot do it in the name of their Master, thus throwing away an opportunity to influence and regain a large population now notoriously beyond their reach. Our Christianity ought to be thoroughly philanthropic and our philanthropy ought to be thoroughly Christian. These two, which the Master joined together, we ought never to have put asunder.

The rules of a certain railroad forbade hackmen, while waiting for trains, to enter the depot. In storms and severe winter weather considerable suffering resulted. A lady moved by a Christian spirit circulated a subscription to build a suitable shelter; and the hackmen said: "See how kind these good people are. The churches care nothing for us. They have allowed us to stand around in the cold, winter after winter, and have never done a thing." It is quite possible that "these good people" were all church-members, but their Christian act gave the churches of the place no influence over a neglected and alienated class.

The church, as the body of Christ, ought as nearly as possible to embody the Christianity in the world. But Christianity in its spirit and work is much broader than the church to-day. Many movements in behalf of humanity which were the manifest result of the pervasive and regenerating spirit of Christianity have been left by the church to struggle alone, and in some sad cases even against her opposition. As President Bascom remarks: "Reforms of the most imperative character meet with hesitating and wavering support from churches, and sometimes encounter bitter opposition. . . . Most of the social questions of the last hundred years have brought nearly as much discredit as credit to religion." [1]   The abolition of slavery in the United States was undoubtedly due to the influence of Christianity, but it won no honor or gratitude to the church.   Principal Fairbairn said before the London Congregational Union a few years ago: "There is one thing I profoundly feel—the way in which churches, taken as a whole, have allowed the industrial classes to grapple almost unaided with their problems, to fight unhelped their way into their liberties and rights."

If the church is willing to teach by her example that Christianity is divorced from philanthropy and reform and social science and the progress of civilization, or that these are broader than Christianity, she must be content to occupy a little place and never dream of conquering the world for Christ.   But if she aims at universal conquest, she must show a universal interest in human affairs.

We are living in the sociological age of the world, the distinctive problems of which spring from the relations of man to his fellow.   When civilization is brought face to face with an age problem it constitutes a race emergency.   If a religion is to prove itself thoroughly adapted to human nature and destined to be final, it must show itself equal to the great emergencies of the race, and able to meet the peculiar demands of every age.

Here is the most serious question of our times: Is Christianity able to establish right relations between man and man?   The skepticism which is most dangerous to Christianity to-day is not doubt as to the age or authenticity or genuineness of its sacred books or distrust of time-honored doctrines, but *loss of faith in its vitality*.   Is it equal to living issues, can it inform our developing civilization and determine its character, can it reconcile classes and conflicting interests, can it right existing wrongs, can it purify politics, can it command

---

[1] Sociology, p. 173.

the public conscience, can it lay the industrial world under its law of love to one's neighbor, thus putting an end to the unnatural duel between capital and labor, can it fit men for earth as well as heaven ?

It has already been shown that the gospel of Christ was intended to govern human relations and is capable of solving the problems which grow out of them. The question, then, becomes this: Will the church enlarge her conceptions and activities to the wide measure of her· mission and apply the principles of the Gospel to the entire life of each community ? Here is the opportunity of the ages for her to gain a commanding influence over the lives of the multitude and fashion the unfolding civilization of the future.

Notice briefly some of the results which would naturally follow the full acceptance by the church of her comprehensive mission.

1. The church would be inspired with a new and unconquerable courage—the courage which springs from a full assurance of final and complete victory. The Christianity of Christ is to conquer all peoples, sweeten all relationships, sanctify all activities. The New Jerusalem is even now descending from God out of heaven and will yet fill the earth. The time is surely coming when in all the world "there shall be no more sorrow, nor crying, neither shall there be any more pain; for the former things shall have passed away." Wrong and wretchedness have their day that seems so long; they have their day, but have their doom. It was spoken when were uttered those divine words, at once prayer and prophecy, "Thy kingdom come, thy will be done *in earth as* it is in heaven." An assurance so great, a hope so glorious, can never know discouragement. A thousand hard-pressed columns that are wavering to-day would rally with fresh enthusiasm did they but see the sure issue of the battle.

A thousand evils exist only because we have become accustomed to them and imagine that they are inevitable. But whatever is essentially unjust or selfish is anti-Christian, and therefore temporary. It will as surely pass away as Christ and his kingdom shall abide. " If we think things cannot be different from what they are, we but add so much to the dead inertia of the world, which keeps them as they are." [1] Once let the conviction take hold that there is no such thing as necessary and permanent evil, and courage will rise to the attack of every evil, however well intrenched.

2. Should the church accept her commission to prepare the way for the full coming of the Kingdom, she would become the champion of needed reforms.

In almost any community you can find the churches living in the midst of evils and at peace with them. Individual Christians may be in conflict with them, but not often the churches, as churches. They are opposed to evil in the abstract all over the world, but here are concrete evils at their very doors, on which they never lay hands. Take, for instance, that abomination of desolation, the saloon, at enmity with all good and in league with all evil. Only here and there is there a church at war with it. One might attend most churches for years and never hear of the saloon, much less be asked to join a campaign against it or provide a substitute. We call ourselves "soldiers of the cross." *Soldiers* indeed! Whose idea of " service " is to " sit and sing ourselves away to everlasting bliss," while there are vice and crime, moral and physical filth, ignorance and wretchedness, within hand-reach of every one. This apathy on the part of a multitude of good people touching a thousand evils would be impossible if the church had a true conception of her mission.

When a Christian is at peace with any sin in his own life, when he is reconciled to any evil habit, or becomes indifferent to anything in his own character which renders him unlike Christ, he is disloyal to his Master. In like manner, when a citizen of the kingdom of God

---

[1] " Ethical Religion," by Wm. Mackintire Salter, p. 155.

is at peace with any sin of society, becomes reconciled to any evil habits of the community or indifferent to anything inconsistent with the full coming of God's kingdom on the earth, he is disloyal to the kingdom.

Are the saloon, pauperism, and crime consistent with the full coming of that kingdom? Surely not. Then they are in the way of its coming, and it is the business of the church to clear them out of the way. If it is the duty of the church to relieve the poor, has she no duty concerning the causes of poverty? Is it binding on her to seek and to save the vicious, and has she no responsibility concerning those conditions which invariably breed vice? Is it her business to save the drunkard, and yet has she no business with the saloon? The attempt to cure the world's evils by such practice is sheer quackery. If it is the duty of the church to put a stop to certain effects, it is evidently her duty to put an end to the causes which inevitably produce them. There must be no compromise, no truce, but a war of extermination. Wherever there is an evil, it is the business of the church to smite it, and with the "perseverance of the saints" to keep on smiting it even to the death. Every wrong on earth is a divine call to the Christian and to the church to right it. When the church gains this conception of her mission and acts on it, there will be a marvellous mortality among the world's evils.

With this broader vision of her mission the church will soon learn that her reformatory work must be constructive as well as destructive. There is an important principle which is often forgotten by reformers, viz., that of substitution. There is a story of a man out of whom an unclean spirit was cast. The evil spirit returned after a time and found his former home *empty*. "Then goeth he and taketh with him seven other spirits more wicked than himself, and they enter in and dwell there; and the last state of that man is worse than the first." The evil spirit regained possession because the man was *empty*. Good had not been substituted for evil. Human nature as well as nature abhors a vacuum. Much of our reform work is an unsuccessful attempt to create vacuums. The way to empty is to fill. Empty of evil by filling with good. Drive out darkness by admitting light. In our warfare against the saloon and immoral amusements we think the victory won when the evil spirit is cast out; but our victories prove to be only temporary. The place which had been full of all filthiness may be "swept" never so clean, and "garnished" never so beautifully; but if left *empty*, it is soon repossessed, with an added contingent of devils.

Strong drink is only one of the attractions of the saloon. There is warm comfort in winter and cool comfort in summer, a newspaper, a bright light, sociability, and oftentimes attractive music. Why not in all these outbid the saloon? Surely, when the question is, Who will offer most for least? in such competition love of fellow-men can outbid the love of self.

3. This leads us to institutional methods of church work, or to what some prefer to call the institutional church, which is a natural outgrowth of a larger conception of the mission of the church.

The church that adopts these methods recognizes its duty to the whole man. It aims to cultivate body and mind as well as heart. The need of these methods is naturally felt by "down-town" churches, which are surrounded by people whose homes have few attractions; to whom, therefore, saloons and places of amusement appeal strongly. In order to compete successfully with these demoralizing attractions, the church emphasizes its social features and keeps its doors open seven days and nights in the week.

The gymnasium, the reading-room, industrial training, the cooking-school, popular lectures, concerts, recreation-rooms, bath-rooms, games, and clubs are prominent features, though not all of these necessarily are employed by the same church. These churches are earnestly evangelistic in spirit, preaching a simple gospel, and pressing men to an immediate decision. The people are not only attracted to the church, but are also frequently visited in their homes.

What of the success of these methods? They seem in every instance to win the people, especially the young men and boys. Dr. Scudder reports that twelve hundred patronize the gymnasium weekly, that the weekly visits to the recreation-rooms run from fifteen hundred to two thousand. He says: " No need of talking about reaching the masses any longer. . . . We have more masses than we know what to do with. When we opened our Boys' Club we had five hundred and seventy applications in less than a week and then we quit giving out any more, for fear of a Johnstown flood of juvenile humanity. We could not accommodate all who want to come, if we had four times the room." [1]

But are those who are attracted by the educational and social advantages of the institutional church brought into its membership? Let the facts answer. The Jersey City Tabernacle has more than doubled its membership in a few years. The Berkeley Temple, Boston, had 305 resident members Jan. 1, 1888, and in three years has received 313 to its membership. The Fourth Congregational Church of Hartford had 337 resident members Jan. 1, 1887, and on Jan. 1, 1892, its membership was 675. In 1882 its Sunday-school numbered 305, and its Sunday-evening congregations less than 100. In 1892 the Sunday-school had over 900 members and the evening congregations nearly 800. Dr. Scudder says: " Institutional work has tremendously increased the congregation. On Sunday evenings we have from 1000 to 1200, and as many as 300 of this number are young men. It has increased the young men's Bible classes, has flooded the Junior Endeavor Society, increased the church membership, and made the weekly prayer-meeting larger than ever in the history of the church." [2]

[1] " The Institutional Church," by Rev. C. S. Mills, in *The Bibliotheca Sacra*, July, 1892.　　[2] Ibid.

When we remember that this success has been won
in localities where churches working along the old lines
have become enfeebled and have died or moved away,
we can better appreciate its significance.

In new work like this, some mistakes will be made of
course. Not all experiments will prove successful, but
the success already achieved certainly indicates that an
important step has been taken in the right direction.

Its wisdom is confirmed by the experience of the
Young Men's Christian Association, whose surprising
success came only after it enlarged its aims and recognized the fact that young men have bodies and minds
as well as souls.

At this point an objection is interposed. Some will
fear that this is turning the churches aside from their
proper spiritual work to caring for bodily and temporal
things.

If the result were to subordinate the spiritual to the
physical, if it practically led to the belief that religion
consists in the service of man and in perfecting the life
that now is, this extreme would be a worse error than
the opposite. While Christ had much more to say concerning this life than the next, he left no room for mis-
apprehension as to their relative importance. "Be not
afraid of them that kill the body, and after that have
no more that they can do. But I will forewarn you
whom ye shall fear: Fear him, which after he hath
killed hath power to cast into hell; yea, I say unto you,
Fear him." [1] Christ taught with entire distinctness that
the spiritual is more important than the physical, but
he did not, therefore, fall into the narrow-minded error
of depreciating the body. He was mindful of bodily
needs and tenderly compassionate of bodily sufferings;
and surely his care for men's bodies gave him no less
influence over men's souls. So far as the Great Teacher
"turned aside" from preaching the Gospel in order to
give sight to the blind, health to the sick, and food to

---

[1] Luke xii. 4, 5.

the hungry, it is quite safe for the church to follow his example. Had his *words* of love any less meaning because of his *works* of love? If the church *lived* the Gospel as well as she *preaches* it, the multitude would have less doubt of the love which she professes. "If the church has become indifferent to the material and intellectual interests of mankind, it has forgotten both the teaching and the example of Christ, it has misapprehended the Christian conception of human nature, it has broken with its own best traditions." [1]

The more nearly normal and Christ-like the life of the church is, the more truly spiritual will it be. Dr. Scudder testifies that institutional work has increased the spiritual tone of his church decidedly. All fear for the spirituality of the church in case she takes an active interest in things temporal is of a piece with the old-fashioned suspicion of a full, vigorous, physical life on the ground that it was unfriendly to piety. But this morbid, worm-ripe piety, once in favor, has pretty much passed out of fashion for the individual, and it is to be devoutly hoped that for the church it will soon follow.

4. The acceptance by the church of this larger conception of her mission would have a powerful influence to carry religion into ordinary, every-day life, and thus by spiritualizing the "secular" afford a further answer to the preceding objection.

It is very difficult to hoe potatoes or build a steam-engine to the glory of God when the occupation of the farmer and that of the machinist are deemed "secular," are not supposed to have any spiritual relations. But when it is seen that the laws of the material world are laws of the kingdom of God, and that on them spiritual results are ultimately conditioned; when it is seen that every act of obedience to the laws which God has established, whether pertaining to mind or matter, that every stroke of honest and well-directed work is laying a stone

---

[1] Schmidt's Social Results of Early Christianity, p. xxiii.

in the upbuilding of the glorious kingdom which shall
one day fill the earth, then it becomes possible, whether
we eat or drink or whatsoever we do, to do all to the
glory of God. In George Herbert's noble words:

> " A servant with this clause
> Makes drudgery divine;
> Who sweeps a room, as for thy laws,
> Makes that and the action fine."

When every act is thus consecrated, the farmer, the
mechanic, becomes a priest unto God, who makes his
entire life an acceptable sacrifice. And religion is seen to
consist not in certain outward acts and observances, commonly called sacred, but in the purpose and motive of
life which may be carried alike into worship and work
and play. True religion is thus seen to be, not something
fractional and incidental, not here and there a little
island of goodness and blessedness in the great sea of
worldly experiences, but rather the salt which pene-
trates every drop of the ocean, is in every wave and
ripple and fleck of foam; sweeping along with the great
gulf stream, running with every tide, found in every
bay and sound and inlet and arm of the sea, filling the
length and breadth and height and depth of the whole,
and cleansing, saving it all. From the ocean's fulness
you cannot dip a single cup of water which is not per-
meated with its salt. And so there ought to be no hour
or moment of life, no great wave of purpose or ripple of
mirth, no deep or shallow experiences of life, no undis-
covered inlet of character, which the salt of a Christian
aim and motive does not penetrate—an ever-present
and all-potent influence.

5. Another result, closely related to the foregoing,
which would naturally follow an adequate conception of
her mission on the part of the church, is a clearer, fuller
consciousness of God. This is one of the supreme needs
of the race.

Animal life is higher than vegetable because it is endowed with consciousness; that is, it is capable of
pleasure and pain. Man is higher than the brute be-

cause he is endowed with *self*-consciousness, without which he would be incapable of a conscience and of moral action. Self-consciousness makes him capable of self-fellowship, capable of conscious harmony or discord with himself, which is a nobler pleasure and a greater pain than any of which the brute is capable. Now the next great upward step is *God*-consciousness. This means a new and higher fellowship, a new motive, new strength, new inspiration, new joy; in short, "a new creature" to whom "all things are become new. And all things are of God." [1] Every Christian has this consciousness of God at times and in measure, and the clearer, stronger, and more constant it is, the more spiritual and Christ-like are his character and life. In Christ this *God*-consciousness was perfect. He could say, "I and my Father are *one*." [2] Moses possessed it in an eminent degree, and "endured *as seeing him who is invisible.*" [3]

To most men God is unreal, and even to most Christians he is far off. The old and false distinction between the sacred and the secular has served to remove him from nature and from the common activities of life, so that he has become to most men what Carlyle calls "an absentee God," manifesting himself only by portent or prodigy. We need to see him in the silent and gradual processes of nature, present in all her beauty, potent in all her life, revealed in all her laws; and hence entering into all our life and activities.

If God makes even the "wrath of men to praise him," all human activities may be said to form a mighty hallelujah chorus. But multitudes join in this praise as did the morning stars when they "sang together," without intention or desert. When men generally have risen to a consciousness of God, the discoveries of science, legislation, business, manufactures, agriculture, art—all human activities will enter into the harmony of the divine plans for perfecting the race,

---

[1] 2 Cor. v. 17, 18.   [2] John x. 30.   Heb. xi. 27.

not because they are *overruled* by infinite wisdom, but because men consciously and intelligently co-labor with God to this glorious end.

6. If the church would accept her full commission, she would soon gain the masses. Let the church return to the Christianity of Christ, and the multitude would soon return to her. Said a workingman before the Committee on Labor of the United States Senate: "Workingmen do not attend the church, not because they are irreligious or are opposed to Christianity, but because the churches have ceased to represent to us the teachings of Christianity."

Charles Kingsley somewhere declares that "If the Christian church were what she ought to be and could be, for a single day, the world would be converted before nightfall." This rightly fixes responsibility for the world's unsaved condition on the church. It is her fault that she has lost her hold on the multitude. She has taught that their occupations were "secular;" and the righting of their wrongs, the relieving of their want, the healing of their sicknesses, she has for the most part turned over to other organizations. They have very naturally gained the impression that she is not concerned with what they consider real life, that her province is the spiritual and the future, which do not appeal strongly to men whose wants are mostly physical and altogether present.

Christianity is misunderstood because it is misrepresented. If we could make the world believe that we are interested in reconciling capital and labor, not simply as economists, but *as Christians;* that we are interested in the purification of politics, not simply as good citizens, but *as Christians;* that we are interested in tenement-house reform, not simply as philanthropists, but *as Christians;* that we are interested in drainage and ventilation and water-supply, not simply as sanitarists, but *as Christians;* that we are interested in commerce, and manufactures, and agriculture, and science, and art because their progress helps to prepare the way for the full coming of the Kingdom; that *because we are Christians* we are interested in men's physical and intellectual soundness as well as spiritual, —would not the world soon gain a very different and much more truthful idea of the Christianity of Christ? And if the church preached and lived such a Christianity, would she not speedily gain a saving influence over the multitude?

7. Finally, the church would not only win the many, who for the most part are living on a physical plane with low ideals, but also the few with high ideals who have lost confidence in the church because she is doing so little for social regeneration.

There are advocates of ethical religion and of theosophy who have a higher ideal of social righteousness than the church, who believe that Christianity can do nothing more for civilization, for humanity, because it has failed to create such an ideal. They do not recognize the fact that for all that is noble in their own ideal they are indebted to Christ's doctrine of the kingdom of God on earth, and that it is an apprehension of a measure of his teaching which gives to these movements whatever vitality they possess, while it is the failure of the church to apprehend the teaching of her Lord which gives to them their opportunity. Such organizations are springing up because the church has failed to grasp Christ's ideal and to apply his teaching to social relations.

The world in this sociological age needs a new social ideal to direct the progress of civilization. Let the church fully accept her mission and she will furnish this needed ideal, viz., her Master's conception of the kingdom of God come upon earth.

CHAPTER XII.

THE NECESSITY OF NEW METHODS.

THE triumphs of inventive genius which have wrought such miracles in the mechanical world are all triumphs of method. No man has ever created a principle or an ounce of power. New inventions are only new applications of old principles or new methods of applying power already existing. Yet method has made all the difference between ox-cart and railroad civilization.

It is a great mistake in Christian work to expect results from *mere* methods. They are nothing if spiritual power is lacking; as well expect results from the water-wheel when the stream has run dry. The prophet Ezekiel saw, in his vision, wheels within wheels, but he saw also that "the spirit of the living creature was in them." Church machinery in which there is no *living spirit* is worse than useless.

But, on the other hand, it is perhaps as great a mistake to underrate, as to overrate, the importance of methods. While method is no substitute for motive, and machinery cannot create power nor organization life, yet life manifests itself by organization, power is applied by machinery, and motive miscarries if method is wrong.

This has been an age of improvement in methods; in education, in medicine, in all branches of science, in manufactures, in commerce, in agriculture, in war, in business, in everything except church work, in which our methods remain substantially what they were many generations ago. There are some churches which are

252

adapting methods to their changed conditions, but as yet such churches are rare.

Surely, methods of church work have not remained unchanged because they were incapable of improvement. Judge them by their results. Look at the power in the church and then consider how efficiently, or inefficiently, it has been applied by the established methods to the work to be done. I pick up a church year-book at random, and turning a half-dozen leaves, find a church of 452 members, which in a year's time received six on confession of faith; another with 445 members which received four. Another with 624 members received two; another with 410 members received one. Such churches, where there is less than one addition on confession to a hundred members, are not representative, but they are very common. During the year 1891, in a large and influential denomination it took, on the average, fourteen church members to win a single convert from the world; in another it took seventeen, and in another twenty-two. These three denominations aggregate four and a half millions of members, and striking the average of all, it took about twenty (19.8) of these Christians twelve months to make one convert![1]

Why should there not be as great possibilities in spiritual as in natural husbandry? Christ used the one to illustrate the other, and talked of thirty and sixty and a hundred fold in a single year—not *per cent*, but *fold*. Thirty-fold (as if that were the lowest natural increase to be expected) means 3000 per cent. The increase of these three denominations on confession of faith (their only accessions to the Kingdom) is about 5 per cent, or *one twentieth part of one-fold!* That is, if the increase had been six hundred times greater than it was, it would then have reached only the lowest standard named by Christ. Is the one-twentieth part of

---

[1] The year-books of other leading denominations do not give data from which to make the computation. There is no reason to think the three referred to are exceptional.

one-fold normal? If a farmer sowed twenty bushels of wheat and harvested only twenty-one, would he not call his crop a failure?

We congratulate ourselves yearly on the hundreds of thousands added to the churches, but if we were not wonted to these small returns we should hide our heads in very shame at their meagreness. The angels of God rejoice over one repenting sinner, and so do we; but when we look on the mighty unchurched multitude we must stay our rejoicing.

If the church had set her heart on saving the race she would long since have become dissatisfied with her accustomed methods, for long since it became apparent that those who are not Christians are on the increase in the world. The Rev. James Johnston, secretary of the World's Missionary Conference in London in 1888, says[1]: "The heathen and Mohammedan population of the world is more by 200,000,000 than it was a hundred years ago; while the converts and their families do not amount to 3,000,000." That is, "the increase of the heathen is, numerically, *more than seventy times* greater than that of the converts during the century of missions." Of our own population at the beginning of the century there were less than 5,000,000 who were not members of some Protestant church; in 1890 there were nearly ten times that number. And as we have seen, extended investigations indicate that one half of the families in the land, or more than 30,000,000 of our population, are quite estranged from all churches.

It appears, therefore, that although the *relative* increase of the churches is greater than that of the entire population, the *actual* increase of population is greater than that of the churches.

We have lost our hold on the masses, and our failure to purge the wickedness and relieve the wretchedness of city slums has become conspicuous. Arnold White, after much study of the social conditions of London,

---

[1] A Century of Protestant Missions, p. 9.

writes[1]: "The present system of the churches, after a course of evangelical teaching extending over one hundred and fifty years, has failed beyond hope of redemption."

It would seem to be sufficiently clear that our methods have been sadly deficient. But even if they had been adequate in the past, changed conditions would now require their readjustment or the substitution of new ones. The problem of the country has arisen, while that of the city has become far more complicated. Immigration has brought us a babel of tongues and a medley of races and religions. Not only has population become more heterogeneous, but classes have grown more distinct. Unbelief has been popularized. The saloon has become an organized institution of immense wealth and tremendous power. The laboring classes have become discontented, and generally indifferent or positively hostile to the church. To absent one's self from church was once disreputable, and even a crime punished by the state; now, few attend except church members and their families. This fact indicates that the growth of the churches in the future will be for the most part confined to the natural increase of Christian families unless some new and effective methods are adopted to bring the Gospel to bear on many now beyond its reach. Past methods will not sustain the past rate of growth, because we have not now in our congregations the material to work on which we once had. The margin of unconverted church attendants had already become so small some years ago that the churches made no such gain on the population between 1880 and 1890 as between 1870 and 1880. During the earlier period, 1870–1880, they gained more than 3 per cent over the population; but during the latter, less than 1½—and this notwithstanding the fact that the rate of increase in population was decidedly less during the latter decade than during the former.

---

[1] The Problems of a Great City, p. 24 (London, 1886).

These changes in the composition of the population and in the ideas and habits of the people constitute a change of conditions which demands a thorough revision of our methods of church work. But far more than all these, a profound change is taking place in civilization; one of the great movements of the ages is distinctly discernible; we have entered on the sociological period of the world, which will witness another evolution of society in the progress of the race toward its high destiny.

Evidence that Christianity is the absolute and final religion is found in its power of adaptation by which it has adjusted its methods and outward forms to changed conditions. Christianity has already had three great transitional periods, and is now passing through a fourth.

During the apostolic age men preached and accepted the simple facts of the Gospel without philosophizing on them. The apostolic fathers were less concerned with theology than with the immediate demands of practical life. But when the rapid spread of Christianity alarmed heathenism and led to acute attacks like those of Celsus, it became necessary to define and defend Christian doctrine. Then Christianity became dogmatic and apologetic. The triumph of Christianity under the empire and the union of church and state marked another transition. The church then entered on a long period of ecclesiasticism and centralization which were doubtless necessary to the preservation of civilization when the empire went to pieces before the inrushing barbarians. Again, when a powerful ecclesiasticism had ceased to protect and foster civilization and served rather to paralyze it by restricting the development of the individual, then came the Reformation of the sixteenth century, which constituted the third great transition. The Reformation was at the same time a return and an advance—a return to Scriptural truth and an advance in the application of doctrine to *personal experience.*

In the new era Christianity will present a fourth new phase, the result of another adaptation to changed conditions; and this new phase, like the great Reformation to which it is complemental, will be both a return and an advance—a return to Christ's teaching concerning man's relations to his fellow-men, and an advance in the application of Christianity to the *organized life of society*.

When the church accepts the second fundamental law of Christ, not as a beautiful and impracticable ideal, but as the practical law of social life, which he evidently intended, her conception of her mission will be vastly enlarged. Instead of aiming only at the salvation of the individual, she will also aim consciously and directly at the regeneration of society. With this larger comprehension and this new aim she will find her old methods wholly inadequate.

Some city churches, as they have gained a larger conception of the meaning of Christianity and of their mission, have adopted new methods, as seen in the so-called institutional churches. But these churches find a large amount of money a prerequisite for their work. The parish house with its appliances costs tens of thousands of dollars. Evidently few churches can command the necessary means for such methods. And it is equally evident that the methods which àre to meet the needs of the new era must be practicable for the *ordinary* church. . For it must be remembered that most of the world's work, in every walk of life, is done by ordinary people. Unless the ordinary preacher and the ordinary church can win success under ordinary conditions, Christianity can never conquer the world. Now the average Protestant church[1] in this country has only about a hundred members; and most churches of that size have to struggle to meet ordinary current expenses. The methods of the institutional church, therefore, however valuable they may be, are quite beyond the ordinary church.

---

[1] The average membership of over 80,000 churches is found to be 104.

It is evident that methods which are to prove successful must be adapted to general use, must overcome the
obstacles in the way of reaching the masses, and must
enable the church to accomplish her social mission.
Methods capable of meeting these requirements can be
developed by the application of two fundamental principles, viz., (1) *the proper recognition and use of personality* and (2) *organization*. These two principles spring
from man's constitution as an individual personally
accountable to God, and as a social being sustaining
relations to his fellow-men. Christ recognized these
two principles when he laid down his two fundamental
laws, and, as we have seen, these are the two principles
which have underlain and governed the development
of civilization. These two principles the church has
neglected, and this is the reason that of the mighty
power which she certainly possesses nine tenths, or
more likely nineteen twentieths, lie latent and useless.

1. We must properly recognize and use personality.

The local church, as a body, feels a measure of responsibility for the evangelization of the community,
but there is little sense of *individualized* responsibility.
The average church hires the minister to love men and
save them in its stead; and the average church member
is under the impression that all personal Christian service may be commuted for a money consideration. He
says not, "Here am I, Lord; send me," but "Here is
my check; send some one else" (and he doesn't *always*
remember the check). He forgets the parable of the
Good Samaritan and its lesson. It follows immediately
the enunciation of the two great laws, and was uttered
in answer to the question, "Who is my neighbor?" It
may fairly be understood to indicate what Christ meant
by loving one's neighbor as one's self. The good
Samaritan not only had compassion on the wounded
man, but "went to him, and bound up his wounds,
pouring in oil and wine, and set him on his own beast,
and brought him to an inn, and took care of him." He
seems to have watched with him all night, for he did not

leave until the morrow. He paid the landlord to give the sufferer further care, but it was *only after he had himself rendered all the personal service in his power.*

The modern Good Samaritan feels for the wounded wayfarer, but he cannot possibly stop because he has a business engagement down town, and so satisfies his conscience when he arrives at his office by sending a check to the Society for the Relief of Travellers robbed on the way from Jerusalem down to Jericho.

Probably not one out of ten professing Christians accepts a personal responsibility for certain ones and makes them the objects of special prayer and effort. A leading business man of one of our large cities remarked that he had not been inside a church for seventeen years, and that during that time no Christian had addressed him personally on the subject of religion, although thousands of them had met him in his store and in social life. This is not at all exceptional. In the popular conception personal Christian work is not a necessary part of Christian living. The time ought to come, and I believe is coming, when it will be deemed as essential to a Christian life as is common honesty.

Individualism has directed its energies chiefly to the establishment of rights; it is high time to emphasize duties, for every right is a hemisphere whose complement is a corresponding duty. The church should adopt methods which cultivate a sense of personal obligation and serve to individualize responsibility.

Most pastors do not know how to set their church members ·to work. Many members are willing, but they are like the laborers who stood all the day idle in the vineyard, not because they were lazy, but because no man had hired them. The multitude lack initiative. It is as true in Christian work as in business, manufactures, or war, that the few must plan and direct while the many are directed. And in Christian work, as in war or manufactures, each one of the many should have a specific place and a recognized duty. "To every man his work."

Again, the church must not only use the power of personality in her membership, she must recognize the personality of those she would help. We talk much of saving the masses; they can be saved, not as masses, but only as individuals. In this day of labor-saving machinery, by which each man's effectiveness is multiplied many-fold and immense results are produced in a few minutes, we look about for some corresponding methods in the moral world, some way of elevating men wholesale; but character must still be made by hand.

If we want to save the criminal class, we must re-member that it is composed of individual criminals, each having his own vicious habits to be reformed, each having his own corrupted character to be re-made or rather re-born. In like manner, the pauper class, being composed of individuals and families, can be elevated only as individuals and families; which cannot be done without a vast expenditure of patient, personal effort, wisely directed. Laws may alleviate or greatly aggravate the disease, but only personal treatment can cure.

Here is the perplexing problem of municipal govern-ment. If we wish to enforce law or reform abuses or effect improvements, everything depends on public opinion. And when we sigh for an enlightened public opinion and an educated public conscience, we are re-minded that it is individual opinion which is the unit of public opinion. Thus the problem of the city is, in its last analysis, the problem of the individual.

The saloon, which as a peril may boast a base pre-eminence, draws its power from the lust of gain on one side of the counter and the lust of appetite on the other —the individual again.

Thus, all of our great moral problems and most others, when reduced to their lowest terms, are found to be per-sonal—problems of the individual.

These problems are in most instances to be studied and solved *in the home*, or what passes for home, be-

cause that is where most people are born and live.
There are the most determinative influences of life;
there are characteristics, temperament, disposition, tendencies, instincts, and often appetites born; there is the
atmosphere, pure or poisonous, in which they grow;
there as nowhere else is felt the force of example and
precept when the young life is most impressible; and
there in nearly every instance are character and habits
formed.

The church and the school, the public library and
reading-room, the gymnasium and the public bath,
may each do much for the home, but they all cannot
solve its problem; that must be solved in the home
itself. And it will be found that many other problems must be solved there too, for all our social
problems have what has been aptly termed a "home
end." There is no more effective place to fight the
saloon than in the home; for the root of the saloon
runs back into it. The wretchedness of the home
causes the saloon to flourish, and the saloon aggravates
that wretchedness. Doubtless it will be impossible to
sink the saloon, in the great cities, until the homes have
been elevated. In all reforms there is occasion for
agitation, and in some for legislation; but all attempts
to elevate the masses, which fail to find the home, are
more or less superficial. A physician who is said to
have made fifty thousand visits among New York tenements remarked: " I think if I were going to uplift the
masses I should first uplift the landlords. I would
make it possible for each human being that lives in the
slums to have a home." We cannot elevate any class
until we have elevated the homes of that class.

If any one asks how the church is to reach the individual and influence the home, we need not go far
afield for the answer. The individual must of course be
found where he is, viz., at his home or at his place of
business, and the influence which is to elevate the home
must be exerted in the home. The answer, then, to the
question is, *house-to-house visitation.* Not a church

census for facts—that is good so far as it goes, but is
worthless unless followed up; not simply an invitation
to church—you might as well expect to transform an
island of cannibals into exemplary Christian citizens
by issuing to them a polite and neatly printed card
inviting them to accept Christian civilization as to
expect to transform a slum by simply inviting its
people to church. The visits must be for actual acquaintance; they must establish friendly and helpful
relations. The visitor must win confidence before he
can acquire influence; and when influence has been
gained it must be used to bless the family in every
possible way.

Octavia Hill[1] urges the importance of knowing the
family life of the classes we wish to help in their own
homes. While recognizing the value of work for boys
or girls or men in clubs, groups of people of one kind
or another, she observes that her workers almost without exception prefer work with families in their homes
to any other sphere whatever. She urges "some system of organized visiting in the homes, by those imbued
with thoughts as to wiser principles of work, and who
should arrange to *do many things for a few families in
a limited area*, rather than one thing for scattered individuals in a larger area."

Such work cannot be done to any considerable extent
by pastors; it is too vast for their numbers. The
church membership must undertake it, and helpful
personal relations must be established between them
and the non-church-goers. This will be the late acceptance on the part of the church of methods adopted a
generation ago by business men. Once the wholesale
houses, manufacturers, and railways waited for buyers
and shippers to find them, just as the churches are now
waiting (though less eagerly, I fear) for non-church-
goers to come to them. But a few men, sent out to
solicit orders, so quickly and manifestly demonstrated

---

[1] *The Nineteenth Century* for August, 1891.

the superior effectiveness of *going* to " disciple " men, that the methods of business were speedily revolutionized.

This change of method was the natural outgrowth of our headlong life. The more preoccupied men become, the more difficult is it to divert thought from their eager pursuits and gain attention to anything else; hence the great increase of personal solicitation in all kinds of business which admit of it.

The church still preserves the waiting attitude. She unlocks the door, rings the bell, posts " Strangers Welcome " in a conspicuous place, and seems to think her duty to the non-church-going public done. Her Example came " to *seek* and to save." The church says to the world, " Come and be discipled." The Master said to the church, " *Go* and disciple."

Personal effort has always been the most effective form of Christian work, but it is more important in this age of intense living than ever before; and it is the only way to disciple the millions who never come within reach of the pulpit.

But this work cannot be successfully done haphazard. If the churches accept the first principle, recognize the personality of the classes they would benefit and use the personality of their membership, they will find themselves forced to make use of the second principle, viz.,

2. *Organization.* In the cemetery of Trinity Church, New York, there are more bodies than there are men jostling each other on the adjoining walks of Broadway. But there is no jostling on the silent side of the fence; no friction there; no need that one recognize the existence of the other. Suppose, however, that on the busy street men forget for one moment that there are others about them; let each teamster drive as if he alone had the right of way, let each footpassenger ignore the existence of every other, and in one instant there would be a dozen collisions, with loss of temper, loss of time, loss of energy.

It is not too much to say (if the reader will pardon the bull) that many churches are living together in peace *because they are dead.* Stir them with a new purpose, give to them the urgency of a new life, let them undertake " to *seek* and to save," to " *go* and disciple," let them accept and use the principle of personality, and if they fail to recognize the existence of each other, if they neglect to come to a mutual understanding and refuse to enter into co-operation, there will surely be collision and confusion, a loss of time, a waste of power.

The lack of such understanding and co-operation in the past has opened the way to competition between local churches and denominations, which has resulted in a congestion of churches among those populations which need them least and a dearth of churches among those which need them most. If all the churches in the United States belonged to one denomination, does any one suppose there would be such a distribution of forces as now exists—three or four feeble and dying churches in a little village of only four or five hundred inhabitants, and in large city populations only one church, and perhaps none at all, for twenty or thirty thousand people or even more? A few years ago in a Colorado town containing about five hundred souls there were three Presbyterian churches, a Northern Presbyterian, a Reformed Presbyterian, and a United Presbyterian church, each struggling for life, each a rival of the others, and all aided by home-missionary societies, while many a frontier settlement was at the same time as churchless and as Godless as a heathen village in Central Africa. Is there not need of mutual understanding and intelligent co-operation among denominations in order to prevent a worse than useless waste of men and means? So great is the task of Christianizing America, so great are the problems of country and city, so great are the perils which threaten our future, that such organization and co-operation as may be necessary to the best economy of power and of all resources have become imperative.

It has been shown in a previous chapter that one of the most marked tendencies of the times is toward organization, combination, co-operation; illustrations of which are afforded in the consolidation of petty states and principalities into empires, the organization of immense standing armies, the growth of powerful corporations, the formation of new political parties, the rise of numerous trusts, the unprecedented growth of cities. A tendency so universal, and which finds such various expression, cannot be accidental or incidental. It is the result of definite causes, and will continue while they remain operative. Organization and co-operation multiply effectiveness many-fold; hence this powerful tendency toward them as soon as rapid transit and ease of communication—steam and electricity—made them possible. The great forces of modern times are those which as *organized* forces have taken advantage of this mighty "tide in the affairs of men," and the church must lay hold of this same power if she would in the future, as in the past, give direction to the development of society. Without it she cannot accomplish her social mission. If she is to take seriously the second law of Christ and accept her full commission to establish the Kingdom, she must apply both of the principles, pointed out above, in order to touch and influence the entire life of the community, physical, industrial, intellectual, social, moral, and spiritual.

These two principles are so fundamental and their full acceptance and use by the churches are so important that each will be made the subject of a subsequent chapter. It remains in this immediate connection only to give a few illustrations of their application.

Christ, even with his miraculous powers, did not attempt to feed the multitude without system and order. He had them seated by companies, "in ranks, l y hundreds and by fifties." The disciples divided the people among themselves, and thus by personal ministration and co-operation under the Master's direction every man, woman, and child was reached and fed and filled.

In our great cities are multitudes, many times five thousand, who spiritually are starving in a desert place. We say to them, "If you want the bread of life, come to the churches and get it"—albeit our churches would not hold the half of them if they came. In effect we say, "Send them away," that is, let them shift for themselves. But Christ's command is, "Give *ye* them to eat." One reason we fail is because we disregard Christ's method, which is as good for the nineteenth century as for the first. Is not his command laid upon us to systematize our work, to divide the multitude into companies, and let Christ's disciples reach them, every one, by co-operation in personal ministrations ?

A modern application of these two principles was only less remarkable in its results than the feeding of the five thousand. At the close of the late war, in 1865, an organization was formed in New York City to aid disabled soldiers, and the widows and orphans of men who had fallen in the struggle. Its membership was limited to twenty-five women, who held a weekly meeting and called weekly on the families they tried to benefit. Their efforts were soon enlisted in behalf of some three hundred soldiers' families, which were divided among the visitors for personal study and endeavor. Soldiers' widows and orphans were found living in garrets and cellars, oftentimes sick and utterly destitute. Medical aid was secured when needed. Situations were found for daughters, widows, or wives. Sometimes a crippled soldier was started in business in a small way. Many pensions were secured. Mothers were taught how to expend their money to the best advantage, how to clothe and care for their children. Girls were taught to sew. Children were assisted to an education. Families were given higher conceptions of the meaning and possibilities of life, and inspired with hope and a worthy ambition. Thus in many ways these families were helped up above the need of help. A few who proved themselves wholly unworthy were dropped, but the great majority were made self-dependent, and some of these families have acquired wealth. Thus in a quarter of a century many hundreds of soldiers' families were rescued from poverty and wretchedness by the personal efforts and self-giving of twenty-five co-operating women. And if such a work is possible to so few, what is impossible to the reserve forces in our churches, when brought to accept these two cardinal principles of personal contact and co-operation? Both are alike necessary. Without the strength, the helpful suggestions, the contagion of enthusiasm which come from co-operation, the courage of these women would soon have failed and their personal work have been abandoned; and without that personal life-giving touch, their co-operation would have amounted to nothing.

Permit one more illustration of the application of these principles—this on a large scale, with correspondingly large results.

The growth of the Salvation Army is so phenomenal as to demand explanation. "It began," says Canon Farrar,[1] "in the labors of a single friendless Dissenting minister, without name, without fame, without rank, without influence, without eloquence; a man poor and penniless, in weak health, burdened with delicate children, and disowned by his own connection: it now numbers multitudes of earnest evangelists. It began in an East End rookery, and in less than twenty years it has gone 'from New Zealand right round to San Francisco, and from Cape Town to Nordköping.' It has shelters, refuges, penitentiaries, food depots, sisterhoods and brotherhoods, already established in the slums. It has elevated thousands of degraded lives. It has given hope and help to myriads of hopeless and helpless outcasts." The official statistics of the Army, under date of October 1, 1891, show 10,795 officers, who give all their time to the work, laboring in thirty-eight countries and colonies, and using thirty-four languages;

---

[1] *Harper's Magazine*, May, 1891.

4595 societies (corps and posts); 2,098,631 meetings held
annually; 2,747,576 homes annually visited; "War
Crys," etc., circulated in one year 43,682,596. The Army
pays over $1,000,000 rental annually. It owns almost
$4,000,000 of property, and has an annual income of
$3,645,000.[1] Its meetings, which are held in the open air
and in 4000 halls, are attended every week by millions,
while something like a quarter of a million of hopeful
conversions have been reported. And it should be remembered that this amazing success, which would be
phenomenal in any class of society, has been had among
those whom the churches have conspicuously failed to
reach. Surely the churches ought to be able to learn
something from the Salvation Army. Accounting for
General Booth's success, Canon Farrar says: "The
reasons are manifold, but the two chief reasons are:
first, that he recognized a tremendous need; and next,
that instead of acquiescing in impotence, as most men
do, he determined to grapple with that need by new
and unconventional methods." [2]

Now, the most essential of General Booth's methods,
or rather the two fundamental principles underlying
them, are aggressive personal effort and organization.
Speaking of the processes by which this great Army
has been made, he says [3]: "The foundation of all the
Army's success, looked at apart from its divine source
of strength, is its continued direct attack upon those
whom it seeks to bring under the influence of the
Gospel. The Salvation Army officer, instead of standing upon some dignified pedestal, to describe the fallen
condition of his fellow-men, in the hope that, though far
from him, they may thus, by some mysterious process,
come to a better life, goes down into the street, and
from door to door, and from room to room, lays his
hands on those who are spiritually sick, and leads them

---

[1] F. P. Noble, *The Missionary Review*, March, 1892.
[2] *Harper's Magazine*, May, 1891.
[3] In Darkest England, Appendix, p. vi.

to the Almighty Healer." The Army thus makes nearly 3,000,000 visits from house to house in a single year.

The other principle, that of organization, is no less essential or obvious. The organization of the Salvation Army would seem to be as complete and effective as that of the British Army. Indeed, Lord Wolseley has declared General Booth to be the greatest organizing genius of these twenty-five years.

The human instrumentalities of this astonishing success are several. Every rescued man is trained to join in the work of rescue, which ought to characterize the church always and everywhere in simple obedience to the command, "Let him that heareth say, 'Come.'" The Army gives expression to the spirit of Christian brotherhood, which the church ought to do far more fully than it does. It utilizes the ministrations of women, which is equally the privilege and wisdom of the church. It appeals to self-sacrifice, which when the church fails to do, it misses the spirit and teaching of its Master. It arouses an enthusiasm for humanity, which makes service glad and persistent; and, as we have seen, it recognizes personality and lays hold of the strength and effectiveness of organization.

The Salvation Army has no patent on these principles or instrumentalities; they are equally available to the church. I am not urging that the church adopt any of the fanciful methods of the Army, but that she recognize and accept the principles which underlie the success of this great movement, whose application would necessitate the methods advocated above. If these principles are generally adopted by the churches, a new movement may be expected to follow, which would be as much broader than that of the Army as the application of these principles would be broader. The Army was intended to reach the lowest classes only: this movement would reach all classes. The Army preaches the Gospel to the poor: by the methods advocated, not only the wretched poor but also the poor rich, the most neglected class in the community, would have the

Gospel preached to them. The work of the Army is remedial: this movement would prove to be both remedial and preventive; for, with the new social ideal afforded by the kingdom of Christ, with the fixed determination of the church to destroy the evils of society, with the strength and efficiency which would follow the organization and general co-operation of the churches, their contact with the entire life of the community, through personal touch, would prove to be *a method of developing methods* by which the teachings of Christ might be applied to all human relations and institutions, so transforming society that the "tenth" or the twentieth would be no longer "submerged."

I believe that I appreciate in some measure the magnitude of the problems which await solution; I am not blind to the perils which threaten us; yet such is my confidence in the saving power of the complete Gospel, that in my very soul I believe a single generation will suffice to solve the problem of pauperism, to wipe out the saloon, to inaugurate a thousand needed reforms, and really change the face of society, provided only the churches generally enter into this movement.

Society is to be regenerated; the earth is to be cleansed from the sweat of oppressive toil, the vomit of vice, the blood of violence, which now cry from the ground unto God. The church has largely "held her peace," and "enlargement and deliverance are arising from another place." Why should not the church accept her mission? Cannot the Bride of Christ be persuaded to put on her beautiful garments, and, like Queen Esther, setting aside conventionalities, appear for the salvation of the people—*her* people? Surely, one would think she had come to the Kingdom for such a time as this!

CHAPTER XIII.

THE NECESSITY OF PERSONAL CONTACT.

DEMOCRACY is not fraternity, and does not prevent the formation of social classes, quite distinct and far separated.

Though we have no hereditary aristocracy in America, we have our aristocracies none the less. There is one of wealth, one of intelligence, one of character; and though members of the so-called higher and lower classes are constantly exchanging places, the classes themselves remain fixed.

It is not strange that in a general way these several lines of cleavage coincide. Of course there are many poor who are of the highest character and intelligence, and many rich who are ignorant and vicious; but as we have already seen, speaking broadly, it is the well-to-do people who are in the churches, and they as a rule are the most intelligent. It happens, therefore, that church lines and social lines very nearly coincide, so that conditions of life and tastes co-operate with religious convictions and habits to separate class from class.

There is very little contact between workingmen and church members except in business, which under competition is more likely to exercise and exhibit a man's selfishness than his Christian character, and there is still less contact between the women of different classes; they are social antipodes, if indeed they do not live in different worlds altogether.

It is not strange that the masses are indifferent toward the church: they are ignorant of it. It is not strange that many hate religion as represented by the church: it has been misrepresented. Richard Baxter's criticism, made more than two centuries ago, is equally applicable to-day. "The work of the church," he says, "is exceedingly retarded by an unworthy retiredness. Christians live like snails in the shell, and look but little around into the world, and know not the state of the world nor of the church, nor much care to know it. . . . Many ministers are of such retiring dispositions that they scarcely ever look beyond the border of their own parishes."

Such separation of the church from the world is Judaic, not Christian. Under the Mosaic régime the idea of purity was expressed by separation. That people which was to be the medium of God's blessing to the world was separated from other peoples, and a wall of exclusion built up by legislation. The tribe especially chosen to serve the sanctuary was *set apart* for that service. The vessels also which were purified for that service were *set apart*, and that portion of the Tabernacle and of the Temple which was holiest of all was farthest removed from the people. This idea of purity by separation culminated in the Pharisee, whose name means *separatist*.

Christ had a different idea of purity. He associated with "publicans and sinners" and by that association transformed them. Moses would maintain the purity of a part by separation. Christ would secure the purity of the whole by contact and transformation His emblem was not water, which is made impure by that which it purifies, but light, salt, leaven; not contamination by contact, but permeation, purification, transformation by contact.

Under the old dispensation goodness was separated and guarded from evil, and needed to be, because it was negative. Moses said, "Thou shalt not." Christ said, "Thou shalt." Under the Mosaic dispensation he who did no evil was a good man. Under Christ he who does no good is a bad man. Note the ground of condemnation in Christ's picture of the final judgment.

In every instance men are condemned *for what they did not do.* The Judge does not say, "Ye robbed me of food and drink and stripped me of raiment," but "Ye gave me no meat; ye gave me no drink; ye clothed me not." He does not say, "Ye cast me out," but "Ye took me not in;" not "Ye thrust me into prison," but "Ye visited me not."[1] Men say, "*Only* a sin of omission;" but in this vision of judgment sins of omission alone appear in the indictment. Christ's parables are full of the same teaching; again and again he emphasizes the guilt of *not doing.* It is not enough that a disciple of Christ go about doing no harm. Like his Master, he must go about *doing good.* Not enough that he do no ill to his neighbor: he must love his neighbor as himself.

Under Moses, goodness, being to so great a degree negative, was put on the defensive. It had not sufficient force to overcome surrounding evil. Contact meant contamination; hence the law of separation; purity must be preserved by isolation. But Christian goodness is positive, active, aggressive, outgoing. To such goodness contact means, not contamination, but *opportunity.* Much of our modern goodness is Mosaic. It is like the goodness of the anchoret, which requires for its preservation that all the world be quarantined from it. We need a goodness of the positive, penetrating, self-communicating sort, more active than the principle of evil; in short, a *Christian* goodness.

Because God is love he is self-giving; because his goodness is of this positive sort he seeks to communicate himself. Because the knowledge and service of God are the highest possible human wisdom, and the love of God is the highest possible human blessedness, and likeness to God is the highest possible human beauty, he has ever sought to reveal himself to men. We imagine that he hides himself, that he has purposely forbidden to the senses any perception of him.

---

[1] Matt. xxvi. 41–46.

On the contrary, he has striven, it seems to me, in every possible way to make himself known. We are like a blind man groping for the light and complaining that it eludes him, while it is pouring about him in a mighty flood, beating upon his sightless eyes and seeking to fill them with day. God is seeking by every possible avenue to enter every mind and heart. He has revealed himself in creation, in his providence, in the Scriptures. But because he is a person he is more clearly revealed through a person than in any other way. He utters himself in nature by a thousand voices, but to most men these voices are inarticulate and even inaudible. *Things* are too unlike God to express him. Jeremy Taylor says, "When God would save a man he does it by way of a man." That is because a man can reveal God better than all created things. They can tell of his wisdom and power, but cannot utter his love. "The heavens declare his glory," but it is the glory of his intellect, not of his heart. Men had gained only glimpses of God's heart until Christ came into the world: he was the Word that fully uttered the love of the Father; and as the Father sent Christ into the world, so Christ sends his followers into the world—as revealers of God, and especially as revealers of the Father's love. Christian living is simply the revelation of the divine Person through a person to persons. As Dr. Parkhurst says,[1] "Every Christian is a divine incarnation brought down to date." Filled with God and his love, the Christian is to save men by a divine contagion, living touch. He is God's leaven, and leaven must be mingled with the meal. He is God's salt, and salt can save only by actual touch. There is salt enough in the world, but it is barrelled up in the churches, and needs to be scattered and applied. It is not enough to yearn over men at a distance. Even God's mighty love could save men only

---

[1] Address before the Evangelical Alliance, Boston, " National Needs and Remedies," p. 313.

as it came to them in human form and uttered itself by human lips; heaven must needs touch earth.

Now, if we are to be God's lips, his revealers to men, the channels through which his love is to flow into men's hearts, we must come into *personal* touch with them, because men's relations to God are personal.

His knowledge of us is personal. We generalize; we know classes, genera, species; we know sparrows, but not the individual birds; we know grasses, but not individual blades of grass. We thoughtlessly imagine that God's knowledge is like our own, but omniscience necessarily descends to particulars; such knowledge must be individual. God knows every sparrow, not one falls to the ground without his notice; he knows every blade of grass. He does not have to lump men, as we do, in order to think of mankind. He calls us each by name; no one of us is ever lost in the crowd.

God's requirements are personal. Human governments enact laws in general terms for the whole people. God's law is personal. The Ten Commandments and the Two Fundamental Laws of Christ are individual in form—not "They" or "Ye," but "Thou": "*Thou* shalt not," and "*Thou* shalt."

God's love is personal. He says, "My *son*, give me thine heart." No relations can be more personal than those between parent and child.

His redemption is personal. Jesus Christ tasted death "for every man." [1]

And God has too much respect even for the finally impenitent to condemn them *en masse.* "Every one of us shall give account of himself to God." [2]

Men who are strangers to God do not feel the closeness and personality of their relations to him. He seems to them unreal or at best far away. His relations to men seem general and vague. The moment they are made to seem personal, the truth becomes real and powerful. How can any man come into right relations

---

[1] Heb. ii. 9   [2] Rom. xiv. 12.

with God until he apprehends those relations as real and personal? He may believe that all men are sinners, and sin on. He never utters the cry of the penitent publican until it has been borne in on him that *he* is a sinner. He may believe that God loves the world and remain indifferent; but when you make him feel that God loves *him*, then the truth takes hold.

The great problem of evangelization is to bring every man of the multitude into right relations with God, to make him appreciate in some measure the closeness and personality of his relations to God, and then induce him to act on his convictions. To do this is pre-eminently the work of *personal* persuasion. Many a man has read with indifference the appeals of the printed page, and listened unmoved to powerful sermons, who has yielded to a single word addressed to him personally. The mind seems to have a mysterious power to reach another mind through some medium other than that of the five senses, and which Sir William Thomson calls a sixth sense. In addition to the persuasion of words, will exerts a remarkable power over will. The laws of its operation are unknown, but the fact is well established. The living man has a power which his printed words cannot possess, *personal* persuasion is effective far beyond all other.

It is life that begets life, love that begets love, character that leavens character. It was not enough that Elisha send his servant to lay his staff on the dead boy: the living prophet must stretch himself upon the lifeless body if he would quicken it. It was not enough that God send his messengers: he must needs come himself in the life-giving power of personality. And this necessity of incarnation is upon us: we must enter into other lives, share their lives with them, give our lives to them, if we would bless.

It is now being discovered in every department of charitable and philanthropic work what an immense blunder it has been to substitute machinery for personal, vital touch. It is being shown that personality is

the great power in all redemptive work; and Toynbee
Hall, in the East End of London; the College Settlement
in Rivington Street, New York; Hull House, in one of
the worst wards of Chicago; and the Andover Settlement, in the slums of Boston, are all outgrowths of this
discovery—points where that which is best and most
Christian in our civilization has, so to speak, incarnated
itself amid the gross and wretched life of our great
cities, that by personal contact the higher might help
up the lower. The heroic Mr. Adams and his wife,
living in the midst of 40,000 Bohemians in Chicago, and
the no less heroic "slum sisters" of the Salvation Army,
sharing the poverty of the lives they long to bless, are
in their own persons revelations of God, and are demonstrating to us what has been demonstrated to every
generation since Christ, that his personal love and sacrifice can be shown by the personal love and sacrifice
of his followers to the most ignorant, hardened, and
vicious, and that with saving power.

Christ in the flesh personally touched the sick, the
maimed, the leprous: so his body in the world to-day
needs to be brought into actual personal touch with the
world's miseries.

This personal touch the church has largely lost. This
personal power is precisely what the great majority of
our church members suffer to lie unused. Its exercise
is not laid on the conscience of most professing Christians as a necessary part of Christian living. There are
hundreds of thousands in our churches who ten, twenty,
or forty years ago professed to give themselves—time,
powers, and possessions—to Christ's service, who have
never even invited a soul to him. Yet they could get
for the asking letters stating that they are in "good
and regular standing." They are supposed, both by
themselves and others, to have discharged their duty to
the unchurched multitude through the contribution-box.

We make societies our representatives, and our bene-
factions flow through established channels to remote
and impersonal objects. We do well to rejoice in such

far-reaching mediums of influence, but we do ill to be satisfied with them; and we do ill to imagine that our money is accepted *as a substitute* for personal service as revealers of God. I know a pastor who said he could get a million dollars from his church for a Christian enterprise, but could not get from them personal Christian service.

The story is told that Pope Innocent IV. was once counting a large sum of money in coin when Saint Thomas Aquinas was ushered in. His Holiness remarked, "You see the church can no longer say with Saint Peter, 'Silver and gold have I none.'" To which the Angelic Doctor replied, "Neither can she any longer say with him, 'In the name of Jesus Christ of Nazareth, rise up and walk.'" Just so far as Christian men make their money gifts a *substitute* for personal service, the church loses the power to lay hold of the prostrate by the right hand and lift them up.

The laity imagine that the minister is their representative in personal Christian work. They attend to the salary, he attends to the religion; religion is his business, not theirs. Just here crops out again that old and pernicious distinction between the "sacred" and the "secular." Laymen think the clergy should be more consecrated than they, should have higher aims, should lead holier lives, should be channels of divine grace as laymen cannot be. Our Protestant churches are only half reformed from the Roman Catholic errors concerning the priesthood.

"Hardly anything has transpired in the history of the Christian church," says Dr. Parkhurst, "that has done more to arrest its growth than the springing up of that kind of discrimination between clergy and laity that distinguishes the two from one another, not simply in function—which is reasonable and scriptural enough —but in their respective relations to the God-spirit considered as a personal tenant, inspirer, actuator in the individual life and activity. . . . The sharp distinction now made between clergy and laity did not exist even in thought in apostolic days, nor for a considerable time after, and when it did come it came as a device of the devil to minimize the number of them who should make large spiritual attainment, to the end of minimizing the number of them who should feel large spiritual responsibility. . . . From that time on the clergy have made it more or less of a business to be holy and preach the Gospel, and the laity have made it more or less of a business to make money, enjoy themselves, pay their pew-rent and solace themselves with an evangelical vicarage." [1]

When our Great High Priest cried "It is finished," " the vail of the temple was rent in twain, from the top to the bottom." There was to be no more priestly monopoly; even the holiest place was thrown open to the people. Sacred offices and places were not henceforth to be common and unclean, but the people were to be set apart for the divine service. There are no *common* people in the kingdom of God, for the sons of the Highest are all kings and priests unto him. It was to all believers that Peter wrote, "Ye are a royal priesthood." [2] The kingdom of heaven is a kingdom of priests.

The clergyman appropriately differs from the layman in certain functions of his office, but as witnesses of Christ, as revealers of God, as saviours of men, clergyman and layman hold one and the same commission and are on precisely the same footing. My obligation to disciple men to Jesus Christ rests on me, not because I am a clergyman, but because I myself am a disciple. "Let him that heareth say, Come." [3] If you have accepted the invitation, there is your commission to extend it.

The great command, "Go ye into all the world and preach the Gospel to every creature," seems to have been addressed, not to the eleven apostles only, but also

---

[1] Address before the Evangelical Alliance, Boston, "National Needs and Remedies," pp. 314, 315.

[2] 1 Peter ii. 9.   [3] Rev. xxii. 17.

to "them that were with them," [1] that is, to the whole body of believers. And this seems to have been the understanding of the early Christians, for when the persecution which followed the death of Stephen scattered the church which was in Jerusalem "*except the apostles*," " they that were scattered abroad [the laity] went everywhere preaching the word." [2] This certainly was lay preaching. They had received the diploma of no theological seminary, they had passed the examinations of no ecclesiastical body, there had been no laying on of consecrating hands. They had themselves accepted the invitation, and were therefore bound to extend it. Their fitness to proclaim the Kingdom lay simply in the fact that they had become citizens of it. That Christ deemed this a sufficient qualification appears from the fact that he said to one who had only just made a profession of loyalty, " Go thou and preach the kingdom of God." [3]

An educated ministry is necessary for the edification of the church. I am not arguing against that, but against the paralyzing impression that only those are under obligations to disciple men to Christ who have had a course of special training therefor. The Franciscan friars in the sixteenth century, the itinerant Methodist preachers in the eighteenth, and the Salvation Army in the nineteenth have all demonstrated the efficiency of generally uneducated men in evangelistic work.

If the millions of church members in this country were each one revealers of God, how soon would he be made known to the multitude ! But there is no such freedom of spiritual communication as of every other kind. The printing-press has been a mighty stimulus to intellectual life because it brings mind into contact with mind. The locomotive and the steamship have enormously quickened our material civilization because they have so facilitated communication. There has

---

[1] Luke xxiv. 38–50.   [2] Acts viii. 1, 4.   [3] Luke ix. 60.

been no corresponding progress in spiritual intercourse. The church and the masses lie apart like two great continents, with an almost untraversed ocean between. When there is accomplished, by means of personal contact between the church and the multitude, a spiritual intercommunication corresponding in some good degree to the freedom of intercourse already established in the intellectual and material worlds, we may reasonably expect results in our spiritual life corresponding in magnitude to the intellectual and material results produced by the printing-press, the telegraph, and the railway.

1. Such personal intercourse is needed for its effects on the church.

It is impossible to have spiritual health without spiritual exercise. It is complained that the majority of church members are spiritually weak and have little appetite for the strong meat of the Word. If they were as inactive physically as they are spiritually, they would soon become helpless invalids, unable to take any food stronger than water-gruel. Exercise quickens respiration and sharpens appetite, and more food assimilated increases strength. The laws of health are much the same for the spiritual and physical man. Increased spiritual activity leads to more prayer, " the Christian's vital breath," and arouses an appetite for the work, feeding on which the Christian grows healthy and strong.

The laity are suffering from a great number of spiritual ailments which are directly traceable to a lack of spiritual exercise. They are hiring the minister and the city missionary to exercise in their behalf; but such exercise does not aid the spiritual digestion of the laity. Spiritual exercise can no more be taken vicariously than physical. And if every man of the multitude could be reached and rescued by a hired representative, the layman would still need to engage in personal Christian work for the sake of his own spiritual health.

Such work in systematic house-to-house visitation is of great educational value to those who engage in it. It enlarges their horizon and saves their lives from littleness; it carries them outside themselves and cultivates an active habit of beneficence; it affords definite objects of interest, effort, and prayer; it gives a practical knowledge of human nature. If the visitation is to the poor, it creates an intelligent interest in the great sociological problems of the times; the visitors touch the great heart of humanity and come into fuller sympathy with it; and by the measure of love and sacrifice with which they enrich other lives they are themselves enriched. One pastor said, ".If you should come into my prayer-meeting, you could pick out the sixty church visitors there by the *shine on their faces.*" This giving of one's self is like mercy,

> ". . . . twice bless'd;
> It blesseth him that gives and him that takes."

Not only does the church need such personal intercourse for the spiritual health and training of her membership: she must come into personal contact with the life of the community if she is to accomplish her social mission. Such contact, by affording a definite knowledge of facts, would serve to overcome the indifference which is now so serious an obstacle to reaching the masses with Christian influence.

When the heart is right (and a man is not a Christian if his heart is not right), what is needed to secure right action is to inform the head. It has become proverbial that one half of the world does not know how the other half lives—not the other half on the opposite side of the globe, but in our own midst—and ignorance is of course attended by indifference.

Indifference must be killed with facts—not guesses, or estimates, or opinions, but solid facts, clean-cut and well-established. In almost every community there are facts enough just under the surface to arouse Christian activity, if only they were known—relievable suffer-

ing, wrongs, violations of law, ignorance, neglected
children who are growing a crop of paupers and
criminals. In a New England city of 75,000 inhabitants, in two months' time, one hundred and fifteen
boys and girls between the ages of seven and twenty
were arrested. The annual report of the State Superin-
tendent of Public Instruction in New York shows that
during the year ending in July, 1890, there were 800,000
children of school age in the state who did not attend
school at any time during the year, and that the average daily attendance was over 1,000,000 less than the
total number of children of school age. The canvass
of a county in Ohio revealed the fact that one third
of the families were without the Bible, and the canvass
of a ward in Brooklyn showed a like destitution on the
part of one half of the families in the ward. Such
facts being interpreted mean that Christians have been
neglecting their duty, and that something ought to be
done by somebody.

Personal contact with the life of the community
brings such facts to light, and more especially yields
specific cases which are vastly more effective in arousing interest than general statements. We know that
in a great city there must be many who suffer want,
but that knowledge does not deeply move us. We
learn that in a certain hovel there is a deserted child,
sick and starving, and we can neither eat nor sleep
until we have carried succor. "It was only the other
day that a little boy who had been carrying beer all
day to an East Side factory was found in the cellar
dead, gnawed by rats. He had crawled down from the
shop drunk, and had perished there during the night." [1]
We know that many children are employed every day
in New York to carry beer from saloons, and with
many bad results. And most men can hear this general statement with indifference; but this specific
instance kindles our indignation to a white heat. It

[1] Jacob Riis in *The Christian Union*, May 16, 1889.

is one thing to read of women starving to death at the point of a needle, and a very different thing to become personally interested in a victim of this wrong. A wrong in print may make you indignant, but that wrong embodied in flesh and blood before your eyes stirs you up to *do* something about it.

I believe it was Mrs. Browning who said, "Most people are kind, if they only think of it." But the comfortable classes are generally too self-satisfied to think very much of the struggles and sufferings of the poor. They make bargains at the store which, if they only stopped to think, would tell them of starving needlewomen; they pay wages which must needs mean underfed and ill-housed families, pinched and hopeless lives, but they do not stop to think. If they were personally acquainted with the lives and homes of the poor they could hardly help stopping to think. Such acquaintance would enable the well-to-do to put themselves, in some measure, in the place of the ill-to-do, which would make sympathy possible. "Half of the cruelty in the world," says Mr. John Fiske, "is the direct result of stupid incapacity to put one's self in the other man's place." [1]

Many Christian people are indifferent to the physical and moral destitution which exists around them because they are ignorant of it, or know of it only in a vague and general way. Personal contact with it will arouse their interest and activity, if anything can. Several pastors in one of the wards of New York met to talk over the organization of house-to-house visitation. They decided before sending out their visitors that they would themselves thoroughly investigate a portion of the ward. Each took a square or more, and agreed to call on every family. When they met again they were full of enthusiasm for the work. One, who I think had been with his church nearly a quarter of a century, was quite overcome with emotion that he had lived so many

---

Destiny of Man, p. 99.

years in the midst of such moral and spiritual destitution without knowing it, and declared that the hours
he had given to that investigation were the most profitable in his ministry, both to himself and to others.
Another who had had a pastorate of twenty years in
that ward bore similar testimony. Bring clergy and
laity into actual contact with the community, and it
will soon be found that light is accompanied with heat.

Again, the church needs this personal contact with
the community that she may *intelligently* discharge her
duty to it. If she is to purify its entire life, she must
know its entire life. The first step toward a better condition of things is exact knowledge of the existing condition of things. There should be made in every city
some such analysis of the population as has been made
of 900,000 people in East London by Mr. Charles Booth,[1]
which shows the number of loafers and criminals, the
number of the "very poor," the "poor," and so on up
to those who are "well to-do." Definite information
should be obtained of every family in city and country
that the church would help. Even in its pauperism
and crime human nature follows certain laws, which
we must understand if we are to solve these great
problems. God's methods are scientific, and ours must
be if we are to be his intelligent helpers. And if the
scientific knowledge necessary to intelligent Christian
work can be obtained of London, it can be obtained
of any city in Christendom.

Without such knowledge, suffering will exist, ignorance and vice will flourish, wrongs and crimes will be
perpetrated, and deaths will occur, the causes of which
the church might have removed.

A knowledge of these causes and conditions can be
gained only by investigation and study. Pauperism
thrusts itself on our attention, but many of the most
worthy poor, who are struggling with genteel poverty
—the most biting kind—are never known unless hunted

---

[1] Labor and Life of the People. (Two volumes.)

286 *THE NEW ERA.*

up. They do not parade their poverty, but rather make the most ingenious and pathetic attempts to conceal it. Many of them would rather starve or freeze or commit suicide than beg. Our public charities do not reach them. They have too much self-respect to accept help from a stranger. Only one who has made himself a friend can aid them; he can enter into their life and find ways to assist without sacrificing their self-respect.

Many of this class are driven to crime or suicide. Miss Alice S. Woodbridge, Secretary of the Working Women's Society of New York, writes [1]: "The story of Mrs. Henderson, who threw herself from the attic window of a lodging-house some time ago, is the story of many another. There have been many such instances in the last two weeks. Mrs. Henderson could not live on the salaries offered her. She could live if she accepted the 'propositions' of her employers."

Early in the morning of July 3, 1890, the body of a comely and neatly-dressed woman clasping a baby in her arms floated into the docks of the Rotterdam Steamship Line, Hoboken. It was soon made known that Mr. Werdtland and wife with their child had jumped into the North River, driven to death by poverty.

Starvation in this land of luxury and in this nineteenth century of our Lord is not uncommon. A young man was found dead on the sidewalk in New York; Mrs. John King was found dead in New Haven. In each case a physician certified that they starved to death. A year or two ago in March a family was found in Quebec which had spent the winter in an attic without fuel, with hardly a bed, and no furniture. The father was maimed and sick. Three of the children had starved to death, and a fourth would probably die. They were "poor and proud." Another family was found in the same city in much the same condition. Henry George says: "In the richest city of the world

---

[1] *The Arena*, April, 1891, p. 640.

the mortuary reports contain a column for deaths by sheer starvation." [1]

The significance of these facts to which I wish to call attention is, not that there is dire want in the world. That is nothing new; there is far less wretchedness now than when Christ came. Then, the "milk of human kindness" had well-nigh curdled into misanthropy in the proud Roman breast. "Humanity," said Sydney Smith, "is a modern invention"—modern because Christian. There are multitudes of humane men and women now who would gladly relieve want, if knowing of it and convinced of its reality. My point is that in our large cities there may be men, women, and little children starving to death, suffering agonies as terrible as if they had been lost in the desert of Sahara; and all this within call of scores who would gladly rescue them if their want were only known. In one block, sickness, starvation, despair, death; and in the next, wealth and generous Christian hearts, all unconcerned because ignorant.

A widow with four children, living in Boston, was told to vacate her rooms because several weeks behind with her rent. Notwithstanding the eldest daughter was sick and the mother very sick, an eviction was ordered in midwinter, and every piece of furniture save the bed in which the dying woman lay was carried out. Not even the stove on which a child was preparing some broth for her mother was allowed to remain. That night in the cold and desolate room the mother died. Boston was indignant when the story was told, and no doubt ten thousand kind hearts thought, "I would gladly have prevented that outrage if I had only known of the destitution."

A similar case of eviction occurred with like result in New York not long after. Such things are possible, not because Christian sympathy is lacking in these cities, but because there is lack of information; and because

---

[1] Twilight Club **Tracts**, p. 37.

of this lack the sympathy might as well be on one side
of the globe and the suffering on the other.

Once cities might suffer starvation while crops rotted
on the ground forty miles away—this for lack of communication. Such famines are no longer possible, but
a family now starves with abundance not forty miles
away but within forty feet maybe—and *this* for lack
of communication.

Spiritual famine is common, and from like cause. A
pastor in Maine, already quoted, said that of seventy-
eight funerals at which he officiated the year before,
forty-one were in non-church-going families, and
"thirty-one of them were of adults, who were sick and
died without a visit from any religious person, a prayer,
or a word of hope." This pastor would gladly have
ministered to this destitution, but he did not know of
the existence of these people until called to bury them.

But it is the business of the church to know. She
might know, and therefore ought to know, so that ignorance is no excuse. "If thou forbear to deliver them
that are drawn unto death, and those that are ready to
be slain; If thou sayest, Behold, we knew it not; doth
not he that pondereth the heart consider it? and he that
keepeth thy soul, doth he not know it? and shall not he
render to every man according to his works?"[1]

The contact of the church with the community should
be so complete and the work of visitation so systema-
tized that if a young man is in arrest, a young woman
in disgrace, a family in want, or if any one has died
from hunger or drunkenness, some one ought to know
the circumstances and feel in measure responsible for
it. If any one has moved out of the district or into it,
it ought to be some one's business to know it. The
church can never fulfil her mission until there has been
established what General Booth calls "a nervous system" for the community, which shall bring her into
communication with every man, woman, and child.

---

[1] Prov. xxiv. 11, 12.

"The charity organization societies do enough to show where the weak spot in our system is, but from the nature of their organization they do not fill the gap which they disclose. I do not myself believe that the gap will be filled till the Church of Christ devotes itself systematically to the business, and when it does, I think it will prove that its success is on the old lines, of personal oversight by consecrated men and women, carried out so far that every person in the district in hand may be under the direct personal and intelligent supervision of somebody." [1]

Thus this personal contact with the community will show the church where and what her work is and enable her to undertake it intelligently.

2. We have seen that such contact is needed by the church; it is no less needed by non-church goers. Without it we shall not solve the problem of evangelizing the masses.

The world is dying of selfishness. "Perhaps the worst devil a man can be possessed withal," says George MacDonald, "is himself. In mere madness the man is beside himself; but in this case he is inside himself. The presiding, indwelling, inspiring spirit of him is himself, and that is the hardest to cast out." Nothing but love can exorcise this devil. Hence God has revealed his love to men, and is trying to love them out of themselves. Isaiah says:[2] "Thou hast loved my soul from the pit." But the world does not know God or believe in his love, nor does it believe in the love which Christians profess. The natural and only adequate expression of love is sacrifice; only by sacrifice could the divine love fully utter itself; and sacrifice must ever be for God and man the mother-tongue of love. But self-sacrifice is precisely what the world does not see in the life of the average Christian. It may be

---

[1] Edward Everett Hale, D.D., *Magazine of Christian Literature*, November, 1890.

[2] xxxviii. 17, Marginal rendering.

there in some real measure, but the world is not aware
of it. He appears as well-groomed, as comfortable, as
self-absorbed, as self-centred, as the upright man of
the world, from whom he is hardly distinguishable.

Nothing is more difficult than to convince a selfish
man of disinterestedness. He has had no experience of
it; he has had little or no observation of it. The Christian professes a disinterested love for his fellow-men,
but profession is not proof. He may give his money
for churches and missions, for music-halls and public
libraries, but the selfish man finds it easy to suspect
some ulterior motive. A money gift cannot certify to
the motives which prompted it. It may or may not be
a sacrifice; but when a man gives *himself*, that affords
proof of disinterested love, if anything can.

And this is pre-eminently true in these times of
popular discontent, when many believe that the money
given by the rich and well-to-do really belongs to the
workingmen. Says the editor of the *New York Evening Post :* "The poor, and ignorant, and barbarous, and
anarchical, and indifferent of this city, or of any other,
are not what they were fifty or one hundred years ago.
They cannot be any longer won, or persuaded, or raised,
by simple preaching, or even by almsgiving. They
have become too knowing for that. They are envious
and suspicious of the rich and well-to-do, and they are
tired of the old gospel of contentment when delivered
by people who have all the comforts this world can
give. Nothing touches them nowadays but the spec-
tacle of self-sacrifice."[1] And this is true because nothing else demonstrates love.

Self-giving is not incidental but essential to Christianity. Christ's coming was an exhibition of God's
self-giving; Christ's life was a perpetual self-giving;
and he made daily self-giving the condition of dis-

---

[1] *The New York Evening Post*, Dec. 4, 1888. When this truth is so
clearly seen by the secular press it is high time for the churches to recognize it.

cipleship. But the average Christian thinks to discharge his duty to a lost world by *money*-giving
instead of *self*-giving. The multitude very naturally
take the average Christian as a fair representative of
the church, and seeing in him no evidence of love, they
disbelieve in the church and its professions, and the
church loses its influence over them.

Governor William B. Washburn believed in personal
Christian work. It was his habit to go into the homes
of the poor people in his village for at least one or two
hours every week, and talk and pray with them and
invite them to church. And the time, sympathy, and
thought given by this busy man to the poor were worth
far more to them than any money he might have given,
and at the same time a much better proof of his love.
It is not strange that Governor Washburn had a large
and successful Bible-class.

What if the best men and women in the churches,
chosen for their tact no less than their piety, should
visit the homes of the masses, not once or twice as
census-takers, but going repeatedly, as friends, to establish intimate and helpful relations, studying spiritual
and temporal needs and seeking to serve in every possible way ? How long would it be before the masses
would regain their faith in the church, and in the sincerity of its members ? "The only conclusive evidence of
a man's sincerity," says Mr. Lowell, "is that he gives
himself for a principle. Words, money, all things else,
are comparatively easy to give away; but when a man
makes a gift of his daily life and practice, it is plain
that the truth, whatever it may be, has taken possession of him."

And it must not be forgotten that the church has a
mission to the rich as well as to the poor. Christ did
not say, Go preach the Gospel to every creature except
the rich. True, it is the well-to-do who constitute most
of the church-going class, but in the aggregate there
are many rich who are as Christless as the benighted
heathen. They are the most utterly neglected class in

the community, as unapproached as if living in the heart of the Dark Continent. There are no societies organized for their evangelization, the city missionary society cannot reach them. Their spiritual destitution does not appeal to us as do the bodily want and squalor of the poor, but a lean and tattered soul is equally pitiable in God's sight, whether it lives at the "East End" or the "West End." The poor rich are by far the most difficult class to help, but they can be reached with Gospel influence by skilful personal work.

Again, personal self-giving is necessary in order to dissipate skepticism. For a supernatural religion unbelief demands supernatural evidence. By all means let it be given. Christ met this demand with miracles, and speaking of them he said to his disciples, "Greater works than these shall ye do." Surely there could be no greater physical miracle than raising the dead to life. Christ's prophecy, then, could be fulfilled only in the doing of spiritual miracles—in the raising of souls, dead in sin, to spiritual life. New lives, therefore, inspired with higher than natural motives and filled with more than natural service, in short, lives filled with the spirit and self-sacrificing love of Christ and manifesting a likeness to him which is truly supernatural, are the miracles with which Christ expected in all ages to convince the world that his religion was from God. Such lives are all-conquering. Unbelief cannot live under their influence. The arguments of infidelity can no more cope with them than words can stay the shining of the sun.

The most mischievous infidelity in the world is not of the philosophical sort, which men read out of books, but of the practical sort, which they read out of professedly Christian lives. When the average church member, by unmistakably giving himself to the service of his fellow-men, proves his love to them, he will show that Jesus Christ is able to cast out the devil of self, and thus furnish the supernatural evidence which the skeptic demands.

Again, personal self-giving is necessary in order to solve the problem of pauperism.

Indiscriminate charity (and up to date most of the world's charity has been indiscriminate) has no doubt done vastly more harm than good. It has perpetuated the evils it has sought to relieve, and created others.

When men discover that begging is at the same time easier and more profitable than work, they beg; when they find that rags and filth pay larger dividends than cleanliness and decency, they invest in rags and filth; when they learn that mutilated and deformed children wring more money from the charitable than able-bodied beggars can, parents maim and torture their offspring into objects of horror. So-called charity puts a premium on loathsome filth and hideous deformity, and by thus helping to create them becomes in measure responsible for them. Unintelligent, emotional almsgiving is more cruel than a pestilence. It means well, but, as Octavia Hill says, "Let us never weakly plead that what we do is *benevolent;* we must ascertain that it is really *beneficent* too.". Mr. Carnegie is of the opinion that out of every $1000 given in charity, $950 do harm. This would be extravagant as applied to all money given away, but hardly too strong as applied to that given in emotional charity; that is almost invariably mischievous. But a small proportion of those who apply for alms need aid, and those who do are probably injured by giverless gifts.

The Charity Organization Society of New York, after investigating many thousands of cases of pauperism, makes this generalization, that of all applications for aid less than one in sixteen requires continuous help, and less than one in four needs even temporary aid.[1] Many a pauper "dispenses with the necessaries of life" only because he is in full possession of its luxuries. Unintelligent, emotional charity supports hordes of hypocrites, and when it blunders into aiding a worthy man,

---

[1] Fifth Annual Report, p. 37.

helps to pauperize and degrade him. It never finds the many who suffer and utter no cry.

Too often the giving of money is only a lazy and selfish way of satisfying conscience. What the pauper needs rather than money is self-respect, self-restraint, industry, economy, judgment, enlightenment, hope, courage, character. But these cannot be passed out of the pocket leaving the giver free to go on his way unhindered, while he rejoices in an approving conscience. To give what the pauper really needs costs time and thought and sympathy and effort. His case must be studied and treated with skill and perseverance. The Psalmist says: "Blessed is he that *considereth* the poor."[1] How few almsgivers are entitled to this blessing? It takes time to "consider," and most men would rather give money.

And even where we do consider conscientiously it is very difficult to give money or material help without doing mischief. Rev. S. A. Barnett, who as founder of Toynbee Hall has had wide experience and observation, says that as a rule it is almost impossible to give people what they *want* without doing injury. Some attempts to benefit the families of workingmen by giving them *things* have been found to be in effect contributions to the pockets of their employers, just as gifts to the families of drunkards are often found to go for drink, and so make the wretched family only more wretched.

But the problem of pauperism can be solved. It *has* been solved. Says Prof. R. T. Ely,[2] "Wherever there has been any earnest and intelligent attempt to remedy the evil, the success has been equal to all the most sanguine could anticipate." The experiment which was inaugurated in 1853 in Elberfeld, and which has since extended to many other cities of Germany, the famous work of Dr. Chalmers and that of the noble company of women in New York City, referred to in the preceding chapter, all show that in a few years the pauper can be

---

[1] Ps. xli. 1.   [2] *North American Review*, April, 1891.

helped up above the need of help; and in all of these instances patient and wise personal effort was the saving power. "Not alms, but a friend;" not silver and gold, but moral healing. Of course material aid must sometimes be given, but it is not remedial. The cure of pauperism is more expensive than can be wrought by the check-book. Its remedy is *self*-giving. "Give for alms those things which are within." [1]

It might be shown, further, that personal contact and self-giving are necessary, if we would solve the problem of vice and crime, but we must bring this discussion to a close.

If, as we have seen, personal effort is necessary in order to win the masses and elevate the degraded, there must be an immense increase of lay activity, for it would be simply a physical impossibility for the clergy and other salaried representatives of the church to reach so vast a multitude. If the church is to leaven the whole community, this universal touch must come through the laity. If she is to accomplish the reforms necessary to purifying and Christianizing all human institutions, activities, and relations, she must remember that back of institutions and laws, back of parties and policies, back of public morals and public opinion, is *individual character*, and character must be wrought upon by character.

Laymen are absorbed by business, but when the Premier of Great Britain and Ireland finds time to talk and pray with a wayward boy, to make a weekly visit to a drunkard who is trying to reform, and to read the Bible to an old street-sweeper in an attic, surely men on whom press only their little private businesses ought to be able to find some time for personal Christian work.

Most of our forces never come to close quarters with "our friends the enemy." The Roman shortened his sword and lengthened the bounds of his empire. We must learn to handle the short sword, if we are to conquer the world for Christ.

---

[1] Luke xi. 41, Revised Version.

CHAPTER XIV.

THE NECESSITY OF CO-OPERATION.

THE most powerful tendency of the times is centripetal. It is profoundly influencing production and distribution—industries of all sorts—and the movement of populations. So general a tendency toward combination, organization, centralization, indicates, as we have already seen, nothing less than a new evolution of civilization, the beginning of a higher organization of society, made possible by steam and electricity and the higher development of the individual.

The development of great railway systems affords an excellent illustration of this tendency to combine. The early railway charters were for short lines. That part of the New York Central road between Albany and Buffalo was originally owned and operated by sixteen independent companies. In France forty-eight companies have been absorbed by six. In England five thousand miles were owned in 1847 by several hundred different companies. Twenty-five years later thirteen thousand miles were nearly all owned by twelve companies.[1] Mr. Charles Francis Adams says that the next move in this country will be in the direction of railway systems of twenty thousand miles, each under one management. Business, open-eyed, has seen and seized the immense advantage which lies in consolidation, organization; but the Protestant churches do not yet appreciate this advantage.

---

[1] Natural Law in the Business World, p. 196.

That they are not indifferent, however, to this greatest tendency of the times appears from the very general
discussion of organic union. The several denominations certainly sustain much more friendly relations
with each other than they once did. But though they
do not now as formerly "hate each other for the love
of God," as Mr. Stead says, they still stand apart and
suffer all the weakness of division.

In rare instances churches co-operate, but so far as
any comprehensive survey of the field is concerned,
and the wise adjustment of supply to need, the denominations generally, like the Jews and Samaritans, have
no dealings one with another. In one city an Episcopal
rector told me that in organizing house-to-house visitation he had met for the first time a Baptist pastor,
whose church was in the same block with his own,
where they had both been laboring for six years. In
another city, one of the smaller of our large cities, a
Presbyterian pastor and an Episcopal rector, each
prominent in his denomination, each of large mind and
fraternal spirit, and each of whom had been settled
in the city for more than a quarter of a century, were
introduced to each other at a parlor conference which
had met to consider co-operative work. Imagine two
military captains or colonels, set for the defence of the
same city, fighting a common enemy for twenty-five
years before holding a council of war or even having
met !

The military maxim, Divide the enemy and conquer,
has in it the wisdom of experience. The Protestant
churches are divided. Notwithstanding the protestations
of friendship on the part of denominations and the actual
love and fellowship of many individual members of
different communions; notwithstanding we have much
more in common than in difference; notwithstanding
there is to a certain extent an underlying spiritual
unity—yet so long as different churches are unable or
indisposed to co-operate for the accomplishment of
common objects, so long as one church is willing to

build itself at the expense of others, so long surely as churches are in competition one with another, they are divided; and while they thus remain cannot hope to conquer the world for Christ.

Consider some of the more obvious and important reasons for co-operation.

1. It is necessary in order to put an end to the evils of competition.

In many small towns, east and west, there are too many churches. If in a community there are three churches where there is room for only one, there must of course be a struggle for existence. If one becomes strong, it is at the expense of the other two; and more likely all three are enfeebled. As there is a great deal of human nature in people, this struggle to live under such conditions naturally leads to competition, jealousies, and strifes. Thus Christ and his religion are dishonored before the world, and the character and influence of the churches are marred.

This competitive struggle to live has many bad effects. Sometimes it seriously modifies the tone of the preaching, rendering it less bold, less faithful to the conscience, less loyal to the truth, for fear that some rich sinner may be offended.

As another result, some churches are led to cater to the rich. When there come into our assemblies a man with a gold ring, in goodly apparel, and also a poor man in vile raiment, does not the usher sometimes say to him that weareth the gay clothing, "Sit thou here in a good place;" and to the poor man, "Stand thou there, or sit here under my footstool"? And is not the family of the man in gay clothing likely to receive more social recognition than that of the man in vile raiment?

When the support of a church becomes a great burden to its members, the financial question demands undue attention. With a great multitude of churches the condition of the treasury is the supreme concern. Their energies are absorbed by church fairs, suppers, and what not, while they lose sight of the real object of the church.

The great question comes to be, not How to save *men?* but How to save the *church?* Instead of making the church a means to the salvation of the community as an end, the community is looked on as a means to the saving of the church as an end, and men are sought for the purpose of building up the church. Of course such a church has little or no influence over non-church-goers. Men who care nothing for the church cannot be induced to attend for the sake of the church. When it seeks them they think it is for some ulterior purpose—believe that it seeks not them, but theirs. An acquaintance of mine, a clergyman, was making an effort, which had been already several times repeated, to induce a workingman to attend church. "Why should you," said the man, "be troubling yourself about me and my family anyway? I couldn't give more than four or five dollars a year, and that isn't worth your while."

The impression that the church is after money is one of the great obstacles in the way of reaching the masses. And that impression is likely to remain as long as competition between the churches continues.

This competitive struggle to live of course intensifies sectarianism. Many become devoted to the church, not because it is *Christ's* church, but because it is *their* church. They may hate some other church of Christ quite as heartily as they love their own. They love it not so much as a church, as an object for which they have made sacrifices. They lay the flattering unction to their soul that they are uncommonly pious, when as a matter of fact they are simply bigoted. Thus the struggle to support superfluous churches, instead of enlarging the heart as all noble sacrifice does, only narrows it and increases sectarianism.

This spirit of competition utterly belies Christianity. "Every church for itself" is as selfish as "Every man for himself." The policy and labors of some pastors and churches are essentially selfish, and whatever is essentially selfish is essentially unchristian and cannot manifest to the world Christ and his self-sacrificing spirit. Such churches utterly misrepresent their Master.

Another evil effect of this competition is the congestion of churches so often seen in our large cities, that is, the multiplication of churches in those wards of the city which need them least, and the neglect of the most needy. A denominational city missionary society, which of course never takes counsel with a "rival" society, looks over the whole field to select the place in which to plant a new church. The secretary says to himself: "If we go down-town we shall find prices very high, and no help on the ground to buy or rent. The people are needy enough; but if we go to work in the slums, as soon as any one is converted and made respectable he will move away, so that the mission will never become self-sustaining. But up-town, where the well-to-do and Christian people are building, there is room for a church. The people will contribute largely toward building it, and in two or three years it will not only be self-sustaining, but will begin to return money to our treasury." And, of course, he goes up town with his new church. The representative of another denomination takes note of the fact and says: "There are some of our people living near that new church, and they will be going into it and we shall lose them to our denomination if we don't build in that neighborhood." So another church is built on the opposite corner, not because there isn't any church in that vicinity, but precisely because there is. Thus the churches are planted not where they will best serve the interests of the city, but where the city will best serve the interests of the churches.

Business men have learned that the remedy for the evils of competition is combination. Surely the evils of sectarian competition emphasize the necessity of substituting co-operation.

2. Another reason for co-operation is that it is necessary to the best economy of existing resources.

The tendency toward organization which is so general

finds expression among Protestant denominations not in comprehensive co-operation as it should, but in an ever-increasing multiplicity of boards, agencies, societies, and the like, many of which overlap and interfere, while a multitude of interests are neglected. Thus the power and effectiveness which would belong to a comprehensive organization covering the whole field are lost in a confusion of efforts which are sadly expensive in time, strength, opportunity, money and men.

The combination of railway properties effects a vast economy over the independent management of many short lines.[1] The same is true in all sorts of business; why should the work of the churches be an exception?

The various Christian denominations have a common aim, viz., to bring all men into obedience to their common Lord. But instead of conference and co-operation so as to make the wisest expenditure of resources, each conducts its work with little or no reference to the others; very much as if it were the only body of Christians in the land. How foolish, not to say criminal, this is!

Here are some 65,000,000 people in the United States living in nearly 29,000 townships. These townships rarely contain less than twenty-five square miles, and many contain several hundred. Evidently one minister in one township would have a large parish, however sparse the population might be; and with such a disposition of ministerial forces the clergyman in each of our 443 cities would have on the average over 40,000 souls under his care.

If now the largest of the Protestant denominations were called on to supply the religious needs of the whole country from its own resources, it could not furnish one half of the organized townships in the United States with a minister. And the smaller of the

---

[1] Under this process, in one instance, the cost of transportation had fallen in 1885 to one fifth of what it was twenty years before.

half-dozen most influential denominations, on which we rely chiefly for the evangelization of the nation, could not furnish one minister for every six townships. The largest Protestant denomination has only one sixth of our Protestant clergy, and the smaller of these leading bodies has only one twenty-first part of them, while the church membership of the latter is only one twenty-sixth part of the whole. Is it not absurd for any one of these bodies to assume that it is *the* Christian force of the country, and that upon *it* rests the chief responsibility for its evangelization? And yet if this responsibility were wholly laid on any one of the Protestant denominations, its policy could hardly differ much from its present policy. Is it not a foolish and unchristian assumption for one of these denominations to adopt a policy which virtually ignores the existence of all others? Ought not the policy to fit the facts? Is it possible to blink the facts and avoid a wicked waste?

This wicked waste of men and means is precisely what we see in many thousands of communities. A letter recently received from a town in Massachusetts says: "Our total population is probably not over 500, yet we have near together a Congregational, a Baptist, and a Methodist church. The average congregation in each is between twenty-five and fifty." Each of these churches receives outside aid. A clergyman in the State of New York writes: "In one town are two houses of worship where the aggregate congregations rarely exceed seventy. In another village are two houses of worship, the aggregate congregations in which rarely exceed thirty." In another community of six or seven hundred are four churches. "All these cases," writes my informant, "are within a radius of six miles. In an examination of statistics, covering some scores of churches, located mostly in agricultural districts and in small villages, I found the average population to the church to be less than three hundred. In a village of some three hundred or four hundred population there are three church edifices having a seating capacity of *eight hundred.*" Horace Mann estimated that ordinarily only about seventy per cent of the population could attend church on a given Sabbath, and as this attendance is spread over two or more services, he thought the places of worship did not need to accommodate more than fifty-eight per cent of the population. Yet in the case before us there is a church-seating capacity for the entire population twice over, while on the frontier there are communities as destitute of churches as any heathen village in the heart of benighted Africa, and we have large city populations where there is only one church to ten, twenty, and even forty thousand souls. I am informed of a village in Kansas where there are ten churches, four or five of them being Presbyterian of varying tint, and nine of these ten churches are dependent on home-missionary societies. Is this investing God's money as stewards who must give an account? Were these appropriations for the Kingdom or for the denomination? Would any one of these nine home-missionary societies think of supporting nine churches of their own order in one village? If such an investment would be poor economy for one denomination, it is poor economy for the Kingdom. Surely we need to introduce business principles into our Christianity about as much as we need to introduce Christian principles into our business.

The instances given above are hardly exceptional, and might be indefinitely multiplied. Such a condition of things is the natural result of a policy which ignores what other denominations are doing. Some churches are much less guilty than others, though probably none is in a position to cast a stone at a convicted offender. And while we waste our resources in competition, we sing,

> " We are not divided.
> All one body we."

Some tell us that we have Christian union now. But if this is union, I wonder what disunion must be. Is not the body of Christ dismembered when the eye says

to the hand, "I have no need of thee," and when the
head says to the feet, "I have no need of you"? When
members of the body of Christ act independently of
each other, and even in competition with each other,
they certainly do not fulfil the Master's prayer that
they might be one, as the Father and the Son are one.

Economy of resources demands not only an understanding between denominations in the distribution of
their forces through the land, but also local co-operation, that there may be the wisest application of effort
in the community. Without consultation and co-operation between denominations there is, as we have seen,
a strong tendency to plant most of the churches in
those parts of the city where they are least needed.
"It is a very important point in illumination," says Dr.
Parkhurst,[1] "to put your light where it is dark. If
corporations did not understand the philosophy of lighting cities by gas better than some of us seem to understand the philosophy of lighting cities by Gospel, the
nights in some of our wards would be as black as the
morals are." When churches are located with as much
reference to each other as are lamp-posts, the moral
darkness of the slums will be less dense.

What is now everybody's business proves to be
nobody's business. When according to the plan of co-
operation suggested in the following chapter each
church accepts a special responsibility for a particular
part of the town, every city ward and every country
school-district can be systematically and thoroughly
reached. Dr. James McCosh says that by the co-
operation of the ministers and churches in a town
where he was once a pastor "every man, woman, and
child in a parish of six thousand was carefully looked
after, and there were not a dozen people who did not
attend the house of God."[2]

---

[1] Address at the Boston Conference of the Evangelical Alliance, "National
Needs and Remedies," p. 317.

[2] Ex-President McCosh in *The Christian Union*, Feb. 6, 1890.

3. Again, co-operation is necessary to develop the latent forces of the church.

Paul chose the highest organism of which we have any knowledge to represent the church. He called it the *body* of Christ. In the human organism every member serves every other, and each increases the effectiveness of all. Your eyes make your one pair of hands worth more than a dozen pairs without eyes. The thumb makes the four fingers more serviceable than a score of fingers without a thumb. A regiment of soldiers represents vastly more than the fighting power of one man multiplied by a thousand. There is a cumulative power in organization which discredits the multiplication-table. Why is it that a company of soldiers can disperse an armed mob of ten or twenty times their numbers? It is not because the soldier is physically stronger or braver than the civilian, but because he has learned to co-operate. That is what drill means. It enables every soldier to make every other soldier more effective. "One shall chase a thousand and *two* put," not two thousand, but "*ten* thousand to flight"—the cumulative effect of co-operation.

We have very little in our Christian work which corresponds to the fighting power of a regiment of soldiers, and nothing at all that answers to the movements of a vast army as it executes comprehensive plans. What we need is, not companies of bushwhackers nor a great Christian mob, but a mighty Christian army, that shall move as one man and strike as one arm.

Military science has laid hold of the mighty power in organization; and never has the world seen such armies as exist to-day in Europe. Politics has seized upon the same principle; and, other things being equal, the party that is best organized wins. Manufacturers and business of every sort are massing capital, thus developing a power which crushes competition. Even sin is organizing. And we see gambling and lottery combinations powerful enough to shake a great state, while the liquor business has become the "liquor *power*" by virtue of organization. The papers give an account of the discovery of a "burglars' syndicate or trust," which according to the story was organized on the theory that burglars, safe-breakers, pickpockets, sneaks, and the like could operate with better success and greater safety if they joined forces. If the churches are to overcome the mighty evils which are contending for the mastery, and mould the civilization of the future, they must develop their latent forces by organization. If bad men can combine for bad ends, surely good men ought to be able to combine for good ends.

The differences between the various denominations need not interfere with their co-operation; they may even serve to increase its efficiency. Differences do not necessarily imply discord; without difference there can be no harmony.

There is such a thing as the polarity of truth as well as of light, which is its accepted emblem. All great truths have opposite poles or sides, and we are so fractional that we seize on a portion of the truth, only a segment of it, and forget or depreciate its complement. Hence the different sects, each emphasizing a different truth or portion of truth, need each other to round out its perfect circle. Different organs with different functions are a necessary condition of all high organization. A hundred hands do not make an organized body. There must be many members in one body having different offices. There is a mighty power in the various Protestant churches as yet undeveloped, because these various members of the body of Christ have failed to enter into true and helpful relations with each other. It is not enough that the separate members of that body be active, each one: "the whole body" must be "fitly joined together and compacted by that which every joint supplieth."

True, some of our differences are not complemental, but contradictory; they are, however, comparatively

insignificant. Missionaries in heathen lands find that
such differences become puerile in the presence of those
who worship the devil; and surely they are too insignificant to prevent our co-operation in the presence of
those who worship the world and the flesh. Christian
civilization is beset with perils many and great. We
need to make every ounce of possible power actual
power. Dare we for selfish and petty reasons refuse
that co-operation which will enable *two* to put ten
thousand to flight?

The Greeks were for generations weakened by their
inter-tribal jealousies and strifes. But when the Persian appeared on their borders with his mighty army
he proved to be the smith who with the hammer of war
welded those separate tribes, glowing in the fires of
patriotism, into a mighty nation. May not the difficulties and dangers which confront us in this transitional
period force the churches by a blessed compulsion to
draw together in close relations and to seek the strength
which comes from intelligent co-operation?

For lack of such co-operation there is every day a
waste of power which in view of the world's needs is
scarcely less than criminal. On a sea-voyage, Mr. Edison, after spending hours on deck looking at the waves,
said that it made him wild when he saw so much force
going to waste. "But one of these days," he continued,
"we will chain all that—the falls of Niagara as well as
the winds—and that will be the millennium of electricity." There is as much unused power in the Christian church as in the aimless winds and waves of the
sea; and it might well make a lover of the Kingdom
wild to see such vast resources run to waste. But some
day this power, utilized by organization, is to be linked
to the beneficent and intelligent purposes of Christ's
church, and *that* will be *God's* millennium of righteousness—the Kingdom come.

4. Again, without co-operation the church cannot
fulfil her social mission.

It is a very large part of the social mission of the

church to effect needed reforms, and the progress of nearly all reforms depends on the education of public opinion. The press has given a vastly enlarged meaning to publicity; and as its meaning has increased so has its influence. Men are growing more and more sensitive to public opinion. Even the Autocrat of all the Russias and the Sublime Porte are not insensible to it. Among occidental peoples, government is for the most part government by public opinion; and in this country, where it is altogether so, evils of every sort are amenable to it. When the popular conscience is properly educated, public opinion like the sun is found to have its rays of heat as well as of light. And when they are focalized by pulpit or press on some iniquity, and steadily held there as by a mighty burning-glass, that evil, no matter how deeply intrenched in human ignorance and prejudice and selfishness it may be, will at length scorch and writhe and smoke and blaze and consume away.

Dr. Thomas Arnold in a letter to Mr. Justice Coleridge said: " I would give anything to be able to organize a society for drawing public attention to the state of the laboring classes throughout the kingdom. . . . A society might give the alarm, and present the facts to the notice of the public. It was thus that Clarkson overthrew the slave trade." All this and much more the churches might easily accomplish. They might compel public attention not only to the evils which Dr. Arnold deplored, but also to a hundred others, and at the same time educate the public conscience while they enlightened public opinion.

Suppose the churches apply the two great principles advocated in this chapter and the preceding. By cooperating in systematic visitation they come into actual touch with the entire life of the community. They see its poverty and pauperism, its sickness and its unsanitary conditions, its prisons and poorhouses; they discover where are its saloons and gambling dens and houses of ill-repute, and gather evidence of their violations of law; they become acquainted with the life of the factory operative, the railway employé, the clerk, the sewing-woman, the working-girl, the mechanic, the miner, the unemployed; they learn what are the wrongs inflicted on classes and individuals, what laws work hardship and what good laws are not enforced; and they find a thousand needs that can be met only by the wise helpfulness of a friend.

The visitors are men and women carefully selected and judiciously assigned to their respective fields. Some of them will drop out of the work when the novelty wears off. Meanwhile recruits will be made of others who see the value of the work and are in deep sympathy with it, so that with this selecting process and the results of experience there is gained at length a choice body of men and women who have the spirit of Christ, the sense of human brotherhood, who know how to give themselves for others, who are living to make the world better, many of whom also have wealth, social position, and influence.

Now would it not be a saving thing to the community for such men and women to become thoroughly acquainted with prevailing evils, not as mere generalizations of which they have read or heard and which as generalizations are powerless to move most men, but as wrongs which have become real to them because individualized—wrongs whose victims are brother men they know or suffering women and children in whom they have become deeply interested ? How long could any popular abuse continue if its victims had each one aroused the intelligent interest and gained the Christian friendship of some good man or woman, back of whom are the churches which control public opinion touching all moral questions, and which are now organized to fulfil their social mission ?

When men who believe that Christianity has a remedy for the world's great evils distinctly *see* those evils they will feel them, and when they feel them they will bestir themselves to remove them. Knowledge, then action! The great evils of our cities are seen and felt by comparatively few. Bring Christian men and women into personal contact with the homes of the city, and with the attics and cellars called homes, and the social wrongs, the industrial abuses, and the nameless evils which now thrive in secret would set Christian blood to burning, and Christian nerves to tingling, and Christian tongues to crying aloud until public sentiment was aroused; and in this country public sentiment is only less mighty than Omnipotence.

Such contact of the richer and poorer classes would be worth almost as much to the former as to the latter. It would be the best possible way to form a right public opinion in the churches on many questions, and at the same time afford the churches the most effective means of educating public opinion in general. Take the saloon question, for instance.

Let a good man become thoroughly interested in rescuing a degraded and destitute family, and when he finds the saloon meeting him at every turn and repeatedly defeating his efforts, he will be very apt to see new light on the subject of the saloon and how to deal with it. There are hundreds of thousands of good men who would like to see this curse removed, but who think that "the time is not yet ripe for it." If these good men should undertake practical, personal rescue work, they would probably discover that they who are waiting for the times are precisely the men for whom the times are waiting.

Suppose, on the other hand, that the churches undertake to push the temperance reform. This must be done by educating public sentiment. But how? Touching this and all other reforms we may divide society into three classes, viz., friends, enemies, and those who are indifferent. The latter class is the large class. Most needed reforms tarry, not because so many oppose, but because so many don't care. It is from the indifferent that recruits and victories must be won. How is this class to be educated? When we announce a tem perance meeting, it is those who are already interested who attend, and the indifferent, because they are indifferent, stay away. That is, the meeting reaches those who need it least, and fails to reach those who need it most.

In like manner temperance books and periodicals are bought only by those already interested. The indifferent, whom we wish to influence, are precisely the ones who will not buy. We print tons of truth every week, enough to effect a dozen reforms in a twelvemonth, if it were only read and pondered by the right persons. The difficulty is that, for the most part, only those who already believe it read it or know anything about it.

If the church is to accept her social mission, if she is to accomplish needed reforms, she must learn to reach the indifferent. How! The answer is sufficiently obvious. If the mountain will not come to Mohammed, Mohammed must go to the mountain. Politicians no longer depend on great meetings to form public sentiment; they divide up city and country into districts, and send workers from house to house with documents to influence men personally. Why should not the churches adopt the same methods? Here is a noble opportunity for the Young People's Societies of Christian Endeavor, the Epworth Leagues, and the St. Andrew's Brotherhoods. What if these societies by intelligent co-operation should sow this land a dozen times a year with wisely selected literature, how profoundly they might influence public opinion on many needed reforms!

Many a vicious propaganda is actively using such methods among workingmen. We have left the formation of their economic and social theories quite long enough to ignorant quacks and conscienceless demagogues. We might by the medium suggested above supply their homes with good, bright, wholesome reading matter which would supplant the lying tracts and the sensational story-papers—the poison and the highly

seasoned sawdust—which so many now devour for
food.   Neighborhoods might be supplied with little
libraries of a dozen books each, which would be read
by working people and exchanged among themselves
when too tired to dress up for a visit to a reading-room
or the public library.

The various societies of young people referred to
have been giving their members good drill for several
years. That is well, but only preparatory. The camp
exists not for itself, but for the field of action. Is not
this the forward movement which these magnificent
Christian armies need to make? It will cost some
effort, some sacrifice; but it would not be worth the
doing if it did not.

The Young Peoples' Societies of Christian Endeavor
are peculiarly adapted to this kind of work. They emphasize the two great principles of co-operation and personal effort. Unlike many others, they are *within the
churches*, and at the same time *inter*-denominational.
The new methods demanded by changed conditions are
far more readily accepted by young Christians than by
their elders; and youthful zeal easily kindles into enthusiasm. Surely this movement is the divine method of
preparing the churches for the new era that is dawning.
In a dozen years this organization has reached the astonishing growth of 1,700,000 members. What may it
not become, what may it not do, in twelve years more ?

Furthermore, co-operation would not only afford the
churches a means of educating public opinion, but also
a medium for expressing it, which is hardly less
needed. Not unfrequently there are bills before our
state legislatures or the national congress which do
violence to the moral sense and the Christian conscience of the people. The obnoxious measure may
arouse popular indignation, but before the storm can
gather and break the bill becomes a law. The dis-
graceful New Jersey race-track legislation in the interest of gambling affords a good illustration.

If now the churches of each city and town were organized for co-operation, constituting what might be called the *collective church* of the community, and these collective churches were knit together into county and state organizations—all of which is entirely practicable—the Christian public opinion of the state could quickly and emphatically utter itself. By means of such an organization an immoral bill, within one week of its introduction, could be crushed with hundreds of thousands of protests.

And Christian men, if they will find each other out and co-operate, can make and unmake not only the laws spread on the statute-book of the state, but also the stronger, unwritten, and self-enforcing laws of society. The church might thus become what it ought always to have been—the controlling conscience of the social organism. This the church must become, if it is to reconstruct society on Christian principles. There is a vast and important remedial work yet to be done, but there is another work still more important. It is more important to prevent pauperism than to cure it, more important to stop producing criminals than to reform them; and if our social system is to be so readjusted and reformed as to remove the causes of pauperism and crime, the churches must take large views of their relations to society, must recognize their obligation to teach the second great law of Christ, and, as the social conscience, must hold all men, all corporations, all institutions, to a faithful observance of that law. All of which is impossible, without some form of organization and co-operation.

Precisely what form organization and co-operation are to take is still something of a question; that they are coming in some form I do not doubt. Some advocate denominational federation, which would make possible an official ecclesiastical co-operation. This would be good so far as it went, but such co-operation would be subject to very serious limitations. It would stop the competition of the various home-missionary societies, which would be a great economy of men and of money and a distinct gain every way ; but such a body would be weak in the prosecution of reforms and in attempts to solve the great sociological problems of our times. On all such questions its position would necessarily be conservative; it could not lead. It could never go faster than the slowest denomination entering into the federation. As there could be no compulsion, the denomination which was least advanced on any question would necessarily determine the position of the federated body on that question. Such would be the result of federation *at the top.*

Federation *at the bottom* promises larger results. By that I mean the federation of the local churches. A half-dozen neighboring churches, representing as many denominations, can be induced to take a much more advanced position concerning needed reforms and new methods of work than the half-dozen denominations which they represent. The conservatism of one community would not keep back a less conservative community; and a conservative church by declining to enter into the federation would not keep back less conservative churches of the same communion.[1]

This federation of local churches, or this collective church, might enter into co-operative relations with other like federations to form county and state organizations. Such organizations would have no ecclesiastical authority, but they would be far more aggressive and have vastly more influence than a federation of entire denominations.

There are increasing indications that if the churches do not soon· organize for the prosecution of social reforms they will lose their opportunity of leadership and with it their great opportunity to regain their lost hold on the masses and to shape the civilization of the future. For good men, representing reforms and philanthropic interests which have sprung up outside the churches, are beginning to feel after some form of organization which will afford the advantages of co-

---

[1] See article by the author in *The Review of Reviews*, Oct. 1892.

operation. Some common centre is needed in the interest of economy and efficiency where efforts to improve
the community may be co-ordinated and adjusted to
each other in some comprehensive plan—a common
centre to which information may be brought and to
which suggestions and complaints may be made—a
common centre, too, where the good citizens of the
community who want a better state of things can find
each other. Elijah was disheartened and God's chosen
ones in Israel were weak because the seven thousand
who feared God were known only to him and not to
each other. In the city there are " seven thousand "
men who have not bowed the knee to the Baal of the
political machine or kissed the Mammon of utterly
selfish living, but who are weak and disheartened because they are ignorant of each other. And they will
remain weak and disheartened as long as they each
one think, "I, even I only, am left." Doubtless there
are enough good men in every community to save it,
if they would only find each other and act together.

5. Again, we need co-operation because it is a necessary step toward organic union.

If we were perfectly frank one with another, I
think it would appear that the most serious obstacle to
organic union is not differences of creed or polity or
ritual, but a lack of entire confidence. The secret of
sectarian competition is the belief (not always unex-
pressed) that the world stands in peculiar need of *our*
church and the type of character produced by it; the
conviction that *we* are a little nearer the Lord and a
little more pleasing to him than any others.

Ignorance naturally breeds suspicion; our lack of
confidence is due to a lack of acquaintance. When
we get near enough to a man to see in him the likeness
of Christ, whether he be white or black, red or yellow,
we must needs love him; whatever be the name by
which he is called, whether Protestant or Catholic, even
though he refuses to fellowship us, we must love him in
spite of himself. But the various Christian denomina-

tions have not come near enough to each other to see distinctly that image of the common Master. Let them join in co-operative work, and they will get acquainted. Let them draw near enough for united action, and with shoulder to shoulder they will feel each other's hearts beating in the same loyalty to the same Lord, and then they will grow in mutual confidence and love.

Organic union involves co-operation and much more; churches, therefore, which cannot co-operate are incapable of organic union. Inasmuch as co-operation is a necessary step toward union, a church or a denomination which advocates the latter and yet refuses to practise the former is like a man standing at the bottom of a flight of steps, longing to reach the top, but refusing to take the first step because it is not the last. He scorns the low level of the first step because, as he says, it is of the nature of a compromise, and a man with his high aims will have none of it. Those who advocate union and will have nothing to do with co-operation show little Christian statesmanship.

Dr. John Henry Barrows writes[1]: "The churches must first learn to co-operate, and then later they will achieve whatever unity seems desirable." And the lamented Dr. Roswell D. Hitchcock said a short time before his death : "If ever organic union comes, it will come through co-operation." Certainly churches and denominations which cannot co-operate cannot coalesce.

Now the best possible field for co-operation is the philanthropic. As Canon Fremantle says[2]: "The surest way to get rid of sectarianism is to find new ground which is unaffected by it." Happily there exist among the churches no historical differences along sociological lines. Though divided in doctrine and polity, and though they might differ widely as to methods of evangelization, they can unite in seeking to solve the problems of labor, of pauperism, and of crime. The magnitude of these problems which confront the

---

[1] *The Independent*, Dec. 15, 1892.
[2] The Gospel of the Secular Life, p. 10.

churches demands their united efforts. Many reforms and Christian enterprises are as impossible to the churches acting independently as they are practicable to co-operating forces. Here, then, in the field of applied Christianity the co-operation of the churches is at the same time the most needed and the most practicable.

All churches known as Evangelical hold the great essentials of Christianity in common; they differ only in non-essentials. Is it not evident that the churches of one community, which are united in the great essentials of Christian faith and experience, and which at the same time share the great responsibility of Christianizing that community, are in reality much more closely related to each other than to churches a hundred or a thousand miles away, with which the only distinctive bond is some non-essential of doctrine or a common form of government or ritual? Are not the common work, the common difficulties, the common responsibilities and opportunities, of churches in the same city or town more than the mere name or the form of organization which they share in common with the churches of distant communities? May it not be that the cordial recognition of this fact and the active co-operation which would follow would do more for Christian union than the official action of ecclesiastical bodies?

We have seen that the great tendency of the times is toward combination, co-operation, organization. Carlyle somewhere describes the insight of genius as a "co-operation with the real tendency of the world." If we cannot claim the "insight of genius" for the churches, may we not at least look for sufficient insight of common-sense to discern the obvious signs of the times, to see the great march of events, and to place themselves abreast of the mighty forces which are moulding the civilization of the new era?

CHAPTER XV.

THE problem of the country and that of the city may
be called generic, so that to solve these two great problems is to solve many.

There have been pointed out two great principles,
harmonious with man's constitution, with the fundamental teachings of Christ, and with the laws of historical development. Of the truth and importance of
these principles I am absolutely sure. That they must
be applied before the Kingdom can fully come, I am
equally sure. That the two great problems before us
are to be solved by the application of these two principles I cannot doubt, but of specific methods of applying
them I speak with diffidence, and of course subject to
the correction of wiser men and to the test of more extended experiment.

Methods must be simple and flexible, and vary with
the varying needs and conditions of different communities. One of the following would seem to be adapted
or adaptable to every city and to every village having
two or more churches.

Let the churches come together by their pastors and
a given number of lay representatives from each
church, chosen as the churches may see fit. In villages
where there are but few churches, it may be desirable
to make every member of any church who is interested
in the objects of the organization eligible to membership. This lay element differentiates the organization
from the ministerial association where one exists,
makes it more representative of the churches, and

318

probably renders its discussions less speculative and more practical.

Its objects are as follows :

1. To afford a point of contact for the churches—a common centre, the need of which was presented in the preceding chapter. The several churches constitute the collective church of the community, of which this is the official board or executive committee.

2. To cultivate the fellowship of the churches. Creeds were once made the chief and almost only ground of fellowship and, hence, of disfellowship. But with the growth of individualism there has been conceded a much larger liberty of belief. Moreover, men are learning to distinguish essentials from non-essentials. As a matter of fact the lay membership of the various evangelical denominations is not separated to any considerable extent by creeds, but rather by temperament, habit, and inheritance. Probably nine tenths of the members of any one of these denominations would to-day be members of any other, if their parents had been. The lack of fellowship and confidence, so far as it exists, is due almost wholly to a lack of acquaintance.

3. To foster co-operation, with all the advantages enumerated in the preceding chapter.

4. To cultivate a broader idea of the mission of the churches, and to study the problems of the times common to all communities, together with those peculiar to the manufacturing city, the commercial centre, the lumber town, the mining camp, the agricultural district, and the like ; thus enabling the collective church to undertake its social mission by consciously and intelligently attempting to apply the principles of the Gospel to the entire life of the community.

Such a committee of the churches enables them to undertake their own proper work instead of handing it over to outside organizations. The collective church is concerned with everything that Christianity was intended to do for the community in which it exists, and its committee is a Sabbath committee, a temperance organization, a law and order league, a society for tenement-house reform, and for every other reform which is related to human welfare, *just so far* as the churches are educated up to their social mission.

The Gospel will prove to be the panacea of the moral, and ultimately of the physical, evils of the world'; and the commission of the church to apply it is as broad as the wide world's needs. When this commission is intelligently accepted, the best brains and hearts of the community will meet statedly to study its problems and to apply to their solution the principles taught by Jesus.

5. To afford a means of crystallizing, and a medium of expressing, the public sentiment of the churches as occasion may require; thus enabling the collective church to perform its function as the conscience of the social organism.

The above represents the simplest form of organization. Another might differ from it only in scope. Formed in the same way, it has the same objects, but in addition undertakes an *annual canvass* of the community.

There are many cities and towns which are not ready to begin systematic visitation, and would not sustain it if they did, but which feel the need of a more exact knowledge of the population and of some concerted action in order to reach the multitude with Christian influence. An annual canvass, properly followed up by each church, is well adapted to the wants of such communities. It shows where the new-comers are. It reveals who are the non-church-goers and what are their church preferences. It finds many laid-away church letters. It makes the churches better acquainted with the condition of the masses and serves to bring them into closer relations. It sometimes reveals needs which had been unknown or at least unappreciated, and furnishes data for the intelligent location of new missions or the inauguration of benevolent enterprises. It affords an annual opportunity to furnish the city or town with the Scriptures and other religious reading, to gather the children into Sabbath schools, and to invite the whole population to attend the church of their preference.

Of course the knowledge gained by a canvass is useless unless used. Every co-operating church needs a committee of visitors who shall assist their pastor in attaching to their church all the newly-discovered families who express a preference for it.

This annual canvass is made by paid, skilled labor or by the gratuitous work of church visitors. In the latter case, discretion must be used, of course, in the assignment of districts to canvassers.

Another form of organization, having the same general objects as those already described, is distinguished by *systematic visitation.* There is an important difference between the canvasser and the visitor. The former is a stranger (in all cities), the latter becomes a friend. The primary object of the one is information, that of the other is influence. The visitor accomplishes all that the canvasser does and much more. He makes the several families assigned to him (or her) a study; he seeks to gain their confidence, to do them good in every possible way, and then uses the influence thus acquired to win them to Christ and the church. Octavia Hill says[1] : "If once you have got a wise and loving heart established in close personal relations with a small number of families, you have got an arrangement capable of being utilized to almost any extent."

The essential features of this method may be stated as follows :

1. The churches of a community agree to divide the territory among themselves, no church taking more than it can work thoroughly. It is far better to work one half of a city or township well than to half work the whole. But what if some very conservative church refuses to co-operate ? That need not keep back the

---

[1] *The Nineteenth Century.*

others. Let them organize and move on. When the church which refuses to co-operate has had her nap out she will wake up to discover that she has been left far behind.

2. Each co-operating church holds itself responsible to carry the Gospel, by repeated visitation, to every non-church-going family in its district. It will commonly be found, I think, that the non-church-goers are more easily influenced if the church-goers are included in the visitation ; the object in calling on the latter being to arouse their interest and to enlist their co-operation in influencing their non-church-going neighbors.

3. *It should be distinctly understood that the district does not in any sense limit the activity of the church accepting it or that of other churches.* The district is not a parish with exclusive rights; its boundary lines may be crossed either way. When a church accepts a district it surrenders no rights in other districts, but agrees to see that at least every family within the assigned limit is reached by Christian influence. It is perfectly at liberty to reach as many more families elsewhere as it is able.

4. The invitations to church and Sabbath-school should be given in the name of all the co-operating churches, and notice of preferences sent to the churches or pastors for whom preference is expressed. It is very important that a church should not discontinue its visits as soon as a preference is expressed for some other, but to continue its efforts in behalf of the preferred church until the family is well identified with it, or until a visitor from that church has taken the family in hand.

5. Each church is left perfectly free to adopt its own method of work. Some will leave the pastor to do it all until he discovers that he cannot. Some will commit it to the officers of the church. Some will employ the paid services of missionaries; but it is to be hoped, for the sake of the spiritual quickening of the churches, that the work will generally be done by the laity. In the latter case the church will select as many visitors and super-

visors as it pleases. The object of having supervisors is
to secure the greater efficiency of the work and to avoid
overtaxing the pastor.

6. The co-operating churches meet monthly, bi-
monthly, or quarterly, to report the work done, to devise and execute plans for meeting the needs which
have been disclosed, and to profit by each other's experience.

The churches may be employing a half-dozen different
methods, but this habitual comparing of results will
naturally lead to the survival of the fittest.

This method of work makes application of the two
fundamental principles of co-operation and personal
effort or personal contact, and is equally applicable to
country and city. But let us apply these two principles
more specifically to—

I. The problem of the country. There are hamlets
where there are no churches, and others where the
churches are pastorless and more dead than alive—quite
too torpid to undertake such a work as has been outlined. Where the need of aggressive Christian work
is greatest, there are the least ability and disposition
to undertake it. To meet such conditions a *county* organization is needed. There are few counties except in
the newer states where there are not several strong
churches. If these churches would accept a responsibility for the whole county, it would be the first great
step toward solving the problem of the country. And
these strong churches may well recognize a responsibility for the rural districts, for they have grown strong at
the expense of the rural churches. The removals from
the villages which have depleted so many country
churches have added just so much strength to the
churches of the county-seat or of some other smart city.
So that if the strong churches should share the labors of
the weak ones, it would be in many instances only the
payment of a just debt.

If it is the duty of the churches of a county to evangelize that county, then the responsibility rests on each

according to its ability. If the churches of the county-seat have grown strong until they contain one half of the numerical and financial strength of the churches of the county, though the county contains a dozen townships, the churches of this one township may fairly be said to bear as much responsibility for the whole county as all the churches of the remaining eleven.

The feeblest churches are in the most destitute districts. So that without co-operation the greatest burdens often rest on the weakest churches. If now the churches of a county will organize and co-operate to discharge their responsibility to the whole county, the work can be so divided as to adapt the burden to the strength of each.

This county organization could foster the formation of local organizations in the several townships, on some one of the plans suggested above. To the most destitute neighborhoods, not reached by the churches, it could send a county missionary, who would visit the people in their homes, distribute religious and temperance literature, hold cottage meetings, and organize Sunday-schools. Such a missionary could make the rounds of these destitute districts several times a year. Young women from Mr. Moody's Training School at Northfield have been employed to do such work in some of the neglected districts of Vermont, and the reports of their success have been very gratifying.

Fellowship meetings might be held throughout the county which would do much to allay sectarian strife and to quicken spiritual life. Lecture courses might be arranged which would be stimulating and helpful. Loan libraries might be put in circulation, different sections being sent to different towns, and periodically exchanged. Such a county organization would be effective in the prosecution of all needed reforms, would make the churches the most powerful agency in every good work, and at length win for them a commanding influence in all departments of human life.

The Andover Band of Maine is a company of five

young ministers, who, having associated themselves, while yet in the seminary, to help solve the problem of the country, were settled near each other over five feeble churches in Maine. This band has been instrumental in organizing a monthly reunion of the ministers of all denominations in the county, which has proved helpful in many ways. It is an all-day meeting, affording opportunity for fellowship, devotional exercises, reports, papers, discussions, and suggestions.[1] While perhaps few such organizations would care to meet every month, a quarterly meeting or only an annual meeting might do much to facilitate co-operation.

Let the churches of a county be inspired with the New Testament conception of Christ's kingdom in the earth, let them gain some sense of their responsibility for the welfare of society, and they would soon recognize the necessity of co-operation in order to discharge that responsibility. Having formed such an organization as that described above, and having gained a clear conception of the problem of the country which springs from the drift of population cityward, they could soon solve it by devising effective measures to prevent the deterioration which attends increasing isolation.

If only a few ministers in the county have seen the vision of the Kingdom and have felt the impulse of the coming social movement, they can make an important contribution to the solution of the problem of the country by forming such a county organization, which would greatly aid in giving currency to enlarged ideas and new methods.

Country communities stand in peculiar need of some of the new institutional methods of church work, the practicability and value of which in rural districts have been already demonstrated. It is to be hoped that the inability of a feeble church to inaugurate such methods alone will lead the churches of many a village to co-operate in making provision for the intellectual and social life of the community.

---

[1] *The Andover Review*, March-April, 1893.

The isolation of dwellers in the country has made them slow to avail themselves of the advantages of co-operation; but they are beginning to learn that by means of it they can secure larger returns for the same or less outlay. For instance, it has been proved by experience that one large graded school centrally located, to which the children are brought by free carriage, is not only cheaper than several schools scattered through as many districts, but affords vastly better training. This new method, which may yet revolutionize the educational system of country communities, originated some years since in Concord, Massachusetts, and is now spreading quite rapidly. "Bedford has taken up the same idea. It has closed its four outlying schools and now has but one schoolhouse, located at the centre, with accommodations for High, Grammar, Intermediate, and Primary schools, all in this building. Instead of seven teachers, four are now found sufficient. The children are daily brought from their homes and returned at the expense of the town, and farmers' wives are hired as drivers, the service costing only six dollars a week for each conveyance. The school is now pronounced by competent judges equal to any in the large cities, while no child has to walk over a third of a mile and the cost of the schooling is no more than under the district plan. By the new method real estate in outlying districts has improved in value, owners recognizing that their children have new advantages." [1]

In like manner co-operation will secure good roads, without which good schools and strong churches are well-nigh impossible. Good roads also give an upward impulse to property and serve to relieve isolation.

Thus it appears that the depressing and deteriorating influences of isolation may be largely or entirely overcome by the principle of co-operation, variously applied, and by Christian visitation.

But the very great and prevalent evil of too many and competing churches in the country requires heroic

[1] Dr. Addison P. Foster in *The Advance*, September 22, 1892.

treatment. Experience thus far does not encourage the hope that union churches will afford a solution of the problem. We need a new and brief age of Christian martyrdom, in which many churches shall suffer death for the glory of God. But who shall select the victims? We can hardly expect many responses to a call for volunteers.

Suppose there were a state committee, selected so as to represent the various denominations concerned and the different sections of the state. Let the character of the committee and the method of choosing it be such as to command the entire confidence of the several denominations. This committee, with the aid of the last census, could easily be made acquainted with the facts concerning superfluous churches. Suppose, after considering the population of a community, the prospect of its growth, the number of churches, the numerical and financial strength of each, the hold which each has on the people, and every other pertinent point, the committee is *unanimously* agreed that a certain church or certain churches ought to be disbanded. As this opinion would be intelligent and disinterested, and shared by those members of the committee who represent the denominations of the condemned churches, there could be little doubt of the correctness of the judgment, and it would certainly have great weight with the public. I do not, however, imagine for a moment that a church whose sectarian spirit has grown lusty by fierce competition would have grace enough to die on the simple recommendation of such a committee. The "dying grace" would have to be bestowed by ecclesiastical authority or by the denominational home-missionary society, which in nineteen cases out of twenty keeps the struggling church alive.

In those denominations, like the Baptist and the Congregational, in which the local church has entire autonomy, there is no ecclesiastical authority that could compel the dissolution of the church. All that could be done, therefore, in the case of such a church which refused to take itself off, would be to withdraw home-missionary aid. If a few people insist on wearing expensive ecclesiastical frills of a certain distinctive pattern, they should be required to do it at their own expense.

If the missionary societies of the leading denominations should agree that they would give no aid to any church condemned by such a committee, the withdrawal of aid would, in most cases, be decisive of the result; and even where it was not, the money which had formerly been worse than squandered would now be saved for fields suffering for the lack of it.

A number of the great denominational home-missionary societies would undoubtedly agree to such a plan. Some would at first refuse, but their refusal would throw on them the responsibility, and I may add the odium, for the continuance of the existing waste. Public opinion on this subject is having a healthy growth, and even ecclesiastical narrowness cannot always resist its influence, especially in view of the fact that the public holds the purse out of which home-missionary societies live. If such state committees were formed, and several of the large denominational societies should come to such an agreement, it would solve the problem in all communities where there were only such churches as represented the communion of the several co-operating societies. And the good results which would certainly appear in due time would constitute an unendurable criticism on those denominations which by their narrowness maintained the division, strife, and weakness of the churches in other communities.

If such a plan were generally adopted, the home-missionary societies would each save many thousands of dollars annually for needy fields in the city and on the frontier, now neglected for lack of funds. While each denomination would lose a number of feeble and dependent churches, none would lose any considerable membership, for losses in one community would be compensated by gains in another. Thus in each of two towns in North Dakota there was a Congregational and a Presbyterian church. As the population in each case was small, it was decided that the four churches were not needed in the two communities. Accordingly at Groton the Congregational church disbanded and joined the Presbyterian, while at Columbia the Presbyterian church disbanded and joined the Congregational; which was no loss of membership to either denomination, and was a positive gain in Christian influence, an economy of ministerial service, and a considerable saving of money to both.

Doubtless there would be some who, mistaking denominational preference for Christian principle, would conscientiously refuse to unite with any communion except their own. Such would be something of a numerical loss, but ceasing to perpetuate these unworthy divisions to future generations in the community would compensate a thousandfold.

Such a committee, in addition to the service suggested, might in many ways facilitate co-operation between denominations so as to reduce friction, economize force, and increase results in the extension of the kingdom of their common Lord.

Let us attempt now to apply the two great principles to—

II. The problem of the city. We have seen that this problem is twofold : that it is divided into the problem of municipal government and that of city evangelization.

1. Remedies for the evil of municipal misrule are being sought in various quarters through a reconstruction of the form of city government, the holding of municipal elections at a different period of the year from state and national elections, the Australian ballot, patent ballot-boxes, and the like. Is it not significant and somewhat startling that we find ourselves relying on mechanical means to prevent fraud ? Method is important in government as it is in business, Christian work, and elsewhere, but it cannot be made a substitute

for character. Let us by all means find the best possible form of city government, let us by all means separate municipal elections from all others, let us by all
means have the Australian ballot. All these may be
efficient, but we shall not find them sufficient. We
need not hope to save the city by any we-touch-the-
button-and-it-will-do-the-rest arrangement. Self-government is not a question of ingenuity. Mechanism
cannot be made a substitute for morals. The solution
of the problem of municipal government must be found
in *men*—men of *character*, men of *intelligence*. The
only way to make the city a law unto itself is to make
the *citizen* a law unto himself. If each of fifty men is
individually incapable of self-government, or if most of
them are, then the fifty formed into an organization
would be incapable of self-government. And this is
equally true of fifty thousand or of five hundred thousand.

The individual must be made capable of self-control;
this is the only remedy which is radical. And here we
see the connection between municipal reform and city
evangelization. That reform will not be fully accomplished until the masses have been brought under the
influence of the Gospel, nor, on the other hand, can the
city be saved morally and spiritually under a government which is in league with iniquity.

Meanwhile much can be accomplished for the regeneration of municipal government by applying the two
principles of individualism or independence and that of
co-operation or organization. Either without the other
is futile, or becomes a positive evil. There is no lack of
organization with the political machine of either great
party; the boss is always an organizer. But the voters
sacrifice the principle of individualism to that of organization. The ignorant and unamericanized voters,
spoken of in a preceding chapter, can be bought and
sold like cattle, and delivered in "blocks" of almost
any required size. And the great bulk of American
voters, who are more culpable because more intelligent,

are brought into line by the party whip. They have not sufficient independence to break away from the bondage of party politics, which is the bane of municipal elections.

On the other hand, many who have become disgusted with the corruption and folly of politics assert their independence, but neglect organization and absent themselves from the polls. If all good citizens would first declare their independence of party politics in municipal elections, and then organize to elect the men best fitted for the desired service, thus applying the two principles commended, the scandal of our rabble-ruled cities would soon cease.

2. We saw in a preceding chapter that the problem of city evangelization was complicated by the mixed composition of the city, the environment of certain classes, the isolation which separates localities, classes, and individuals, the lack of homes, and the rapid growth of the city. The two great principles which have been discussed are admirably calculated to meet the needs which arise out of these conditions.

The mixed character of the population and the isolation, which springs from it and from other causes, call for personal contact and friendly, Christian intercourse. Such intercourse, by winning confidence, would do much to remove the suspicion, prejudice, dislike, and even hatred which are now common between different classes and races, thus opening homes and hearts to outside influences. It would do much to assimilate and Americanize foreign elements. It would show the victims of the city's "crowded loneliness" that somebody really cares for them. It would convince multitudes that there is such a thing as disinterestedness in the world. Thus this little thread of friendly visitation, insignificant as it may seem, running back and forth between the many fragments of society, would at length suffice to stitch it into something like a whole.

The lack of homes also emphasizes the need of Christian visitation. A very large proportion of the popula-

tion of the city, and especially of that class not reached
by the churches, moves every year or oftener. This is
one reason why the churches fail to get a permanent
hold upon them. If church ties begin to be formed,
they are soon broken by removal. If this class were
followed up by friendly visitors, church relations might
be easily re-established.

Moreover, of the great army which every year
marches up from country to city a very large proportion are young men and women, who by the change
become homeless. Old associations are uprooted. Un-
accustomed to city ways, they are peculiarly exposed to
temptation. Many yield, and help to swell the human
wreckage of the great maelstrom. What a blessed
thing it would be if the churches so worked their fields
in the country that when John or Mary goes up to the
city to live, the friendly visitor at once learned it and
sent word to the Young Men's or Young Women's
Christian Association in the city, or better yet to the
churches so organized that they could quickly find the
new-comers and be the first to put an arm around them!

The environment of the slums constitutes an obstacle
to city evangelization the removal of which will require
co-operation in the largest sense.

The slums are the "putrefying sores" of the city.
They may be mollified with the ointment of missions
and altogether closed at one point, but it will be only to
break out at another until there is a constitutional treatment which shall purge the poison of the social system.
As long as men violate the divine laws for the individual and for society there will be slums, for they are
the perfectly natural outcome of sin.

Though the mission brings the most abandoned men
and women into right relations to God, as long as men
sustain wrong relations with each other—as long as
society is based on the existing law of selfish competition instead of Christian law of brotherly love—there
will be the weak, the wretched, and the vicious, who
will gravitate to the horrible pit called the slum.

The last of the above-enumerated factors of the problem of city evangelization, viz., the rapid growth of the city, obviously demands the co-operation of the churches to prevent overlapping and the waste of resources, which must be used with the best economy if church provision is to overtake the growth of urban population.

Thus each of the several conditions which help to complicate the problem of city evangelization calls for the application of one or both of the two principles of co-operation and personal contact, the necessity and value of which have been already presented.

As soon as the churches perceive and accept their social mission, they will lay hold of these two principles as absolutely indispensable, if they would accomplish it. When they really undertake to save the city thoroughly they will see the necessity of knowing it thoroughly. The friendly visitors will be seen to be the needed points of contact between the churches and the multiform life of the city. They will serve at the same time as mediums of information and channels of influence. They will reveal the magnitude of the needs of the city, which the organized strength of the churches alone can supply.

The forms of organization and work suggested at the beginning of this chapter would seem to be suited to any city. If the city is large, it will be well to form separate branches of the organization in the several wards.

When applying these two principles to the evangelization of the city, we must remember that so far as religious work is concerned every considerable city is two cities—what we call the residence portion and the business portion, though the latter is perhaps more densely populated than the former. Conditions differ so widely in these two parts of the city that they must be recognized by corresponding adaptations in our methods of work.

In what is called the residence portion is to be found most of the American element of the population. In

what is called the business portion the population is
chiefly foreign. There is a constant drift of the well-
to-do element (which is generally the church-going
element) from the business portion of the city to the
residence portion. This makes it easy to plant churches
and to bring them to self-support in the latter, unless
conditions favorable to church growth have resulted in
overstocking localities, thus producing a sharp denominational competition. Of course this drift of church-
going people away from the business portion produces
conditions there precisely opposite those created in the
residence districts. The down-town churches, once
strong, are depleted until they die or follow their membership up-town or become missions dependent on up-
town churches. The pastor of a down-town church in
New York informs me that in a district including four
wards he has seen ten churches die, three remove, two
become missions, and three unite with other churches.
Thus in a few years eighteen churches have disappeared
from a densely populated district.

The business portion of the city with its tenement
population is not desired by the churches, and comes to
be known as the field of the City Missionary Society,
where one exists.

The suggestions made above in regard to organization
are `applicable only to the residence portion of the city,
where churches are numerous and strong. The problem
of city evangelization in the business and tenement-
house districts is much more difficult, and requires a
different solution, which, I believe, is to be found in the
methods of the McAll Mission and in the institutional
church.

The popular idea of city evangelization in this country
has been to hire a large hall or build a tabernacle, and
employ famous evangelists to preach to thousands. But
the work is temporary, and the results are usually
rather disappointing. And, however gratifying the results may be, such work must always be limited, because
the number of great evangelists will always be small.

When we make the work permanent by establishing a mission, we plan for large numbers. We say that the preacher can as easily speak to a thousand as a hundred; and accordingly a large audience-room makes the first cost of the mission heavy. Then we must have a man who can fill the room and keep it filled; and any one who can thus sustain himself year after year will probably be an educated man, with the tastes and necessities of an educated man, which means that he must have a salary of two thousand or twenty-five hundred dollars a year. There must be a number of helpers to make the most of so expensive a plant, so that the continued cost of the mission is heavy. Manifestly no city will support more than a few such missions.

Some eight or ten years ago Professor Curtiss of Chicago declared that a hundred missionaries were needed to give that city the Gospel. But at that rate of supply, or one half that rate, it would be impossible to find the educated men and the millions of money which would be needed to evangelize our cities.

With the present or any prospective supply of men and means, our existing methods must prove inadequate. We need many points of contact with the churchless multitude of the city, and the able men who are capable of conducting great mission enterprises cannot be sufficiently multiplied to meet the necessity. Most of the world's work is done, and must always be done, by ordinary men; and this is as true of Christian work as of any other. The best methods, then, of reaching the multitude must be those with which ordinary men can succeed.

We are now prepared to note several important particulars in which the methods of the McAll Mission are in contrast with those commonly used in American cities. The promoters of that mission aim at many small meetings rather than a few large ones. In many of their missions there are meetings every night, and in all several meetings a week. Our Gospel meetings are too often confined to the Sabbath, with one or two midweek prayer-meetings. They have two speakers, who *talk* fifteen minutes each; we have one, who preaches thirty minutes or more. They frequently have different speakers every night; we commonly think that a change of speakers is almost as bad as a change of congregations. By admitting a change of speakers, they are enabled to make use of a vast amount of volunteer service, having six or seven stations for a single paid missionary. Thus they can conduct a hundred missions at a total expense for salaries of only $18,000. With us a hundred city missions would mean more than one hundred paid missionaries, at an expense of not less than $200,000. Of course salaries are larger here than in France, but that is only an added reason for adopting cheaper methods.

If the methods of the McAll Mission are less expensive than ours, they are no less effective. Indeed, I do not know where to look in this country for missions of like evangelistic power. Mr. McAll began his work in the worst quarter of Paris, where, during the reign of the Commune, only a few weeks before, cart-loads of priests had been shot down like dogs. The police repeatedly warned him that his preaching there might cost him his life. But this quarter, once characterized by lawlessness, lewdness, and drunkenness, and famous for desperate men and furious women, has been so transformed by these missions that it is now one of the most orderly sections of the city.

There is no reason why the same Gospel, applied in the same way to meet the same human needs, should not produce the same results in New York, or Chicago, or San Francisco as in Paris. Of course conditions differ, but, excepting the higher rents and salaries required in the United States, conditions seem to be more favorable here than there.

There is one embarrassment to which mission work in halls is subjected, and which the McAll Mission has not escaped, viz., the difficulty with which converts are induced to identify themselves with some church. The best remedy will be found, I believe, in uniting institutional methods of church work with those of the McAll Mission. The remarkable success of the so-called institutional churches in down-town districts, already cited, is sufficient evidence of the power of these methods to attract the masses.

But how are these expensive churches to be provided? Here is an opportunity to apply the principle of co-operation, both between different denominations and between churches of the same denomination.

Divide the business and tenement portion of the city into districts, each as large as could be properly cared for by one church. Let the uptown churches build in each district a church thoroughly equipped for institutional methods of work. Such churches in such districts would require a large outlay. Let the expense be divided between three, four, half a dozen churches— as many as may be necessary—*all of the same denomination.*

Suppose, for instance, that several Methodist churches have thus accepted a certain district as their especial field. The pastors can say to their people: "Here are so many thousand souls assigned to us. If we do not give them the Gospel, no one will. Our several churches propose to plant a church in that district; and when planted it will be a *Methodist* church. Now, how much will you give toward it?" When a definite amount of money is needed to do a specific and a *denominational* work, I think about ten times as much can be raised as could be secured for an undenominational city-missionary society needing an indefinitely large amount.

When the church is built, these several churches having a special interest in it can send down members enough to form a nucleus for the new organization.

Around this institutional church, at appropriate distances from it and from each other, let there be opened mission halls on the McAll plan—as many as the district needs. Each one of these halls, being operated from the church as a centre, becomes a recruiting station for it. Let these halls be on the ground-floor, of course, and large enough to accommodate only from one hundred to two hundred people, which would insure a comparatively low rent. If there are only five or six of these halls in a district, one man, the pastor or a helper, can take the general charge of them all; and he will need for his work the McAll spirit and a double portion of sanctified common-sense.

With proper supervision most of the work may be volunteer service and unpaid. Ministers who are adapted to such work (and it is a pity that all are not) and other effective speakers are asked: "How many evenings can you give us this month?" A schedule is made, in which each hall is supplied with two speakers each evening. As the work progresses a large amount of lay talent will be developed, much of it in the class of men among whom the work is done. There will be not a few plain men who are unable to speak to edification except as they tell the story of their conversion; and this they may be able to do very effectively. Such men, judiciously paired with others who can instruct, may be used at a dozen different halls on as many different nights. In the course of time there would be raised up from among the people men with special adaptations for such work, whose whole time could be secured for salaries equal to the wages they have received. Such men could do the gathering far better than men who have been educated away from the people, and who must be paid two or three thousand dollars a year for *not* reaching them. As rapidly as recruits are gained, let them be turned over for drill to the church, whose pastor is a trained man and able to build them up in the most holy faith.

After this manner each strong denomination in our large cities might take several such districts, contiguous or otherwise, and make adequate provision for them. The strongest churches would each be able to take a district. Thus, by common understanding and

co-operation between denominations and churches of
the same denomination, the neglected parts of the city
might all be cared for.

One great advantage of such a plan would be the
localizing of responsibility. This responsibility for the
evangelization of the city, which is acknowledged by
all, is accepted by few because it is general. Localize it
and it will be felt.

But it is asked, "What becomes of the city-missionary society on this plan? I would treat it precisely as
if it were a denomination—give it as large a section of
the city, as many districts as it can work and work
thoroughly. I have never heard of a city-missionary
society which had means sufficient to do one half the
work suffering to be done.

We have seen how the principle of co-operation may
be applied to advantage in the evangelization of the
business and tenement portion of the city. House-to-
house visitation is no less important; indeed, it is more
needed in this quarter of the city than in the other. It
would do much to relieve the isolation of the many
foreign elements, and do much to assimilate and
Americanize them. It would afford the only effective
remedy for pauperism under the existing social system,
and would exert an influence on all social, moral, and
industrial reforms. But not many down-town churches
have the membership from which to draw a sufficient
number of visitors of the right sort.

Every such church needs a number of consecrated
and trained women who will give their whole time,
some to visitation, some to nursing the sick, others to
kindergartening.

Among the tenement-houses there are swarms of
children under the school age who might be blessed for
life by a Christian kindergarten training; and such
training diffuses a blessed influence through the homes
from which the children come.

There is always need of the ministry of healing,
freely rendered in His name who had compassion on

bodily as well as spiritual suffering and need. Every institutional church ought to have its corps of trained nurses and its corps of trained visitors—call them deaconesses, if you please—who know how to minister to sick bodies and sick souls, and who will give their service freely for Christ's sake and for the sake of humanity.

The order of deaconesses was instituted in the early Christian church and continued for more than a thousand years until it disappeared in the Dark Ages. It is occasion for rejoicing that the order or office has been re-established in modern times, and it has fully demonstrated its worth in many parts of the world. The deaconess is given a home, a habit, and spending money, but not a salary. It is safe to say that there would be no lack of noble women who would devote themselves to such work if only a training-school and a home were opened to them.

Why should there not be in every considerable city such a school and such a home founded and sustained by the co-operation of the various denominations? There is no sectarian way of nursing the sick, no sectarian way of kindergartening, no sectarian way of lifting families up out of pauperism by personal influence. Why should not the various denominations unite in training a body of women for personal Christian ministration?

Such women, manifesting the love of Christ in their self-devotion, by their sympathy and helpfulness, their tact and skill, win their way into the families of Romanists, of Jews, and of all classes.

Surely these two principles of personal service and of co-operation, if applied as they might be applied, are equal to solving the difficult problem of city evangelization.

Chalmers applied these principles to work in the worst section of Edinburgh, and with what result the world knows. He opened his mission in an old tan-loft, opposite a place notorious as the scene of fourteen murders. The whole community seemed given over to idleness, drunkenness, lewdness, and crime. The police warned him that his life and the lives of his visitors were in danger. But in five years he had established a self-supporting church, an industrial school, a washing-house, and a savings-bank; and the people, one fourth of whom were on the poor roll when the work began, now contributed £70 a year to benevolent work outside their own community, while the police declared their occupation gone.

When Dr. Guthrie once looked down on one of the most squalid, abandoned, and wicked quarters of the same city, he exclaimed, "A beautiful field!" Our great cities have many "beautiful fields" for demonstrating the saving power of the Gospel of God, provided only that it is faithfully applied according to these two principles which he has implanted in man's constitution.

CHAPTER XVI.

AN ENTHUSIASM FOR HUMANITY.

THIS generation is gaining what Walter Besant calls the sense of humanity. The family, the community, the clan, the nation, can no longer live wholly unto itself. The oneness of the race is being forced upon us in many ways.

We saw in Chapter VII that the changes in methods of production and distribution are leading up to a world-life. This means, of course, that the interests of different classes and of different nations are being bound together into one bundle. In the "age of homespun" each family was industrially, though not socially, a little world living apart, supplying almost all of its wants by its own industries, and needing very little money. There are women still alive in this country who in their youth could take the wool from a sheep's back, card, spin, and weave it, and make it into a coat. When most people built their own houses, produced their own food, wove their own clothes, made most of their own tools, utensils, and furniture, it made no difference to them whether the fortunes of people over the mountains or beyond the sea were rising or falling. They were independent ; they lived a separate life.

But the cheapening of manufacture by machinery destroyed home industries ; there was a division of labor, and money became necessary as a medium of exchanging the products of labor. The farmer must now not only make his crops feed his family, but clothe and house them as well. That is, he must produce for the market. His world is no longer confined to his farm; he is now interested in the ability of other men to buy what he has to sell, and he is vitally concerned with the crops and their cost beyond the mountains and over the sea. If on the other side of the world there are lands that can produce wheat much cheaper than he can produce it, and the product of five acres can be brought to his market for less than it costs him to fertilize one acre, it becomes an economic impossibility for him to raise wheat. And of course what is true of wheat is equally true of other crops. Thus economic conditions in one country may drive people from their homes in another country; and this is actually taking place.

Says Mr. Wells : " If it were desirable to search out and determine the primary responsibility for the recent large increase in the number of the English unemployed, or for the distress and revolt of the Irish tenantry, or the growing impoverishment of the French and German peasant proprietors, it will be found that it was not so much the land and rent policy of these different countries that should be called to account, as the farmers on the cheap and fertile lands of the American northwest and the inventors of their cost-reducing agricultural machinery, of the steel rail, and of the compound marine engine." [1] But if these advances in our agriculture and in transportation have wrought hardship for English, Irish, French, and German peasants, we must not forget that by cheapening food they have conferred a blessing on well-nigh the civilized world. Thus both producers and consumers in Europe are made to feel the reality and closeness of their relations to us.

Prices are now based on the whole world's supply. The yield of wheat in Russia, India, Australasia, and the United States together determine the price of every loaf of bread in London. A coal-miner's strike stops the work of 200,000 operatives and mechanics. The passage of a bill by our Congress throws thousands of

---

[1] Recent Economic Changes, p. 378.

men out of employment in a single European city. Financial distress in South America is keenly felt in England and the United States. American workmen and intelligent Americanized foreigners have been thrown out of work and their families brought to the very verge of starvation because degraded immigrants whose families were willing to live in one room and to fish their bread out of ash-barrels had underbid them in the labor market, which they were able to do because of their few wants. Here are people in our midst ruined because certain other people whom they have never seen and who were reared on the other side of the sea are ignorant and brutish.

When before the days of travel peoples were isolated from each other, one city or nation might be smitten with pestilence and it was no concern of another. But in this day of travelling millions, of crowded steamships and cars, when in a single great city hundreds of thousands daily use the same public conveyances, the possibility of contracting contagious diseases is such as to make us interested in the health of all the world. The cholera knocking at our gates reminds us forcibly that we are intimately concerned with the moral degradation and accompanying physical filth of peoples on the opposite side of the globe. The unsanitary condition of some tenement-house may cost life in a palace many miles away. At a meeting of "sweaters" in London it was stated that a suit of clothes ordered for a member of the royal family was made in a small room in which there were two cases of typhoid fever. Before a joint committee of the Illinois Legislature, appointed to investigate the "sweat-shop" evil in Chicago, Mrs. Florence Kelley of the Hull House testified that she had been in a room "where four people were working on cloaks, and every one had the scarlet fever." To find typhoid fever in these "sweat-shops" was a "daily occurrence" in her experience. The head of the Visiting Nurses' Association testified that she had "traced some satin-lined and fur-trimmed ladies' cloaks from a hovel infected with black fever to the best class of retail stores."

The conditions of modern civilization are bringing different classes and nations into ever closer relations. Steam and electricity are making the whole world a neighborhood and every man a neighbor; and as people touch at an increasing number of points, each is becoming more and more concerned with the condition and character of others. God in his providence is making human relations so intimate and complex that they will become simply intolerable unless they are *right* relations, adjusted in harmony with the laws of the kingdom of God. Our close relations with the ignorant, the degraded, the vicious, which it is impossible to escape, are forcing us to do them good in self-defence. The very progress of civilization will yet make it impossible for good and respectable men to live in peace and comfort unless other men also are good and respectable and comfortable; and may God hasten the day !

But further: the race is united not only in all its nations and families, but also in its succeeding generations. Each generation is of course as much the parent of all subsequent generations as it is the child of all preceding; we are as obviously the cause of what follows as we are the effect of what has gone before. The reason that we are civilized and the inhabitants of Central Africa savage is that our ancestors were civilized and theirs savage. Surely our ancestors did more for us by being what they were than they could possibly have done for savage Africa by any means. And if, long before we were born, they could affect our lives for good or ill far more powerfully than they could the lives of their contemporaries on the other side of the world, then they were far more responsible for us than for them. In like manner we are far more responsible for the character of our descendants a dozen generations hence than we can possibly be for our heathen contemporaries.

This is said **not** to poultice the conscience of the

church for neglecting the heathen world, but to arouse a sense of responsibility to the race for its future generations.

Heredity is not always decisive of character, but we know that it exerts a profound influence. The case of "Margaret, the Mother of Criminals" and her descendants is often cited in illustration. She was a pauper child, born about a hundred years ago in one of the villages on the upper Hudson. "In one generation of her unhappy line there were twenty children, of whom seventeen lived to maturity. Nine served terms aggregating fifty years in the State prison for high crimes, and all the others were frequent inmates of jails and almshouses. It is said that of the six hundred and twenty-three descendants of this outcast girl two hundred committed crimes which brought them upon the court records, and most of the others were idiots, drunkards, lunatics, paupers, or prostitutes." [1]

Our lives strengthen or weaken the tendencies which we inherit; and doubtless in some instances we may entirely eradicate them. We therefore become responsible for the strength of the tendencies which we transmit. And so far as we influence or might influence the character and conduct of others, we become in measure responsible for the tendencies which they transmit.

Thus in the complex and intimate relations sustained between nations, communities, and classes, and in the still closer relations of succeeding generations, appears the oneness of the race. The long lines of ancestry which run back through the ages are the warp in the great loom of time; while the steamship, the locomotive, and the telegraphic message are the swift shuttles flying back and forth and weaving in the woof of commerce and communication, thus drawing close the countless individual threads into one vast web of humanity.

The race has always been one in a sense, but it is now becoming one in a new sense, recognized by hard-

---

[1] E. V. Smalley in *The Century*, July, 1882.

headed business men as in no respect sentimental, but
thoroughly practical. Science and commerce are forcing men to accept in a lower sense what Christ taught
in a higher, viz., the neighborhood and brotherhood of
the race. Civilization is compelling an interest in
others for *our own* sakes. Christ inculcated an interest
in others for *their* sakes. Christian brotherhood springs
from something higher than common interests. In an
ocean steamship the steerage and the cabin passengers
have a vast deal in common during the voyage. If the
steerage goes to the bottom so does the cabin. If deadly
pestilence breaks out in the former, the latter is immensely concerned; but all this may be without one
brotherly heart-beat between the two. Modern civilization is fast getting us all into one boat, and we are beginning to learn how much we are concerned with the
concerns of others; but the higher social organization of
the future must have some other and nobler bond than
an enlightened selfishness—even such a love for one's
neighbor as will fulfil the second great law of Christ.

But that is the organic law of a *normal* society, and
before we reach such a social condition there must be
done a vast remedial work. If, therefore, the church is
to accomplish her social mission by applying the principles of the Gospel to the saving of society, her love
must be measured, not by the rule of justice—"*as thyself*," but by the rule of sacrifice—"*as I have loved you.*"
Such love is remedial; and such a love widening until
its arms embrace mankind becomes *an enthusiasm for
humanity.*

Let us at this point pause a moment to gather up
results. We have seen that man's constitution and history afford a presumption, which is confirmed by Revelation and science, that humanity is to be perfected,
"body, soul, and spirit." We have seen that a perfected race amid perfected conditions would constitute
the kingdom of heaven fully come on earth; that in
preparation for the inauguration of this kingdom God
wrought in and through the three great races of an-

tiquity; that Christ came to inaugurate it; that the authoritative Teacher laid down its fundamental laws; and that Christ founded his church to complete the work which he came to inaugurate.

It has been shown that we have come upon the sociological age of the world; that we shall not have social peace and ought not to have it until we have social righteousness—until right relations have been established between man and man; that a higher and more complete organization of society would be in harmony with the laws of historical development which have been pointed out, and is demanded by the logic of events; that the great movements of this century all seem preparatory to still greater movements in the next; that popular discontent is significant of important changes soon to take place; that, in short, the indications seem unmistakable that we are about entering on a *new era* in the progress of the race.

We have also seen that the masses, who are to determine the future of civilization, have become separated from the church; and that the church has lost her hold on them because she has not accepted her social mission —has not exemplified or inculcated as the organic law of society the second fundamental law of Christ.

We have seen, further, that the existing methods of the church are inadequate; and that if she would solve the great problems of the times, if she would win the masses and mould the civilization of the new era, or, in a word, if she would fulfil her mission, she must gain a new conception of it, must make the KINGDOM the object of endeavor, must adapt new methods to new conditions, and enter on the work with a burning enthusiasm for humanity.

This leads to the inquiry, How is such an enthusiasm to be kindled and sustained? We can get the sacred fire and the oil to feed it where the early Christians got them.

Their enthusiasm for humanity, which was something quite new in the world, was kindled in part by the new estimate of human nature made by their Master. He put a new valuation on every human being : "What shall it profit a man, if he shall gain the whole world, and lose his own soul ?" [1] "A man ; " that is, any man ; the meanest, the most shrivelled specimen of the race is beyond price.

We honor great men for those powers or deeds which distinguish them above their fellows, and respect human nature because of the possibilities which we see realized in the noblest specimens of the race. But the highest honor ever paid to human nature, the noblest estimate ever made of it, was in the fact that Jesus Christ "tasted death for *every* man." He did not die for Socrates because he was a thinker, but because he was a *man*. He did not die for Charlemagne because he was a mighty ruler or warrior, but because he was a *man*. He did not die for Shakespeare because he was a genius, but because he was a *man*. Christ offered himself for these men not because of those qualities which distinguished them above their fellows, but because of those qualities which they possessed in common with the wayside beggar.

Twice at least Christ preached to an audience of one —to Nicodemus, an honored member of the Sanhedrim, and to the woman of Samaria, a despised member of a despised race; and of these two extremes of society he honored that in each which was common to both.

Again, Christ kindled an enthusiasm for humanity by the revelation which he made of human nature. He showed to men such moral strength and matchless beauty, such unsearchable riches of love, such unmeasured sacrifice, such sublimity of purpose, as had never been ascribed to man or God. To eyes that could see he was a vision of human nature perfected. And when it was learned that the vilest could become partakers of his life and likeness, then his followers were able to love and venerate the possible Christ in every man.

---

[1] Mark viii. 36,

Christ taught that human nature, even in its most debased and abandoned estate, was savable. And this seems to have been an entirely new truth to the world. The Old Testament Scriptures tell of good men who sinned, repented, and were forgiven ; but I do not find in them the story of a single vicious, besotted, bestial man's being transformed, purified, and made godlike. Turn to the New Testament, and what a revelation of hope ! Christ received into his kingdom publicans and magdalens, and delivered them from the power of sin. He told the story of the prodigal who had sunk into the mire of vice and there wallowed with the vilest, who yet returned to himself and his father's house, penitent and purified. And from that hour to this repenting prodigals have been receiving the Father's kiss of reconciliation.

With Christ there came into the world a new saving power; and hope for humanity made possible an enthusiasm for humanity. To have seen the radiant beauty of Christ and then to see in the vilest the possibility of Christ's likeness, was enough to make love and hope flame up into enthusiasm.

Another source of this enthusiasm which so characterized the early Christians was their love for their Master. He who had shown such beauty and sublimity of character, and especially he who had manifested such love for them and wrought for them such salvation, kindled a passion of love which was overmastering, and which embraced not only their Lord, but also the humanity with which he identified himself.

Furthermore, he revealed the brotherhood of the race, and made every member of it—Jew and Gentile, Greek and barbarian, bond and free—eligible to citizenship in the kingdom of God. Such a kingdom, blest with righteousness and peace, whose fundamental law was love and whose sway was to be universal, might well kindle the imagination and inspire an enthusiasm whose object of devotion could not be less broad than humanity itself.

Now observe that all of these sources of enthusiasm save one may be said to have been opened afresh in modern times. Christ's teachings in regard to the value of every human being were too paradoxical and profound to be fully understood and appreciated by the early Christians. Those teachings are the roots of modern and Christian individualism, which has differ- entiated occidental civilization from oriental. They have produced modern democracy, whose spirit is now almost as pervasive as modern civilization; and with the growth of democracy in this age has come such an estimate of man *as man*, such a valuation of the *common* man, as was hardly possible in any other age.

Again, the most scholarly and fruitful thinking of the past half-century has been focalized on Christ himself, and has resulted in what might be called a restoration of the historical Christ. We cannot claim for this generation any greater love or loyalty to him than has belonged to the Christian heart of every age, but our clearer vision of Christ enables us to see more distinctly and to appreciate more fully the exalted possibilities of human nature which he revealed.

Again, the church seemed almost in danger of forgetting that human nature was savable and that the Gospel was remedial. As the masses drifted away from the influence of the church the impression became common that, with here and there a rare exception, the case of the vicious and criminal classes was desperate, and that the most the church could do was to save the children before they had gone hopelessly astray. And with few efforts in behalf of the worst classes, there were few instances of wonderful transformation to correct this growing impression, until the Salvation Army appeared to convict the church of unbelief and demonstrate once more that the Gospel is indeed the power of God unto the salvation of the most depraved and desperate. Probably during no hundred years in the history of the world have there been saved so many thieves, gamblers, drunkards, and prostitutes as during the past quarter of a century through the heroic faith and labors of the Salvation Army.

It was remarked above that Christ's preaching of the kingdom of heaven, organized on the earth, was a powerful stimulus to the enthusiasm for humanity. For many centuries the church has lost the meaning of Christ's teaching concerning the Kingdom, but it is now being restored by the return, in recent years, to Christ and his words. And these teachings concerning the kingdom of God may well come to this generation with all the power of a new gospel, for, interpreted in the light of modern science and civilization, their meaning is made vastly richer and more comprehensive than they could possibly be to the early Christians. Science has revealed to us ten thousand laws of the Kingdom of which they knew nothing.

We have learned that the physical, intellectual, and spiritual are so wonderfully interlaced in man that society cannot be fully saved in any one of the three until it is saved in all. So that as citizens of the Kingdom we are concerned with all the conditions of life which affect the physical and the intellectual as well as the spiritual life of man.

In like manner, in the world-life which is being organized, different classes, nations, and races are becoming so dependent on each other that it will be impossible to perfect in character or condition any one class or people until all are perfected. So that as citizens of the Kingdom we are bound to be interested in mankind.

We learn from the solidarity of the race that service to one is service to many. This view of the race as a whole, together with confidence in its ultimate perfection, greatly strengthens the motives to service. Isolated need ought to be sufficient to enlist our endeavors; but to the belief that we are helping the individual add the assurance that in blessing him we are blessing unborn generations, making some contribution, however small, to the perfecting of the race, hastening forward, however little, that glorious consummation, and our heart is enlarged with a greater hope and fuller joy, is fortified with a more persistent patience, is inspired with a more ardent enthusiasm.

Moreover, there is inspiration in the knowledge that we belong to a far-reaching organization. A great engine refused to do its work, the machinery of a factory was still, and all the operatives were idle for hours because a little pin less than an inch long had dropped unobserved from its place. Taken by itself, that pin was of the smallest consequence; but as a part of a great mechanism, it was found that the work of the whole factory depended on it. Our lives may seem very insignificant, but when we remember that because we belong to the Kingdom they are part of a vast plan, they at once assume importance; we cannot tell how far their influence may extend or how great may be the issues which depend on them.

And direct influence as well as indirect is immensely augmented by organization and facilities for communication. Had Paul lived in this day, he might have impressed a thousand minds for every one that he influenced during his lifetime. Unprecedented opportunities to aid our fellow-men ought to inspire unprecedented zeal; and beyond peradventure this generation enjoys such opportunities. We have seen the significance of popular discontent; we are evidently in a transition state; our social institutions are in flux; in due time they will recrystallize. This is such an opportunity to give them Christian form as may not come again for ages.

Surely with the highest estimate of the worth of human nature which the world has ever known, with the noblest conception of its possibilities, the clearest demonstration that there is no utterly hopeless degradation, with a growing sense of the brotherhood of man, and a restored vision of the coming Kingdom, and with such opportunities and facilities for blessing mankind as were never before offered, this generation of Chris-

tians ought to glow with enthusiasm for humanity as
no other has ever done.

And if this is true in general, it is thrice true of
Anglo-Saxons. We have seen that for the coming of
Him who should inaugurate the kingdom of heaven in
the earth, three great races wrought until the necessary
spiritual, intellectual, and physical conditions were
made ready. We have seen that these three spheres all
belong to that kingdom; that it cannot fully prevail
until men are brought into glad obedience to the harmonious laws of these three spheres. And we have seen
that those characteristics, which enabled these three
races to fulfil their mission of preparation, all unite in
the one Anglo-Saxon race, indicating that this race is
pre-eminently fitted, and therefore chosen of God, to
prepare the way for the full coming of his kingdom in
the earth.

We have also seen that America is ultimately to be
the seat of the Anglo-Saxon's power, the centre of his
influence. Surely, to be a Christian and an Anglo-
Saxon and an American in this generation is to stand
on the very mountain-top of privilege. We are, it
seems to me, even more favored than those who are to
follow us. Some one has said that he would rather be
his own grandson than his own grandfather; and so
would I: but I would rather be myself than my latest
descendant, because I would rather have part in the
glorious work of creating the Christian civilization of
the future than to bask in the full radiance of its glory.

Yes, this generation in America *ought* to exult in its
transcendent opportunities for service. But it is possible to see these opportunities and yet feel no thrill of
new life unless there is added the quickening touch of
the divine Spirit. These great truths which have been
pointed out are the fuel. If it is to be kindled into
a blessed conflagration of Christian enthusiasm, the
heavenly spark must fall. Let us gain a profound conviction of the worth of every human being, a profound
conviction of human need, a profound conviction of the

saving power of Jesus Christ and his truth, and surely we shall not wait in vain for the cloven tongue of Pentecostal flame. And then there will be a new enthusiasm for humanity, for enthusiasm is conviction on fire.

Such an enthusiasm unites the three Christian graces, faith, hope, and love—a mighty faith in God, a glorious hope for humanity, a burning love for both. It is therefore no mere gust of feeling, but is as constant and as permanent as its elements, of which Paul says[1]: "Now abideth faith, hope, and charity, these three." This is a threefold cord that cannot be broken even by a strain that snaps life itself. It has held the great heroes of humanity to their beloved toil till death. After three years of lonely labor in Burmah, unencouraged by even a single interested listener, Judson wrote: "If any ask what prospect there is of ultimate success, tell them, as much as that there is an almighty and faithful God. If a ship were lying in the river, ready to convey me to any part of the world I should choose, and that too with the entire approbation of all my Christian friends, I would prefer dying to embarking." And again after *five* years he wrote: "I know not that I shall ever live to see a single convert; but notwithstanding, I feel that I would not leave my present situation to be made a king." If such an enthusiasm were common in the Christian church, how speedily would its fire enlighten the night of heathendom !

Should such an enthusiasm take possession of the church in America, how soon would she stretch forth hands of benediction over Africa and China ! These are the two great strongholds of heathenism remaining, for India is already honeycombed with Christian influence; and to the 500,000,000, inhabitants of China and Africa we in the United States sustain exceptional relations of opportunity and obligation. The greater part of the work of evangelizing these many millions must

---

[1] 1 Cor. xiii. 13.

be done for Africa by negroes and for China by China-
men. Men of the same race can better endure the
climate and can more easily establish close relations
than men of foreign blood. The providential significance of thousands of Chinese and millions of negroes
in our midst is obvious. If we had a Christian enthusiasm for mankind, we should be preparing them by the
thousand to go as missionaries to their brethren. But
instead we are debauching Africa with our New England rum, and outraging China by our brutal legislation.

An enthusiasm for humanity is needed to transform
the church; and thus transformed, the church would
soon transform the world. Such an enthusiasm would
speedily make active the latent power of the church.
The conventional Christianity of the day has never
dreamed of the spiritual power asleep in pulpit and pew.
Says the author of *Ecce Homo:* "It is not possible to
set bound to the restoring and converting power of virtue, when, as it were, it takes fire, when, instead of a
rule teaching a man to do justice to his neighbors, and
to benefit them when an occasion presents itself, it becomes a burning and consuming passion of benevolence,
an energy of self-devotion, an aggressive ardor of
love."[1] How would such an enthusiasm vitalize our
preaching! I think it was David Garrick who said:
"We actors present fiction as if it were truth, while you
preachers present truth as if it were fiction." Such acting has more power than such preaching. Moreover,
a Christian enthusiasm, by impelling men to personal
Christian work, would make preachers of the laity. As
long as the laity hire the minister to love men in their
stead, the church will make only the present slow rate
of progress.

Whether that progress seems to us great or small,
occasion for joy or shame, will depend on our standard
of comparison. As compared with nothing at all, the

---

[1] Page 274.

work is gloriously great and unspeakably precious. As compared with what it might be and, therefore, ought to be—as compared with Christ's standard, its progress is painfully and disgracefully slow. We have seen tha. taking 80,000 churches together, their annual additions on confession of faith are only five per cent of their membership. Instead of an increase of thirty or sixty or even a hundred fold, of which the Master talked, these churches, if they had the same number of additions every year—even though they suffered no losses by death—would require twenty years to make an increase of *one* fold, six hundred years to gain thirty fold, twelve hundred to gain sixty fold, and two thousand years to gain a hundred fold !

We have seen that, averaging four and a half million church-members, it takes twenty of them twelve months to win a single convert. And these twenty church-members have all professed to give themselves, body and soul, time and substance, to God and his service. What if twenty politicians pledged themselves for a year to the service of a political favorite ? The great object of these men every day in the year and every hour of the day is to win adherents to their candidate. To this end they have consecrated not only their time and energies, but their money also. After a twelve-month they meet to sum up results, and find that in one year they have together made *one* proselyte ! What occasion for mutual congratulation ! Would not one spark of enthusiasm make such a result impossible ?

When we look at the black cloud which envelopes 800,000,000 heathen, and think of the heathenism which still clings to Christendom, we are oppressed, perhaps appalled, and cry: "Who is sufficient for these things ?" The church of Christ is fully sufficient if aroused, if her latent power is made active. Look at the beginning of the Christian era when Roman society was one mighty ulcer before God—a stench unto heaven. The foundations and framework of civilization were heathen. Ideas, habits, customs, laws, all were heathen. There was no mass of Christian literature with which the world has since been enriched. The New Testament had not taken form. Except for the favored few the Old Testament did not exist. There were no Christian institutions, no Christian laws, no Christian atmosphere, which modifies where it cannot transform. And there was sent out to face this heathen world a little band whose equipment was an enthusiastic love for God and men, together with the good news which had kindled their enthusiasm. Yet look at results. Into this mass of heathenism the salt of Christian truth was cast, and that rotting civilization was penetrated with Christian influence, its corruption arrested, its heathenism destroyed.

We, with a Bible for every home, with our Christian press, our Christian literature, our Christian schools and millions of Christian hearts, are ten thousand times more equal to our work than were they to theirs, provided only we have a like Christian enthusiasm, making the latent power of the church active.

An enthusiasm for humanity would lead the church to see and to accept her social mission. The conception of the church is common, and I believe general, which deems it a spiritual transfer company whose business it is to receive souls on earth and to deliver them in good condition in heaven. But an enthusiasm for humanity means far more than a strong desire to save as many individual souls as possible. It means also a longing for the uplifting and perfecting of humanity as a whole, for the saving of society, for the sanctifying of all human institutions and the sweetening of all human relations. Such an enthusiasm would give to the church a profound interest in all the conditions of life which affect the upward or downward tendencies of races, all that works the improvement or deterioration of the human stock. Many good men are as little concerned for future generations as was Sir Boyle Roche when he asked the Irish Parliament: " Why should we put ourselves out of the way for posterity ? What has

posterity done for us?" But he who is inspired with
the enthusiasm for· humanity is as ready to toil and to
sacrifice for generations far removed in time as for
nations far removed in space. The Kingdom extends
not only outward to other lands, but also onward to
other ages. Would that the millions who daily pray
"Thy kingdom come" might fill this vast petition with
a mighty longing for the perfecting of humanity, of
which our Lord's prayer is a prophecy,—a longing so
genuine as to lead forth effort. For as John Ruskin
says: "If you do not wish for His Kingdom, don't pray
for it; but if you do, you must do more than pray for
it; you must work for it." An enthusiasm for humanity would lead the church to work for the full
coming on earth of the kingdom of heaven, which
would be the acceptance of her social mission by the
church.

And this would bridge the chasm between the church
and the masses, for, as we saw in a preceding chapter,
the refusal of the church to accept her social mission
has been the chief cause of their alienation.

The enthusiasm for humanity also bridges the social
chasm for all who feel its thrill. When the heart has
become hot with the God-enkindled fire of love it refuses to regard any class, however ignorant or degraded, as human rubbish. It looks down on no being
for whom Christ thought it worth his while to die. The
essential dignity of human nature belittles the artificial
distinctions of social rank. Caste can no more survive
the awakening of the spirit of universal brotherhood
than night can outlive sunrise. Any one who feels the
enthusiasm for humanity recognizes the possibilities of
humanity, and with Charles Kingsley longs and labors
for "the time when the ordinary man can be a saint, a
scholar, and a gentleman." He who sorrows over men's
ignorance and sin and wretchedness, and longs to lift
them out, finds no social barriers obstructing his way to
the slums. An enthusiasm for humanity inspires not a
few men and women in London, Bristol, Liverpool,

Edinburgh, and Glasgow to give up their whole time, strength, and fortunes to working among the poor and outcast. "There is a merchant in Glasgow who refuses a seat in Parliament, lest it imperil his work among the Glasgow poor. London can show earls, lords, gentlemen, ladies by the score, who have no other business but seeking to save the lost. There are wealthy members of the aristocracy who, with their wives and daughters, go habitually into the low abodes of poverty and misery, and who conduct missions of every conceivable kind." [1] And there are high-born women who for the love they bear to Christ and humanity have made their homes in the vermin-infested tenements of the slums.

The Earl of Shaftesbury was once talking to Frances Power Cobbe of the wrongs of young girls. The tears came to his eyes, his voice trembled, and after a pause he added: "When I feel how old I am, and know I must soon die, I hope it is not wrong, but I feel I cannot bear to go and leave the world with all the misery in it." Shaftesbury's enthusiasm for humanity made it painful for him to be separated from the wretched so long as he had any power to relieve their misery.

Again, such an enthusiasm would overcome difficulties and successfully apply the two great principles which have been discussed. Undoubtedly their application presents difficulties; but pretty much everything that is worth doing does. Discovery and invention and science and art and Christianity have not advanced thus far toward the conquest of the world because they met with no difficulties. Difficulties have been yielding to enthusiasm ever since the world began. For a long time Mr. Edison's phonograph refused to say the word "specia." It would drop the *s* and say "pecia." And Mr. Edison says he worked from eighteen to twenty hours a day for seven months to secure that single sound, until he succeeded. The material which he originally used for

[1] Dr. A. T. Pierson, *The Missionary Review*, Nov., 1889.

his cylinders did not prove satisfactory. He wanted something delicate enough to receive impressions not more than a millionth part of an inch in depth, and yet rigid enough to carry the needle up and down, exactly reproducing the vibrations which had made the impressions. Scientists told him there was no such substance in existence. "Then we must produce it," was the reply. They insisted that it could not be done, because the qualities which he demanded were inconsistent and exclusive of each other. This modern Aladdin declared that it *could* be done because it *must* be done, *and he did it.* Enthusiasm is always accomplishing "the impossible." It was Paul's enthusiasm which declared that with Christ strengthening him he could do anything. This spirit of enthusiastic determination, of sanctified wilfulness, is as effective in Christian work as elsewhere. I knew a city missionary in New York who was determined to reclaim a certain family. They suddenly disappeared. He followed every possible clue until he found them. They moved again and again, ten times; and ten times he hunted them up until at length he won the success for which he had labored.

The great wrongs of the world persist because human appetite and passion are enlisted in their behalf. They are opposed by the spirit of benevolence. As long as appetite and passion are stronger in wicked men than benevolence in good men, these wrongs will continue. Hence the necessity of arousing Christians to an *enthusiasm* for humanity if we are to overcome the difficulties which beset Christian effort. When the average Christian is inspired with an enthusiasm which is more watchful, more persistent, more eager in doing men good than is selfishness in doing them evil, then the full coming of the Kingdom will not long tarry.

Again, an enthusiasm for humanity would make the discovery, which so many need to make, that consecration to God means service to man. Thousands have thought to serve God by withdrawing themselves from the world and by living as nearly as possible out of all relations with their fellows. As Dr. James H. Ecob puts it: "The notion has prevailed that to become a truly spiritual man is to sign a quit-claim to this world and take a mortgage on the next." But God has immense interest in this world, and an immense work to do here, and as an old proverb says: "God loves to be helped." The best way to serve him that I know of is to help him do his work; that is, to help him perfect humanity, and thus to hasten the coming of his kingdom. Christ, the same yesterday and to-day, would still seek the lost, but he must now do it on *our* feet. He would still minister, but he must do it with *our* hands. He would still warn and comfort and encourage and instruct, but he must do it with *our* lips. If we refuse to perform these offices for him, what right have we to call ourselves members of his body, in vital union with him?

> " ' Why, God,' thought Marian. ' has a missing hand
> This moment; Lucy wants a drink, perhaps.
> Let others miss me! never miss me, God!' " [1]

Moreover, Christ teaches that the needs of men are *his* needs, that he is in the world hungry, naked, sick, in prison. If we wish to serve him, how can we do it better than in the person of those with whom he identifies himself? [2] Self-giving is the law of Christian living; but self-sacrifice for its own sake is not good, and is no more pleasing to God than to human nature. To teach that God requires it or is pleased by it is to caricature him. But self-denial *for the sake of others* is Christlike, Godlike.

Again, and finally, enthusiasm for humanity inspires sacrifice. When a man has what Clement of Rome called "an insatiable desire of doing good" it makes sacrifice not only easy but blessed.

It is as true of the church as of her Lord that only sacrificing power is saving power. It is said that Napoleon once stood before his guards and asked for a hun-

---

[1] Mrs. Browning's "Aurora Leigh."   [2] Matt. xxv. 40, 45.

dred men to lead a forlorn hope. He explained that every man would doubtless be killed the moment the enemy opened fire. Now who would die for the emperor? "A hundred men, forward! Step out of the ranks!" And not a hundred men, but the whole regiment, as one man, sprang forward in solid line and rang their muskets at his feet. And shall Christ and country and humanity fail to command an enthusiasm which Napoleon kindled? Is there nothing worthy of supreme sacrifice to-day? There are many who would die for Christ, but in these times he calls for men willing to *live* for him. Human nature can summon itself with high resolve and in one supreme act lay life itself on the altar. Thank God, the heroism of martyrdom has not been rare in the history of his church; but what is needed to-day is a higher heroism, a nobler, more costly martyrdom—that of the *living* sacrifice, the *sustained* resolve, the *renewed* self-giving, the *daily* consecration. Only a living sacrifice can, like Paul, "die daily."

The Captain of our salvation summons his church militant to-day, not to a forlorn hope, but to certain and glorious victory. Oh that the whole church with unbroken line might spring forward to offer the *living* sacrifice, until the Kingdom is fully come, and God's will is done on earth even as it is in heaven!

INDEX.